W9-CRV-784

IN NECK DEEP

STORIES FROM A FISHERMAN

Jay Zimmerman

Harmony Series
Bottom Dog Press
Huron, Ohio

0-933087-90-X
$15.00

Bottom Dog Press
PO Box 425
Huron, OH 44839
Lsmithdog@aol.com
http://members.aol.com/Lsmithdog/bottomdog

Credits
Cover Art & Drawings:
Kendall Zimmerman
Cover Design:
Eva Zimmerman
Editorial Assistance:
Susanna Schwacke
Ann Smith

Supported in part by
The Ohio Arts Council

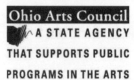

Ohio Arts Council
A STATE AGENCY
THAT SUPPORTS PUBLIC
PROGRAMS IN THE ARTS

CONTENTS

The Orchard Pond — 7

Sands of this Great Lake — 17

Eating It Up — 25

Into the Jungle — 41

Two Pantherville — 55

Fort Bragg Bass — 81

Working Nights — 91

River Rats — 109

The Pisgah Pilgrim — 125

Freedom and Rocky Mountain Trout — 145

Mind Sludge — 159

Road Trip — 167

Halibut Hotel — 187

Office on the Buskin — 211

Salmon Mints — 227

Silvers and the Styrofoam Hatch — 237

End of the Run — 249

Author Photo & Biographical Sketch — 256

The Orchard Pond

May had been too dry and the locals were starting to become concerned when, in the last hours of the month, a thunderstorm rolled through. It has given the recently planted fields a much needed soaking and caused everyone's lawn to grow at least three inches overnight.

Northern Ohio lets out a long sigh of drought relief–all but me, the punk kid standing barefoot in a patch of poison ivy. I couldn't care less. I'm eighteen years old and graduating from high school today. Twelve long years of sustained torture and forced obedience. My sentence ends today. After being trapped for so long by ridged constraints, I feel that both my imagination and I deserve some room to roam. My name is probably being called right now. But, I'm not wearing a cap and gown and I'll be going nowhere near that podium.

There are many more pressing things at hand. *Fish.* They are out there and I have to find them, although the situation is looking exceptionally grim from where I now stand.

It had seemed like a good idea to me a few seconds ago. I could've saved some time, avoided trudging through a muddy corn field and gotten to the old Orchard Pond in no time. All I had to do was barrel through the largest patch of poison ivy in Erie County. *No problem*, I thought. *I'll worry about the consequences in a day or two.* All this would have been fine, but an eight-and-a-half-foot graphite fly rod doesn't barrel through things with quite the same zeal as an impatient eighteen-year-old with fish on the brain.

I could have broken the two-piece rod down and picked my way through the briars, brush and vines. That would have been the sensible thing to do. Instead, I turned the fly rod around so the tip stuck out behind me. With a firm grip on the cork handle, I charged head down into the poisonously lush abyss. I made it a bit further than halfway before the reel began losing line.

So here I am, my line snagged up somewhere behind me, and I am stuck, exactly where I don't want to be.

The greenery is too thick to clearly see where the problem has originated. I tighten my grip on the rod, hook the line and leader firmly with my finger and give the thing a yank. The mystery shrub a few feet behind me does not let loose; my #10 dry fly does. It pops off the back of the reel and shoots directly into my finger. The rod is dropped as I recite my usual prayer, "GOD DAMMIT! SHIT!"

The damage is not all that bad. The barb is still exposed and blood pressure alone has pushed the tip of the thin wire hook nearly to the surface. I pluck the fly from my finger and secure it back in the reel. The sharp pain has eased and all that remains is a small spot of blood, which I dab off on my mud-smeared and tattered shorts.

Now pissed off and in an even bigger hurry, I stomp back to where the rod tip lies and yank my fly and line loose. I grab my rod again and plow forward, stumbling as I break free into an open field.

I stop a few rows into the new field to gather my bearings, adjust my eyes to the sunlight and try to calm down. I don't need to be in such a hurry, there's plenty of daylight left. It's hard sometimes, though, not to feel the need to run, because the sun sets so fast, and tomorrow always promises to come and be busy. There'll be no time for a deep breath and a sunny day then.

There are soybeans planted and the soil is better drained on this side of the poison ivy thicket, making for much easier traveling. With beans you don't have to be nearly so careful walking as you do with corn. No guilt-inducing popping sounds as you change lanes, snapping off a half dozen young stalks. Besides, woodchucks love beans and usually chew the young plants away from the edge of the woods, leaving a clear trail to my destination.

My pulse begins to settle as I trudge along this varmint made clear-cut with my head down and eyes alert, attracted to anything neat, be it an old stone arrowhead or just some fresh deer tracks to report back to Dad. I stop occasionally to poke at glossy flakes of flint–left by a hunter maybe? My mind conjures up an ancient scenario: a buckskin-clad native kneeling near a downed deer, chipping a sharp, new edge on his favorite skinning knife. The flakes are a deep blue; from nodules mined miles distant, hoarded, traded and coveted, but not valuable enough to merit a place in my collection. So I move on, and they remain where they have been for thousands of years.

Of equal interest are the footprints. There is the usual assortment of raccoon, deer, opossum and woodchuck, but it is the sign from other humans that I look over carefully. Some are old boot prints that look familiar and I assume that they're Dad's. The rest were made with bare feet and are a few days old, a fact that pretty much confirms their origin. They're mine.

The walk is a fairly long one for a Midwestern fishing trip, through woods, fields and an old overgrown apple orchard. I know this walk well, having walked it alone many times over the years of my mainly solitary adolescence. I always enjoy the suspense and expectations that build with every step, knowing that I'm free, unhindered and unaffected by anything man-made. I'm voluntarily lost and alone in my own world, for a little while anyway.

The Orchard Pond must not seem all that spectacular to anyone else. The only company I ever have are a pair of Canada geese and an equally shy muskrat. This only makes the place that much more grand and mysterious, one of those pockets of water that seem to speak to the deepest, most intimate reaches of my fish-infected soul, pleading for me to come near and cast a fly upon her, and promising to divulge to me alone, the most wonderful of her sleek little children. I oblige as often as possible.

On the best and last part of the trek I clear the final stand of young poplar trees. They surround the pond on all sides, leaning in with frail, outstretched limbs and small, quivering leaves, protecting their hidden treasure as best they can. It's less than an acre, not the largest treasure, but the only one they have.

At the edge, where the trees end and the cattails begin, I can see the luring, calm water as I peer breathlessly over a dense green wall of long stalks and sharp, slender leaves. There are no rise-forms or other movements that might give away or suggest the presence of a fish, as if the pond were still keeping its secret, not saying a word.

I carefully part the first layer of cattails as I move forward. The tea-colored water is cold against my bare skin. It's nice after the long walk on this "sure is hot for June" afternoon. My sense of hurry and impatience are soothed as I navigate my way slowly out into the knee-deep water, submerging myself into the mud and aquatic forest. I have become part of the pond.

The clicking of the reel has an almost ominous sound as I strip line from it, like a camouflaged sniper chambering a round, preparing for that one well-placed shot. My fly reel doesn't have the same–very distinctive–sound and authority of a high-power, bolt-action rifle, but in my mind it sets the same mood. If panfish made movies, I'm sure they'd start the scary music now and maybe do one of those three-stage, B-rated close-ups on my reel. I'm feeling quite lethal.

I strip out the line and it coils in the water by my legs. The fly is unhooked and I pull out just enough so the entire leader and a foot or so of the actual fly line has cleared the tip top. The fly is then held with my left hand while I wave the rod slightly over the water with my right. With the rod now in motion, the hook is let loose, and two short false-casts get more line in the air. The rod tip stops and my dry fly comes to a graceful rest upon the water, followed by the line and leader. During all of this, only my hand and the rod have protruded from the cattails.

The dry fly is a home tied number I've done myself. Its hackle is dark brown, plucked from a feather duster hanging in the pantry. The wings and tail are tail hair from a chipmunk left as an offering on the doormat, courtesy of the family cat. The gray, dubbed body is shed hair from that same, very convenient, family cat. I've not gotten around to assigning a name to this particular pattern. If I ever become good enough to tie two dry flies that look even remotely similar, I'll then worry about a pattern name.

The ripples fade away and the surface is smooth once again. I hold the rod motionless over the water, studying the innocent looking, artificial bug that has just landed. Long moments pass with nothing visibly happening. There is something serious about to go down though, I can just feel it. A slight jerk of my wrist gives the fly a twitch. The surface boils violently. The vulnerable fly disappears. I raise the fly rod and give a quick downward jerk on the line. The rod bends with the weight of the fish.

The bluegill is a small spawning male, only a half-pounder, but he's scrappy. I pull the fish, still fighting doggedly, into my hideaway and undo the metal stringer from around my waist. Only now, with the fish safely secured, do I hold him up to admire his colors. He has a dark back and a deep orange underbelly–such a beautiful, fresh piece of life. His spiny dorsal fin is splayed out, his anal fin and soft-dorsal pulsating slightly and tail curving toward me–wet, glossy and alive.

I repeat this ritual over and over. There is not a new fish for every cast, but I never have to wait long for another opportunity. After every cast I have to squeeze the hackle with my T-shirt to keep it dry enough to float. Soon this gets tiresome and I let it sink, fishing it as a wet fly, and adding a few more twitches to my retrieve.

I fish less than halfway around the pond, sneaking into five or six makeshift casting-blinds. Most of the time is spent getting myself comfortable and situated as stealthily as possible. The locals never take kindly to trespassing and they have yet to detect me. Their eyesight is second to none and I'm not sure how much longer I can pull this off. Two of them have been puttering around by the far bank all day. They'd spotted some movement right from the get-go but are not quite sure what I am yet. Although some nervous honking and a little neck stretching is a darn sight more desirable than the god awful, holy hell that would break loose if the Canada geese decide to split.

I'm not so much concerned that the commotion of the birds leaving would spook the bluegill. I'm sure they would resume feeding shortly after a cement truck were somehow launched into the middle of the pond. I could see them coming out from the moss ten minutes later to check out the inside of the drum, and drifting through the cab pecking bubbles off the dashboard, proud and cocky in their new home. But the Orchard Pond contains largemouth bass as well, and *they* can be skittish.

The bluegill, as with most farm ponds in the area, are stocked alongside the bass, not for added sporting opportunity, but as a renewable food supply for the more prestigious and lofty largemouth. I'm not ignorant of this, having spotted several nice sized fish cruising predatorily past me while I was wreaking havoc on the bait fish population. They had shown no apparent interest in my dry-turned-wet fly though (believe me, I gave them *more* than ample opportunity.) The bass were there, then gone again, in only a matter of seconds, never allowing me any time for a fly change. I'd been reassuring myself after these brief encounters that *their* time would come. Or maybe it was a threat–either way, the fish were oblivious.

The water here is fairly open although toward the very end of summer the level drops a foot or so and the surface algae gets a bit out of hand. But, even at its worst, there is plenty of clear, open space. The bass drift idly and unattached along the edge, looking for mischief or something fun to swallow, but with an ever watchful eye for any sign of me. The bluegill, on the other hand, crowd around anything interesting, like a bunch of bored groupies after a rock concert, even if it's a dangerous kid with a fly rod. These naive congregations of three-to-five-inch youngsters give the bass plenty of food to choose from, so they're never desperate. And this makes tricking them even more difficult.

There's only one empty clip remaining on my stringer, and that's the one hooked to the belt-loop of my shorts. All the others have at least one bluegill attached and some contain a double load. Fifteen fish should be enough for the meal I've promised, this means five for each of us–because my sister is off at college, there will be only three of us at the table. I'm sure that Mom will have something to add from the garden as well, fresh asparagus and some of last year's potatoes will be perfect.

Now, with my meal obligations fulfilled, I have some time to devote all of my fly-fishing prowess on the elusive, local bass. I also have a new batch of streamers, hot off the vice so to speak, that are itching to get out on the water and prove themselves. I pull the cheap aluminum fly box from my back pocket and look over all the new, feathery creations. What I need is a good, life-like baitfish imitation. Not something too big or gaudy, something just right...I think.

I settle with a long-shanked, #8 Yella Belly. This is a new pattern I've developed with these specific bass in mind. The fly has olive-drab feathers over his back and a black yarn body with white ribbing–dental floss from the bathroom medicine cabinet. The yellow neck and tail (hence the name) are from crest feathers of a cockatoo. My aunt is a breeder of parrots–of various shapes, colors and awful noises–and also a gracious supplier of all my *exotic* fly-tying material. Although, watching her brother's kid dig around in the crap-coated wood chips at the bottom of an aviary, looking for pretty feathers, seems as if it would appeal to her strange sense of humor. So her motives may be suspect.

The decision is made. I clip off my now thoroughly pulverized dry fly and tie on the new streamer. The battered veteran is hooked in my sleeve as a reminder to salvage him upon my return home. His hackle has unwound and his fur body has been pulled down onto the bend of the hook, his tail hidden somewhere in the mess. The exhausted fly seems content to sit out the rest of the day with a good view from my shoulder.

I close the fly box and tuck it back into my pocket. The new fly is perfectly dry, so I hold it underwater for a moment, ensuring that the streamer sinks on the first cast. Now there's nothing left to do but catch some bass.

Because there are no structure or other obvious bass hangouts upon which to concentrate my attention, I'm left casting blind–cast after seemingly unnoticed cast. Occasionally a lone bass swims by, but my timing is never right. Either I have just begun a retrieve from the opposite direction, or my cast is too close and I spook the fish back into the depths when my fly line splashes down a few inches above their nose.

This type of fishing takes a lot more patience than piddling with the bluegill, and I'm trying real hard to pay attention, to make every cast count. I'm keeping the coiled line under control and my eye on the leader. I have to make sure the rod is angled correctly for the retrieve, off to the right a touch and low enough to keep the slack line between the rod tip and the water at a minimum, ready for a strike at any time.

After a while, I find myself watching the sun more than concentrating on the fishing, trying to guess the time. The later it gets, the less enthusiastic my casts become. My back-casts sag too low and are getting closer to the overhanging poplar branches behind me. I'm also quite sure I've managed to put a few knots in my leader, but don't have the energy to check. My retrieves are now boring and repetitious, lacking the excited energy they had an hour ago.

I still have a long walk home ahead of me and a full stringer of bluegill to clean for supper. It has already passed the time when I *should* have called it a day. My mind, on the other hand, already has, and is now wandering around out in the bean field waiting for me to reel in and catch up. I let my thoughts piss around out there, unchaperoned by concentration.

Suddenly a largemouth bass decides that the funny minnow with the yellow tail might taste good, catching *me* completely off guard. The swirl is huge on the calm water. The bass takes my fly in one swipe and heads for the cattails. I'm so surprised and momentarily confused that I forget to set the hook. I just hold the rod and watch stupidly as the end of my line races across the pond. By the time it dawns on me what is happening the fish has safely buried himself in the protective mass of vegetation. If I hold the line tight I can still feel a little movement, but there is no use, the bass is long gone, along with any of his buddies, by the time I wade over to retrieve my fly. This craziness is the final straw for the two geese, who add to the commotion as they take off, surely scaring away the last, if any, of the braver fish. The six-pound-test leader is wrapped tight around a clump of dead cattail stalks, and my streamer is no longer at the end of it, only the remains of my clinch-knot.

The last cast of the day is always difficult to make. More accurately, it's always difficult to decide what cast *will be* your last. "All right, a couple more casts right over there...then I'm outta here." And everyone knows that those two casts automatically roll over if you feel, or see, anything that could *possibly* be construed as a strike. This includes the ones that leave long strands of grass on your fly.

There isn't much to keep me on the water any longer tonight though. My fly is gone and my nicked-up leader needs to be replaced. The sun is low, my shorts are wet, and I'm hungry. The line and leader get wound into the reel, leaving no excuse not to break down the rod. I do, undoubtedly saving time and aggravation on the way home. I undo the stringer from my belt-loop and twist the end of the chain twice around my wrist, lifting the mess of fish from the water as I head for shore.

It's nice to have solid, dry ground under my feet. Cool water and mud between my toes is fun, but the novelty wears thin after the third hour or so. My legs have become shriveled and tender from their long soaking. I'll have to watch my step.

Looking down at the lively stringer of bluegill, I smile. Then a deliberate glance toward the Orchard Pond with a quick nod and salute with the rod tips.

My mind begins to drift again. Pondering, only now, questions of my uncertain future. I turn and lead with my left . . . *left . . . left, right . . . left. . . .*

THE KISHMAN FISH
KZ

Sands of this Great Lake

George Zimmerman was young, fit, with a head for hard work and adventure. The rich woodlands, vast fields and gorgeous beaches bordering the southern shore of Lake Erie were his stomping grounds. There were plenty of opportunities for a young man of George's temperament, right in his own backyard. Huron, Ohio, was a small but rapidly growing town in the 1940's, built around the mouth of the Huron River. The coal and iron-ore dock was more or less the town's hub and employed the majority of the working-age men who lived on the east side of the river.

George's father, Frank was a commercial fisherman for the Kishman Fish Company on the west side of the river. He ran one of the three boats in Kishman's small fleet of trap netters. There were many other independent trap net and gill net fishermen operating out of Huron and selling their catch to the Kishman and Lay Brothers fish companies. Lay Brother's large fleet ran out of Sandusky, a few miles to the west, but their Huron and Vermilion locations (to the east) served the independent fisherman.

George would have liked to join the United States Marine Corp., but by the time he graduated from high school in 1942, he was convinced he had flat feet (although he didn't) and assumed he would be barred from enlisting. With that dream temporarily dashed, he took a job on the lake. But not as a fisherman. During the summer of '42, he worked as a coal passer in the boiler room aboard the *Crawford.* The next season, he sailed again, this time as a fireman on the *Mudge.* Both Hanna Co. ships hauled iron ore from Duluth, Escanaba, and other cities along the shores of Lake Superior and Lake Michigan to ports down along the southern shore of Lake Erie.

During the winter of 1943–44, two things happened that greatly altered George's life. On the frozen waters of Sawmill Creek–a favorite spot to ice-skate at the time–he fell in love with a tall, dark-haired woman named Mildred Mitchell. Then, in the middle of January, he received his draft notice, and their wedding plans were postponed. The big war was in full swing and Uncle Sam was short a few good men.

George was sent to Toledo, Ohio, along with 350 other draftees, for their complementary physical and in-processing. There were three recruiters present to review the paperwork on these prospective young warriors–one each from the Army, Navy and Marines. The Marine Corp. needed only seven men, so George figured between that and his supposedly flat feet, he wouldn't have a chance. Maybe, if he were lucky, the Navy would take him.

The Army recruiter looked at his papers first. "Well," the man said. "Looks like this one would make a good soldier."

"See that anchor on his forearm?" the Navy recruiter said, pointing to the tattoo George had gotten while sailing the Great Lakes. "That means he likes the water."

"Let me see those papers a minute," the Marine recruiter said. He glanced through them, then quickly looked up. "Oh, you would make a much better Marine. I need one more man and you're the guy!"

George was flying high the entire train ride to Paris Island. After boot-camp, it was off to the Hebrides Islands and then farther north: Guadalcanal, Bougainville, Mindanao and Luzon. Between beach-landings, booby-traps, Japanese air-raids and his buddy Nick Zupan, there was enough trouble and adventure to go around.

The first Bomb was dropped on Hiroshima while George was on the boat home. Nagasaki was hammered three days later, when he was on the train to North Carolina to out-process. Mildred was waiting for him at Cherry Point and took him back home. They were married shortly after.

After the war George worked at a local lumber yard for a couple years, but Lake Erie was still there, and so were the fish. In 1948, he quit his job and began commercial fishing with his father. They ran the *Kennith K*, trap-netting walleye, yellow perch, white bass, catfish and the now extinct blue pike.

Their trap nets were quite involved set-ups. A long lead net guided the fish into the large holding net, or *crib*. Once they were there, the fish could stay alive for a few days. The nets were checked daily, if the weather permitted, so there were usually no problems. This system was much more ecologically sound, allowing the fisherman to release any small or otherwise illegal fish. The gill nets, on the other hand, were equal opportunity fish killers. This hurt commercially as well. If the weather turned sour, the fish filled nets had to be left. The catch would rot and it would take the crew days to rid their nets of the foul remains.

George's father was hurt on the job and then retired. Not too many years later George quit as well. The fishing was slowing down and the lake was getting dirty. Kishman payed a salary of about fifty-five dollars per six-day work week, so the lack of fish didn't affect the pocketbook, but it was discouraging, none-the-less, and the net cleaning chores were becoming quite gruesome. Lake Erie had become a cesspool of garbage, toxic chemicals and other pollutants. The nets would come up with the bottom five foot or so covered in a smelly, brown goop. At one point biologists claimed the lake to be officially "Dead."

When George quit fishing commercially in 1960, he took a job doing engine maintenance and repair at a SOHIO gas station. Close to his home and family. Mildred and he had four children by then; one daughter: Katy, and three sons, John, Jim and Larry.

George retired in 1980, but he was still almost five years away from collecting his Social Security checks. So, until that time came, he set trotlines in the Huron River and the nearby marshes. He would check and re-bait the lines every morning, and the sale of the turtle and catfish caught on them held the family over until that first retirement check came in the mail.

And, in his own words, "I've been loafing ever since."

* * *

John Zimmerman was born about two hundred years too late. My dad was meant to be a mountain man, but fate has had a knack for these kinds of errors. What's more, this slightly crazy, misplaced soul was born a Baby Boomer.

Even as a young boy, John had come to grudgingly accept this plight. Huron, Ohio, was not an out-post in the foothills of the Rocky Mountains. The Yukon river didn't flow through town, either, just the muddy old Huron. There were no beaver to trap, no bears to wrestle and no Indians to shack up with. Just a shallow lake, with a shallow river, and a shallow town. So, this young boy took to the woods, and in a sense, never came back.

John loved to hunt, fish and just about any other outdoor adventure. His beagle named Banjo would accompany him almost everywhere: through the thickets after rabbits, across the fields and hedgerows for pheasant, and into the woods for squirrel. John learned to shoot a bow, hunt deer, run a trapline and sell the furs of muskrat and the occasional mink. He learned to walk unheard and move unseen, to swim in angry spring currents and climb forbidden trees. He knew where the best fish lived and what plants to eat, which way was North and how to skin a limit of squirrel faster than anyone around.

John graduated from high school in 1966 and, like his father twenty-three years before, received his draft notice. He took the news well, in fact, unwilling to wait, he enlisted. The Army sent him to Fort Benning, Georgia, for Basic Training and then into the jungles of Viet Nam. Cam Ranh Bay, Saigon, Khe Sanh, Hue, Da Nang, Phu Bai, a strange and interesting place and predicament. John spent one tour-of-duty *in country* and extended twice before he left. Two years of convoys, sieges, patrols and shit-burning details in a stifling hot, war-torn country can wear thin, even to the most dedicated adventurer.

Like a lot of vets, John came home in August of '69 with a deep-seated *"I don't give a fuck"* attitude. He was more wild and reckless than ever. All his off time between various jobs was spent in bars or in the woods, planning or enacting some new, outlandish and barely feasible plot that he had cooked up.

In the Spring of 1970, John went in on a business venture with his older sister KaTy and her new husband, Jim McElroy. The three of them–along with another married couple–flew to Perth, Australia in hopes of starting an electrical contracting company. Although, by the time October rolled around, all hopes of a company start-up were gone. Money was running low and archery-season was already open back home. His father's good words from deer-camp in Pennsylvania, were too much for him to resist.

George picked up his son in Huron and took him straight to camp. John needed to get lost and unwind in the hills of beautiful western PA. His life had gotten a tad complicated in the last six months and was about to get even worse. He had met a woman. She had long, flowing black hair and an easy laugh.

The next two years are a jumbled story, and I'm short on all the details. His younger brother Jim–who had been drafted as well– came home severely wounded from Viet Nam. And of course, there was still this beautiful, brown-eyed *Aussie* woman. It was a time of love, healing and then for good measure, a wedding. John Zimmerman married Kendall Hart in September of 1972 and they have been happy and together ever since.

That same year John started working in the mailroom of a nearby newspaper, the *Sandusky Register*. A couple years later he moved to the pressroom of that same newspaper. He and Kendall rented an old farmhouse outside of Huron until they had saved enough money to buy land. John still had this dream of building a log cabin in a woods he could call his own.

They found a rural, wooded lot nearby, and by hand, built their dreams.

* * *

I know I'm sure going to miss this old wooded lot when I'm off in the Army, or wherever I wind up. I'm extremely lucky to have strong people in my life, and to have had a great childhood. I'm sad that it's about over. I've waited all my life–or at least as far back as I can remember–to be done with school and old enough to do whatever I want. I've heard stories of all sorts at the dinner table– hunting, fishing, travel, war and other grand adventure–since before I could feed myself. I need to get out there and have adventures and wild times of my own.

Heck, if Dad *had* been a mountain man, then I'd be more than willing to stay. I could've kept the meat box full and the bears away, or checked the trap lines and helped flesh out the beaver pelts. It would've been a good life.

I've done what I can while I've lived here, though. I've split firewood and brought back as much meat for the table as I could put my grubby, adolescent hands on. Every year around September I help Dad scout and put up tree stands for deer season. If he or Mom decide to hunt out-of-state for a few weeks, then Eve (my older sister) and I would be allowed to miss school to come along. Dad taught us–Mom, Eve and I–how to shoot shotguns, rifles and bows. He showed us everything he knew about the woods and how to live comfortably within it.

It was Mom who took me out hunting in my early years. At first she had me follow close behind and fetch any squirrel she shot. I had to prove that I had the patience and discipline to be quiet in the woods before I was allowed to carry my own squirrel rifle. And oh boy! Once I was allowed outside with a .22, there were no critters safe! The only stipulation that came along with this armed and dangerous childhood free-ranging, was that I ate everything I shot. The catch–and there always was one–was that Mom would only cook the things that were considered *game* in most first-world countries. I imagine robin and starling wouldn't taste bad if they were stuffed with mushrooms and marinated. They taste really bad burnt-on-a-spit though, and that's what eventually weaned me of plunking anything, and everything, that moved.

I wasn't such a quick study when it came to fishing. You could stock a small hardware store with all the spinning rods and tackle boxes I lost in the Huron River. Dad never lost his temper or sense of humor though. He would reel in all the lines, rig up a rod with a sinker and a few treble hooks, and dredge the boat basin–or wherever else we happened to be fishing–until he came up with the missing gear. Somehow he usually managed to retrieve what I had lost. He would shake the water from the reel, re-bait the hooks and tell me to catch the sneaky old catfish that tried to rob us. I would wipe the snot and tears on my sleeve and try–really hard this time–to pay attention to the end of my rod. I would, until of course, the next weird bug or pretty leaf captured my curiosity.

When I was about twelve or thirteen years old, I found something in the toolshed that would completely erase any remaining chances I had of leading a normal life. It was a two-piece fly rod covered in dust and spider webs. The reel was different than what I was used to, and when put together the rod was long and magnificent. I stood in the driveway for hours, amazed with my discovery, waving the old fiberglass rod around like a sword.

Luckily Dad came home from work before I embedded every tree and telephone pole along the driveway with fiberglass splinters. I just *had* to know how to use this thing, no matter what. Dad dug up some old fly line and took me onto the lawn and gave me my first (and last, as it turns out) fly-casting lesson. After only ten minutes or so I was convinced I knew all I needed to. Dad tied on a few feet of monofilament and gave me a handful of moth-eaten Muddler Minnows. Then I ran all the way back to the Orchard Pond!

I don't think anyone who has ever held a fly rod for any length of time hasn't found themselves dreaming of beautifully festooned trout and scenic mountain streams. The Orchard Pond was always fun, but I was the dreaming sort of kid and I had the affliction pretty bad. There were no mountains laced with ice-cold trout streams within walking distance of my house, but there *was* Chappel Creek across the street, which to me was the next best thing to the Big Hole River. If I held my rod tight and squinted just right, it could be anywhere: Montana, Alaska, New Zealand...anywhere. I would pretend the clouds were snow-covered peaks on the horizon and the palm-size creek chubs were madly leaping rainbows. If I fished the creek long enough and the clouds seemed high enough, I would squint harder and, wow...my rod would bend to the weight of a mighty silver salmon!

I've spent so much time knee-deep in that creek that I feel as if I own it. I know where every sharp rock is, and the exact depth of every riffle, pool and eddy. They all have names too. There's Crawfish Run, Jay's Hole, Shady Hole, Cow Shit Hole (this one happens to be in a pasture) and they all hold fish. I can even tell you the best fly patterns and drifts for each one–if you're interested in catching some real dandy cohos that look an awful lot like creek chubs.

I'm going to miss those creek chubs.

Eating It Up

I never cared much for school. I would've much rather been wasting my precious childhood on any number of other endeavors, like losing my latest dozen homemade flies in the willow and boxelder branches that overhang Chappel Creek. Forced to attend, I tried to make the best of an awful situation. Although, this didn't involve actually studying or trying to learn something.

I employed many of the same survival techniques practiced by inmates of Federal Corrections Institutes or P.O.W. camps. I always traveled in a group and kept my back to the wall, facing the nearest exit. To ease the emotional stress of captivity I would come up with rude nicknames for all the wardens and draw grotesque depictions of them on the walls of the bathroom, all the while counting down the days until my release.

The group I traveled with was a small but motley one. We wore dirty work boots, faded flannel shirts and most of us chewed tobacco (the stains in the school's carpets may still be there). There was Steve Barnett, Jason Tillinghast (who stained far more carpets than the rest of us put together), Ray High, Josh Kramb and myself. Besides attire and disposition, we had one other major similarity: we all loved to hunt and fish. Two or three of us were usually in a class together and would manage to sit by each other for the first week or so before the warden-in-charge got wise and split us up on opposite sides of the room, usually one in the corner and the other with his nose in a circle drawn on the chalkboard. If there had been a third, he was sent to see the principal.

It was at lunchtime that we gathered en masse to spit and throw food at each other, and haze the poor slobs sitting at the adjoining tables. After these social pleasantries were exchanged we would get down to the more run-of-the-mill sort of things like eating, trading cheat-sheets and reminiscing about our latest fishing trip, raccoon hunt or case of beer. Then the fun would be cut short by the angry wardens herding us back to our assigned dungeons.

It was during one of these chaotic lunch breaks that I first met the kid who would eventually introduce me to trout and thus be responsible for advancing my fishing addiction to an incurable level. I had gotten my bag lunch from the lockers and returned to find a strange underclassman in my seat. After I politely explained my situation and desire to accompany my friends, the strange kid left my seat with the apologetic parting remark; "Whatever, asshole."

When I finally took my seat I wasn't greeted with the usual jeers and Jell-O flinging that symbolized our peer affection, but with strange looks and accusations.

"What's your problem today? Why ya being such a prick?"

"What's the big deal?" I asked. "Who was he?"

"That's Matt Stashic," they told me. "He's cool, he likes huntin' and fishin' too."

Naturally I felt terrible for insulting a fellow outdoorsman, but it wasn't until almost the end of my senior year that I could apologize. I was in the hallway outside the vocational-agriculture class when I finally had my chance. It's against some unwritten teenage moral code to come right out and say "I'm sorry" so I settled instead with "Hey, what's up?" We were soon deep into a conversation about great places we knew to go fishing. One place in particular winning top-shelf: the trout laden streams of western Pennsylvania, where, by chance, a friend of his dad owned a cabin they happened to be visiting the very next weekend.

Needless to say, Matt and I were friends by the time the next bell rang. I was even invited to accompany them on their opening-day trout expedition! Just the thought of flailing my flies at *real* trout sent goosebumps down my back. I was so exited that I nearly wet myself eight times before school let out for the day.

That Friday after school, Matt and his dad Dale stopped by to pick me up. I loaded my fly rod and gear in the back of their pick-up and clambered into the cab. I was so keyed up that they threatened to strap me to the spare tire back in the bed if I didn't calm down. But, *come on!* We were going trout fishing!

We made it into Oil City sometime after dark and stopped to get gas, a bite to eat, and our licences and trout stamps. The latter had a gorgeous painting of a brook trout that I rubbed with my thumb and stared at all the way into Forest County.

I expected "the cabin" to be a rustic one-room shack with log walls and a bark roof. But it wasn't, and I was disappointed. It was a small place, with an outhouse at least, but looked neat and well maintained. At the front, by the door, was a fancy wooden plaque that read: "WETSU."

Two men already at the cabin greeted us with cold beers in their hands. It wasn't until much later that night, and after a few cases of Old Milwaukee, that I learned their names. The bigger, surly one was Banks and the shorter guy with the greying beard and low, raspy voice was Vic, the owner of the place.

I guessed Vic to be in his mid-fifties but with the look of a man who has had a hard life and drank too much. He was a decent, laid back guy and seemed interested in my fly rod. I noticed an old wicker creel on the wall and a few books about fly-fishing stacked haphazardly in a cardboard box at the end of a sagging couch. Two books, John Gierach's *Trout Bum* and Richard Brautigan's *Trout Fishing in America*, lay on the cushion beside the box. I admired all these things and Vic provided a seemingly limitless supply of Pennsylvania trout-fishing lore in return.

As we sat around the table drinking beer and plotting our opening morning strategies, it began to rain. Everyone quit talking and listened to the rain softly drumming the roof. This light drizzle quickly turned to a raging downpour. I nervously glanced over at Vic and Dale who were looking at the floor with blank expressions and shaking their heads. I took this to be a bad sign.

Trout season didn't open until 8:00 the next morning but we had planned to be on Oil Creek well before then. As it turned out, we wound up drinking beer and cursing the rain well past 1:00 in the morning. We all woke up late, and with dreadful hangovers. It didn't matter much anyway, Matt and Dale had forgotten to buy bait, and the clear, freestone streams of yesterday had evolved into riley brown monsters that threatened to swallow the entire opening-day crowd.

Vic and Banks didn't bother going out, choosing instead to stay back and tinker with the cabin. Dale and Matt climbed into their waders and we set out to brave the raging beast. My waders were the more practical, multi-purpose, lace-up ones that could be worn to gym class or to the movies, as well as in a bass pond or trout stream.

They were both using light spinning rods with a worm and split shot, so their only high-water strategy change was to add more lead to their lines. I was an inexperienced fly-fisher with a pounding headache, standing next to his first real trout stream, without a clue as to what to do. While they were turning several dozen lively nightcrawlers into lifeless rubber bands, I was whipping the foamy, brown water with everything I had. Nothing came through for me– the trout didn't like Yella Belly streamers, Black-Backed Chomper nymphs or my soggy-hackled Little Bastards–a dry fly that earned its name after it buried itself into my finger. But I don't think my flies were within ten feet of any fish, anyway. The creek was so high on its banks that there wasn't much room left for a back cast, and all my roll casts got eaten alive by the current.

Sometime later in the afternoon someone had the bright idea to leave Oil Creek and try one of the smaller creeks in the area that were at higher elevations and maybe less affected by the rains. We all piled into the truck and roared off down the road with renewed enthusiasm. After seven hours of fishing, we only had one trout to show for our troubles–a small rainbow that Dale had lucked into. All I had to contribute were a few vaguely fish-shaped hunks of flotsam and two thoroughly wet and smelly wool socks, which were very unpopular in the confined space of the crowded pick-up.

After a short but twisty ride, we came to West Hickory Creek. It was everything I had dreamed of in a trout stream. If I closed my eyes and took a mental paintbrush to my favorite stretch of Chappel Creek, I could only hope to duplicate some of the magic I felt as we stepped out of the old Ford and into this lush and vibrant dreamworld. The water was higher than usual but instead of an ugly brown soup, the pools echoed the deep green of the hemlock that crowded the banks and engulfed everything below them in a dominating yet passive embrace. The turbulence of the riffles momentarily laced the streams subtlety with a noisy, white froth that added urgency to our movements and a faint sense of volatility to the pristine surroundings.

Our clothes were cold and damp by the time we made it down the trail and to the water's edge. The trees we passed along this narrow gauntlet gently brushed us with their lower branches, soaking us with a sweet smelling wetness, as if they were secretly blessing us. I felt both chilled and blessed.

Matt and his dad said they knew of a deep hole a ways upstream and encouraged me to come along. But the small run and riffles in front of me looked so alive that I couldn't even *think* of passing it by. "No," I said. "I think I'll stay right here."

It took me many minutes and deep breaths before I calmed myself down enough to tie on a fly. My hands were shaking and I dropped the last of my Black-Backed Chompers into the dense carpet of leaves, but I didn't complain. Digging around in the damp earth and decaying flora felt even more therapeutic than my breathing exercises. *Why am I so damn nervous?*

After a short search I came up with the missing fly and knotted it to the end of my leader. I took another long breath and made a shaky-handed cast to the head of the run. Before I could take up slack or mend my line the surface currents snatched my line and took off down stream with it, yanking my fly through the worst of the riffles, dragging it over the deeper pocket of water where I was convinced the trout were, and then deposited it in a shallow eddy a few feet downstream from where I stood. This didn't discourage me. I kept my eyes narrowed and lips pursed, persistently raking the creek with my jet-skiing nymph.

After more than two dozen of these ridiculously fast drifts, my fly got momentarily snagged under one of the more voluptuous boulders at the end of the riffle. This slight hesitation was enough to allow the undercurrents to suck my fly into the depths of the intended pocket water. I saw a sudden flash of white belly underwater and felt the trout hit my fly.

I only had him on for a nanosecond, but it was sufficient in fraying the last of my already jittery nerves. Just after dark Dale and Matt came by on their way back to the truck and found me shaking wildly and violently snapping the far bank with a now fly-less leader.

"Was that you cussin' and shoutin' about an hour ago?"

* * *

It has been almost six weeks now, but seems as if it's *still* happening. My heart and mind are still parked somewhere along West Hickory Creek. I don't even have to close my eyes to see that greenish water rushing past me, that little pocket of water behind the boulder. It looked so alive, I knew a trout was there. The image of that fish taking my fly is forever burned on the insides my eyeballs, projecting itself over everything I look at. When I do close my eyes, that is all I see.

The fishing wasn't great but was my trout fishing debut and I believe I learned a lot; mainly that trout aren't creek chubs–or bluegill either. I think next time I will be more relaxed. How is it that a foot-long, spotted fish can intimidate the piss out of someone and reduce their otherwise fully functioning brain to a worthless cranium full of mush?

Matt has been promising a return trip sometime next week. We're both out of school–him for the summer, me forever–so we'll be able to stay for more than just the weekend. (I like the way that sounded...out of school forever) In the meantime I have nothing to do but prepare.

From our trip into Pennsylvania I kept mental notes, and as soon as I got home I scrawled down in my journal everything I had picked up or remembered. I had some advise from Vic, and at one point the three of us had stumbled into a fly shop along Oil Creek and I took the opportunity to get a crash course on trout flies and anything else worth knowing. The guy behind the counter wasn't too helpful. I figured it was because I had just left a small puddle of Oil Creek in front of the fly display and obviously had no money. The fact that the two guys I came in with had asked about nightcrawlers and mealworms and then walked out, probably didn't help either.

I remember a thing or two from that fly shop, even though most of it sounded Greek to me–or was it Latin? I drew pictures of some of the neatest looking flies he had for sale and *all* the aquatic bugs I had noticed along the creek. For hours everyday I've studied these notes and drawings; while sulking at the dinner table, or hunched over my fly-tying bench, growing only slightly wiser, but noticeably cross-eyed.

After great lengths and many failed attempts, I've created three new flies to add to my small, but growing arsenal. Two are nymphs and one is more of a wet fly. One nymph is *supposed* to resemble the larvae of a stonefly–or, in a pinch, a dragon fly nymph –and the other, the larvae of a green drake mayfly. The wet fly looks like an abstract version of a tiny bug I found clinging mummified to my pant leg a few days after I got home. I suppose it could have hitched its fateful ride at any time, and even an experienced entomologist would need dental records to identify it, but it looks like prime trout food to me.

I named these patterns too. For me, this process is easy: I remove the creation from the vise, hold it up to the light and use the first word that comes to mind. If I draw a complete blank, which happens from time to time, I name the fly after the animal whose fur or feathers were used. In this case I had tied a half dozen #8 Super Stoneflies, a dozen #10 Soggy Coons and a dozen #12 Black Birds.

Although, I think more than fly selection, it was my presentation that hurt me most. I'm learning that fly selection does count big-time with trout, but first I have to get the fly *to* the trout. Once that's achieved I need to make the fly appear as though it's unattached to anything that's significantly larger than a trout. Looking back, I can see where I went wrong. The trout weren't feeding near the surface at either creek, and that's where my fly was. On Oil Creek I was not using enough weight on my line. I could have loaded my leader with split shot or used a sinking-tip fly-line. I noticed some six-foot sections of sinking line for sale at the fly shop that cost only a few bucks. But having blown my wad on the license and trout stamp I was left broke. I guess I'll have to steal some more split shot from Dad's tackle box.

Hooking the trout at West Hickory was pure luck. The water was shallow enough as not to warrant the use of extra lead–the nymph I was using was already weighted. What killed me was the collage of varying currents having access to my line. If I would have made shorter casts or somehow held the rod and line above as many current changes as possible, or maybe....

Ah, hell, we can't rehash every bloody cast. I need to get back on the water.

* * *

"Are you sure you have everything?" Mom asks.

"Yep" I reply, looking at the pile of gear by the door.

"Your license, are you sure it's in your wallet?"

"No, Mom, it's not, it's pinned to my vest where it's supposed to be."

Dad comes over with his hands in his pockets. "You've got your rod, that's the main thing," he points out.

I nod, still looking at the pile by the door. I'm taking a lot more crap this time. *Dad's right*, but I still feel I'm forgetting something.

"How about your reel?"

"Mom, I got my reel," I say and then bend down and squeeze the circular lump in my vest, just to be sure.

"Thanks for letting me borrow your hip boots, Dad."

"No problem," he says with a wave of his hand. "I thought I had some extra split shot you could take too, but I can't find them."

"Uh...no worries Dad, I'll get a hold of some if I need 'em."

"Someone's pulling in," Mom says from the window. "I thought they were in a truck last time?"

"Matt's driving. His dad's coming out tomorrow night."

Mom leaves the window and comes over to give me a hug. "Well, good luck and have fun."

"Yeah, I'm ready this time." I load the gear onto my shoulders. "I'll catch every trout in the state!"

"Don't say that," she says. "You'll mozz yourself!"

After the last "good-byes" I bound out the door and off the end of the porch, the feet of my new hip boots doing a dance on the small of my back. Matt hasn't made it all the way back to the house yet, so I stand by the turn-around and wait. *Outstanding! Going trout fishing, again!*

When the car rounds the last bend in the driveway I can tell there is more than one person in it. The guy in the passenger's seat looks like an older version of Matt. *Must be his brother.* I don't recognize the guy in the back seat either.

The car stops next to me and Matt rolls down his window. "You can put your stuff in the trunk if there's room." He gets out, walks to the rear of the car and unlocks the trunk. "Found some boots, huh?"

"Yeah, they're my dad's."

The trunk pops open and I cram in my hip boots, over-night bag, vest and sleeping bag. I try to squeeze my rod case in too.

"I'm gonna have to keep this up front," I say, holding up the long silver tube.

"Yeah, sure. Jump in."

I get into the back seat and look at the guy sitting next to me.

"How's it goin'?" I ask.

"It's goin'."

Matt gets back in. "Everybody, this is Jay. Jay, this is everybody."

"Hey everybody," I say.

The guy in front turns around. "I'm Mike, Matt's brother. That crazy guy next to you is Clay." Then looking at Matt he says; "Vic told me you guys needed someone to show you how to fish, so I had to come."

"Piss off," Matt says. "I'll have my limit and be back at the car drinkin' a beer and waitin' for you guys"

"He always talks trash like this before we do *anything*," Mike says and looks back at Clay. "Doesn't he?"

"And I always back it up too," Matt says, trying to look past his brother for oncoming traffic.

Mike turns and looks. "You're good this way."

We pull out of the driveway and head to Pennsylvania, the cussing and joking never slowing down. All three of them take turns claiming that they are indeed the best trout-fisherman to ever live and if everyone else in the car is lucky, they might get better just by being in such close proximity of greatness. These self declarations are followed by put-downs and pillow-throwing from the other two.

Dammit! That's what I forgot – my pillow!

We have our usual pit stop in Oil City to refill the gas tank and beer cooler – and to let the bait fisherman buy bait – before the last leg of the trip. When we arrive Vic and Banks come out the front door of the cabin to see what the commotion is but go back inside after seeing that it's only us. Everyone dumps their belongings on a bunk, jumps back into Matt's car and we head for the creek. There are still a good two hours of daylight left, and we feel lucky.

Oil Creek is very low and clear, obviously affected by the dry spring. I stand on the wide rocky bank and try to recognize the places I had fished before, but I can't. Everything looks so different from almost two months ago. All of the creek's features have become smaller and more defined. Where there had been a two-hundred yard stretch of broken water, there are now at least three different pools, separated by long riffles and countless little pockets. It all looks wonderfully fishable.

I step up on one of the log-size pieces of driftwood and survey the surroundings. Everyone else chooses a pool and starts working it over with their worms and spinning rods. I had stopped to admire the natural beauty of the place, to savor the moment, and subsequently lost my shot at the best water. I slowly and deliberately string my rod and walk to the head of the large pool Matt is fishing. My fly box is held open for what seems an eternity. Mike and Clay have a couple good hits apiece and Matt has already netted his first trout by the time I select a fly.

I occasionally look up from my meager assortment of furry bugs and squint studiously at the water. From a distance someone might think I'm deeply contemplating my next move or trying to "match-the-hatch" to a tee, but my brain has drawn a complete blank. This delay is only thinly disguised procrastination. After all those hours of reading and brainstorming, I still haven't the first clue where to begin. The moment of truth and testing is finally here, and what happens? I turn the light on in my head only to catch my brain trying to escape down my spinalcord with a suitcase full of entomology notes and a "who-me?" look frozen to its face.

Matt announces another hit. This breaks my trance and I pull out a Super Stonefly and tie it on. There are no visible hatches and the trout appear to be on the bottom. *Gotta go deep.* I pinch on a piece of split shot and make my cast.

Matt and Mike give shouts as they simultaneously hook fish, and my fly zips out of the riffle and into the pool without being touched. I can see Matt's rainbow clear the water a couple of times before he lands it. I cast again and try not to panic. My fly gets to the end of its drift and surfaces unharmed, leaving a little white wake behind it as I drag it back to add more weight. Clay hooks a big brown trout and loses it on the first jump. *Nice fish!* My hands are shaking and my breathing has become erratic. *Gotta get my fly deeper!*

I pinch on another piece of lead and make the same cast. The split shot skips on the rocky bottom of the riffle and I jerk the rod–hard. *Damn! I could have sworn that was a hit!* Matt hooks another rainbow next to me, fighting the fish nonchalantly and loudly claiming to be the best fisherman to ever walk the banks of a trout stream. I cast again, this time letting the weights bounce on the bottom of the riffle and then plunge into the head of the pool. My line slows down and the fly begins to sink. WHAM! A trout takes it hard and I tighten the line. *HOLY SHIT!* My line races to the middle of the pool and a rainbow trout launches from the water. *OH SHIT! OH SHIT! OH SHIT!* I give him line and he makes a run back to the head of the pool. I gain some line and he jumps again. *Please don't throw the hook!* He can't, he's still on! I can tell he's tired so I put on more pressure. I turn him and pull him gradually closer to shore, finally beaching him. I drop my rod on the rocks and grab the flopping fish and run up the bank, dragging the fly rod behind me. *HOT FRIGGIN' DAMN!*

"Hey Jay," Matt yells from the other end of the pool. "A big one?"

"Ten inches...*at least!*"

The trout are really active for the first twenty minutes and then turn off. I've gotten myself calmed down and organized enough to start fishing again but none of us have even a bump the rest of the evening. We leave the creek shortly after dark and begin the evenings festivities. Everyone's feeling really good about themselves, especially me. I'm stoked. I've caught a rainbow trout. Yes. I. Have. The real thing.

We haul in the beer cooler and a few lawn chairs and commence "living it up" in the main room of the cabin. This soon leads to "falling down" outside on the lawn. As we lay there, belly-up, gazing at the clear night sky, we have many life-changing insights and mind-boggling revelations. We try to express these to each other as coherently as possible, while those listening offer support.

"Man, I don't remember *ever* seeing *this* many stars before."

"You're drunk, shut up."

"Have another beer, you'll see even more."

"Hey Clay, that was a nice brown trout you had on today."

"Oh Clay, you got such a big *brown trout*!"

"Oh Clay, baby, show us your big brown trout!"

"Hey, fuck you guys."

"He was big wasn't he? Did you see him jump?"

"Yeah."

"Just think, Jay, this time next month, you'll be doing push-ups in the mud."

"Yeah."

"Why? You go and join the Army or something?"

"Yeah."

"Hey, check it out, I think my brother just passed out."

* * *

"WHISKEY BOTTLES. . .AND BRAND NEW CARS. . . OAK TREE YOU'RE IN MY WAY."

What the hell? Where am I? What's that noise?

"THERE'S TOO MUCH COKE. . .AND TOO MUCH SMOKE. . .LOOK WHAT'S GOING ON INSIDE YOU."

Oh my god, my head. Who turned the radio up so friggin' loud?

"OOOO THAT SMELL. . .CAN'T YOU SMELL THAT SMELL."

Yeah, what is that smell? I smell bacon cooking.

Someone turns the radio down and I peek out from my sleeping bag. The lights are on but I can see it's still dark outside. Matt is already dressed and trying to shake Mike awake. Clay is sitting up in his bag, holding his head. *Oh, yeah. I'm in Pennsylvania.*

"What time is it?" I ask.

"Already past four," Matt says. "Banks is making breakfast, get up."

"Well fuck me runnin'," Clay grumbles, still holding his head. "I just had a dream I was trying to strangle Ronnie Van Zant."

"Wake up girls!" Matt yells, shaking his brother some more. "It's time to go fishing!"

We all have a plate-full of greasy eggs, bacon and hot coffee before dragging ourselves out to the car and get going. No one really sure why we wanted to get up so early. No one wanting to admit they feel like their head has been repeatedly run over by a rubber-bladed Bush Hog.

I look around the inside of the car, Clay has his eyes closed and his head in his hands again. Mike is asleep with his mouth open, his head banging the car door window every time we hit a rough patch of gravel. A Picasso is gradually being created on the glass with his tongue and lip prints. The bigger potholes adding movement to the piece. Matt seems to be the most alert. He wakes up every now and then with a startled, wide-eyed look, which is good, because he's the one driving.

"Let's try West Hickory like last time," I say.

Matt opens his eyes, looks over at me and blinks a few times. "Na, it's probably almost dried up by now."

"Mmm...where we going then?"

"Get some more bait and try Fry's Landing."

"Where's that?"

"Oil Creek. Just different place."

I rest my head on the dash for only a second, but when I look up again Matt is parking the car in a gravel pull-off. There's sunlight peeking through the trees and the sound of running water nearby. *Here already? That was quick.*

"Decided not to get bait, huh?"

"I did get bait," Matt says through gritted teeth. "It took me an hour but I found a place open. You were drooling on my dash."

I wipe my mouth and look out the window. "No shit, really?"

Matt lays on the horn for a full twenty seconds, then looks in the rearview mirror to see if it has had any effect. "Wake up. Check out time. Let's go, come on!"

"Let 'em sleep man."

"No, cause then they'll wake up all pissed off because we left 'em here."

"Well, it looks like they're gettin' pissed off already. I'm outta here."

I get out, grab my stuff and follow the sound of running water, along the beaten trail with a big wine-barrel trash can and a sign-memorial for a canoeist, Randy Fry. Once there I sit down and put my hip boots on, enjoying the solitude and view of the river. From where I sit I can see about four-hundred yards downstream to a one-lane, iron trellis bridge. As I watch, a car slowly drives over it and I can hear the hum of tires on the open grate. A little ways past the bridge I can see the dark figure of another fisherman standing up to his waist in the water. Every so often I catch a glimpse of fly line over his head. *That's cool. I'm not the only crazy one.*

I can't see that far upstream. There's a bend in the creek about eighty yards up and I can see the top of another bridge trellis, probably railroad. The bend of the creek is the only broken water around. The rest looks wide, rocky and even deep in places.

After I get myself together I take up position just below the bend. I see a few trout rise to something I can't see, but they don't take my dry fly. A couple fish accidentally hit one of my Soggy Coons, but I'm not on-the-ball, so nothing comes of it. Matt and the other two finally show up, but head downstream to fish.

At noon the clouds come over and I have another hit. Then the rain comes. It isn't a downpour but it comes soft and steady, the beginnings of an all-day soaker. I'm already wet from the armpits down so the rain just evens me out. My new boots let me wade out a lot further than before. After filling full of water they act as stabilizers against the swift current, anchoring me to the bottom. This makes moving around a bit slow, but it keeps me from spooking fish.

After awhile Matt comes by without his rod. He stands on the bank and looks out at me from under the hood of his raincoat.

"What are you doing?" he asks loudly over the noise of the rain. "We're all in the car waiting for you."

"You guys do any good?"

"They didn't," he says. "I got five."

Well, Sonovabitch!

"We're going into Titusville for lunch. You coming or not?"

I make another short cast upstream. "Na, pick me up later."

He shakes his head, still looking at me. "You fell in over your waders again didn't you?"

"Yup. Big ol' hole. Didn't even see it."

Matt says they're going to stay at McDonalds until the rain lets up, then come back and fish some more. I nod, not looking back at him. A few moments later I hear the car door slam and I'm alone again. The fly-fisherman on the other side of the bridge has left, as well.

The rain never stops, but I manage to catch two trout about the same size as my first. Later in the afternoon the guys come by and threaten to leave me overnight if I don't get in the car. I'd think about taking them up on it, too, if I wasn't so close to hypothermia. I lay on my back with my legs in the air to drain my hip boots, then Mike and

Clay help pull them off me. I put most of my wet clothes in the trunk and get myself into the car. The feeling won't completely return to my legs for several days, I'm sure, and my lungs will probably fill with phlegm and kill me in my sleep tonight, but it's all been worth it.

Matt's dad and uncle come in the evening and find us all on the verge of severe drunkenness. They've brought along a full keg and this doesn't help matters any. The rain keeps us inside, for the most part, but occasionally one of us younger guys stagger out to relieve ourselves. The retching sounds that sometimes follow are greeted with howling laughter and applause from inside.

The rain lasts all night and well into the morning. We use this as an excuse not to go fishing, but I don't mind, I feel like my body is trying to reject me. Tired of all the abuse I suppose. Matt and I manage to get to the creek for a couple hours later in the afternoon and we each catch a trout. This pleases me immensely. I'm learning how to do this.

I don't carry on too much when we decide to go home either. Although, I do make them promise to plan another trip before I go off to Basic Training.

As we pull out of the cabin's driveway I look back and laugh to myself. *What a time! What a place!*

I can barely make out the fancy wooden plaque in the glow of the tail lights. "Hey Matt," I say. "What does 'WETSU' mean anyway?"

"Huh?"

"The sign by the door. What does it mean?"

"We Eat This Shit Up," he says.

Into the Jungle

"AT EASE!"

The four privates lying on the floor beside me jump up, go to parade rest and try to force themselves awake. The sergeant who yelled the command is angry because one of us didn't call "at ease" when he came into the room. He quickly forgets this infraction and focuses his attention on the skinny young soldier still asleep on the floor.

"WAKE YOUR SORRY ASS UP!"

I roll onto my side and tuck my hands deeper into my armpits. *I'm tired, don't wanna go fishin' right now.*

The duffel bag I'm using as a pillow is kicked to the other side of the briefing room and my head makes a funny sounding thud on the hard, waxed tile. Suddenly I'm awake, and standing at parade rest with my eyes sticking out like a head-shot squirrel. Feel like one too; a goose egg already forming on the back of my head. *Oh, that's right. I ain't in Pennsylvania no more.*

"WHO DROPPED THE BALL?"

The five of us stand as straight as we can, our feet shoulder-width apart and hands locked flat behind us.

"Uh, what?" one of us asks as bravely as possible.

The sergeant lunges toward the nearest private. "ARE YOU TALKING TO ME SHITBIRD? I'M A SERGEANT IN THE UNITED STATES ARMY!"

No one is brave anymore.

"NOW WHICH ONE OF YOU WAS PULLING SECURITY?"

No one moves. We stare back at the NCO, with ever-widening eyes. The ballsy private who answered the first time, speaks again. "Uh, we just got to the unit this morning, sergeant."

The sergeant walks over to the private and leans in to his face. It looks like the kid might get bitten.

"Sergeant...we where told to wait in here...wait until, um . . . someone gives us a ride to the airport...sergeant."

"GET YOUR SORRY ASS DOWN! ALL OF YOU! FRONT LEANING REST POSITION! MOVE!"

Oh, hell. Here we go.

We do pushups until our brown undershirts are drenched with sweat and our arms are shaking almost to the point of collapse. No one is allowed to quit. A size ten, black leather boot is more than suitable motivation not to. The lecture on the importance of security continues at high decibels, the pissed off sergeant never taking a noticeable breath. I briefly wonder if he'll turn blue and faint in mid-sentence. He doesn't, and I try hard not to smile.

"HAVE YOU ALL BEEN THROUGH BASIC TRAINING?"

"Yes, sergeant," we reply.

"HAVE YOU ALL BEEN THROUGH AIRBORNE SCHOOL?"

"Yes, sergeant."

"Well then, what the major malfunction?" This change in voice level means the abuse is coming to a close. *Good thing, too.*

"You little maggots ain't trainees anymore. You ain't legs either. You're part of the *real* Army now. Ain't no time to get stupid around here."

We look up at him with blank expressions.

"Let me be the first to welcome you to your new family. Welcome to the 82nd Airborne Division. If no one has told you yet, you're all assigned to 2nd Battalion of the 505th Parachute Infantry Regiment. If you noticed, these barracks are empty. That's 'cause all your new brothers are down in Panama. Getting real good tans."

My blank expression becomes slightly animated. *Outstanding!*

"Now get your pathetic, wimperin' little asses up and get on that Humvee parked out on the rocks. It'll take you to Pope Air Force Base. There's a C-5 waiting on you."

"Uh, sergeant?" the private next to me asks. "Do we need a plane ticket?"

"SHUT UP, PRIVATE DUMB SHIT! NOW MOVE OUT!"

We sling our rifles over one shoulder and drag our rucksacks and duffle bags outside. A specialist is leaning against the camouflaged Humvee, smoking a cigarette and looking impatient. We load ourselves and our gear into the back. I slide into the passenger-side seat and prepare a mental list of questions for the driver. *How does he like the 82nd? The 505th? What are they doing down in Panama? How long have they been there? Are any of the rumors true?*

The specialist takes a long drag on his cigarette, flicks it into the gravel formation area and gets in. He turns the toggle and waits for the glow plugs to heat up.

"Hey man, how's it goin'?" I ask.

He turns the toggle further and the diesel engine fires up. "I'm not your buddy. If you need to ask me something, address me by my rank."

"Yes, Specialist."

"Now get back there with all the other cherries."

I crawl back and find a spot on one of the two bench seats with the other privates. None of them are talking. They all sit still, making unwavering eye contact with the toes of their boots.

Am I the only one who's excited to be here?

The Humvee pulls out onto Grave Street and turns left. Some of the lumps next to me come to life briefly, digging newly-issued field jackets from their duffle bags. Technically we're "down south," North Carolina, but it's already December and there's no cover on the back of the Humvee. I don't bother digging for mine, I'm too jazzed up to feel the cold.

The ride from Fort Bragg to Pope Air Force Base only takes a few minutes. We pull into an area next to the tarmac that has the same mock-door training facilities I recognize from airborne school. The driver tells us this is Green Ramp, and that we will all become *very* familiar with it. I notice a grin on his face and wonder what kind of crazy memories he has of the place.

We unload and are told by the specialist which bird is ours– "The big one." It's easy to find, looming over all the smaller C-141's and C-130's that I also recognize from airborne school. It's neat looking out over an airfield full of dark grey, sleeping monsters and being able to say to myself: "Yep, jumped out of one of *those* before." I feel really cool.

The entire nose and cockpit area of the C-5 is flipped up like the cap on a plastic catsup bottle, exposing its huge, gaping interior. The flight crew has lowered ramps and a convoy of Humvee's and duce-and-a-half's are being loaded. I lead our E-2 entourage up to someone who appears to be in charge (hands on hips, pissed off, but not doing anything.) I try to ask him if this is our ride to Panama, but one of the duce-and-a-half drivers revs the engine going up the ramp and we can't hear each other. He motions us on though, so we board. Another crewman spots us pitching camp between two trucks and points us up to the passenger seating.

A separate section, above the cargo area, is strictly for personnel. It doesn't have the long rows of canvas bench seats like all the other military aircraft I have been in. These are normal-looking, airline-type seats. Except they are all facing the wrong way.

I stow my gear and try to get comfortable, maybe I'll even get some more sleep.

* * *

Damn, these seats are uncomfortable! They felt so nice when I first sat down but now that we're in the air it's impossible to lean back. The airplane's angled slightly nose up, but all these seats are facing backwards! I can lean back, but soon as I relax, I fall forward and head butt the seat in front of me.

I'm bored and I can't get to sleep. And there's no one up here to interrogate either. Got a million questions. What happens when we get to Panama? Rumor has it the 2nd of the 505 got deployed there less than a week ago because some Cuban guys killed some U.S. Military Police in the Canal Zone. What are Cubans doing in Panama anyway? None of this makes sense. But, really, I shouldn't complain. I'm on an airplane heading to a foreign land, with an M-16 on my lap. These are all the ingredients for the adventure I've been looking for.

I'm glad I got some sleep before we took off. I didn't look at my watch when we got onboard, but it had to be around dinnertime. It's well past midnight now and I'm still hungry; wonder if they have in-flight meals? Yeah, right.

I felt like an idiot in front of that sergeant this afternoon. I wanted to make a good impression, show them I was good enough to wear these wings and beret. Not a good start. Had thought for sure I was back in Pennsylvania; thought Banks had the radio turned up again.

What a summer, though! Matt and I drove up to the cabin one more time before I left for basic training at Fort Benning. No one else could get time off work, so it was just the two of us. There was no older brother there to buy beer, so we stayed sober the entire time. This, as you can imagine, greatly increased our skill on the river. Oil Creek was even lower than it had been in June. The water was clear and there were hatches every evening, it was great.

Both Matt and I caught a lot of nice sized trout. I should remind you: when used in the context of fishing, "nice sized" is a relative term. So is "a lot" for that matter. I landed over twenty fish during the three days spent on the river, all were between ten and thirteen inches and hooked on my own nymph patterns.

On the evening of the last day we had decided to try Fry's Landing during the last hour before dark. My trout fever had eased a little more with each fish landed, so by this point I was only *jogging* down to the river. Within sight of the water, I slowed down to catch my breath and look nonchalant as I passed the two strangers already there. One was holding out a small fly box and they were both peering intently into it. I noticed fly rods under their arms and assumed, because I carried one as well, we were family–silly me. I stopped and said "hello," but was ignored. They never said a word, and they didn't have to, I could hear the unspoken sentiment–*"Scram, you stupid kid."*

After realizing my presence wasn't welcome I left and found a more receptive place a ways downstream. The creek must have been between hatches; nothing buggy or fishy was moving. Judging by the frustrated expressions on the two snots upstream, the bad luck wasn't solely mine. I was priding myself in being as equally unsuccessful, with my rather primitive gear and knowledge, as two grown men who obviously knew their ass from an Adams fly–indicated by their snazzy, breathable waders and top-dollar rods. Their casts were long and crisp too, not short and borderline catastrophic like mine.

The stage was set for a world-class fishing miracle. The sun was setting on the last day, there was no breeze and a thick layer of mist was forming above the water. And then, the best part, the part that qualifies it as "world-class": *there were eyewitnesses!* Yes, the stage was definitely set.

My nymph reached the end of a drift and began to rise to the surface, then a fish took. He hit hard and gave a wonderfully acrobatic fight, showing only glimpses of himself through the mist as he danced. The two strangers stopped casting and watched–in awe, maybe–as it unfolded. Then, as I brought the foot-and-a-half-long fish near, I saw a problem. He wasn't a rainbow trout. Before me, defeated and exhausted, lay my prize– a big, white sucker!

As I passed the two strangers on my way to the car, one commended me on the catch. The other wanted to know what fly I'd used. (They, too, had been fooled by the trout-like antics of the sucker, and probably assumed I'd just caught and released a rainbow trout larger than any they'd seen all season.) My dismissive sideways glance was perfect. I'd been practicing from the moment the fish was hooked.

Matt had witnessed the event from a greater distance, but was suspicious of my strange behavior. My holier-than-thou facade lasted almost the entire trip home, but I did eventually tell him the truth.

* * *

My head comes away from the hard plastic backing of the seat in front of me. I rub my eyes and feel deep creases in my forehead. We've just touched down and now the pilot's laying on the brakes.

I check to make sure all my gear is still in the two seats next to me. It is, I knew that; it's more nervous movement than anything else. My M-16 is still comfortably between my legs. None of us had been issued any ammunition before we left, but I do have a bayonet attached to my load bearing equipment. I doubt there will be any need for hand-to-hand combat on the runway, but I'm ready, just in case. No one has told us anything. From the sound of the rumors back at Ft. Bragg, the entire Panamanian countryside is crawling with murderous Cubans.

I peer out the window closest to me and get my first glimpse of Panama. The morning sun is almost to the horizon and I can see the black silhouettes of palm trees against the gradually widening, red sky. I whisper the word "Panama" over and over keeping my face to the little round window. It sounds so unreal...and intriguing. *Panama. Welcome to . . . Panama.*

Finally stepping off the C-5, we're hit by what feels like a 90 degree wall of water. We boarded the plane during an eastern U.S. winter and walk off into a tropical rainforest. The humidity wraps its big, warm arms around us and threads its long, damp fingers into our lungs. Some of the privates are still wearing thick field jackets and have to stop in the middle of the tarmac to stow them into their bags. It's hot. Sweat is forming a hanging reservoir at the end of my nose. I notice all the Air Force and Army guys hanging around the flight strip aren't wearing their BDU tops. I suggest we all get in uniform and try to blend in. We were told to remove our maroon berets before we stepped off the bird. No one had told us why, but we did it. Now, with a standard issue soft cap and brown T-shirt, we fit right in.

As we stand at the edge of the tarmac and pack away the already sweat-damp upper halves of our camouflaged, battle dress uniforms, we're approached by one of the nearby soldiers. He isn't wearing a beret either, but we assume he's a paratrooper because of his super-short, high and tight haircut. He isn't wearing his uniform top either, so we're oblivious of his rank. We all go to parade rest anyway, to be safe.

The soldier stops abruptly, still several paces away. "Whoa. At ease men." He smiles and shakes his head as he comes closer. "I don't even need to ask. You guys are the newbies for Second Battalion. Aren't you?"

"Uh, yes...." We all nod.

"Relax, I ain't brass." His smile gets even bigger. "You all would shit if I turned out to be a fullbird or something, huh?"

We all snap to attention and one of us starts to salute.

"Whoa!" He jumps back a few steps and looks around. "Damn. You guys scare me." He shakes his head again. "I was kidding. I'm Specialist Adair. I'm supposed to take you guys home."

"Home?" one of us asks.

"Yeah, Two Pantherville. It's a long drive. Let's get going."

Specialist Adair helps us haul our gear over to his Humvee. We pile in, attach the troop safety strap across the back and get ready for the long drive into uncertainty. The passenger-side seat is left empty this time. Specialist Adair finds this funny.

"Do I stink or something? Are one of you gonna sit up here or not?"

I slide into the seat and laugh along with him, not bothering to explain. I've felt like a human pinball since the first day of basic training. Always getting bounced around from one place to another without any idea what was going on. Never being in the right place at the right time. And being told to double-time from one place to the next, only to be stuck for hours in a line of other privates. "Hurry up and wait" is our motto.

The sun is definitely making its presence known by the time we get on our way. It's already over 90 degrees by the time we make it out of the military installation and onto the main road. The canvas top and doors of the Humvee have been removed, so the heat is bearable. But I'm too caught up in the passing scenery to pay close attention to my comfort level anyway.

Everything's so different. I can't even recognize many of the trees. This feels strange, having become used to knowing the names of every form of flora and fauna I'm surrounded by. This ignorance of my surroundings here is intimidating, yet at the same time, exhilarating. I feel naked and out of place, but deep down confident in my ability to adapt.

Real palm trees. It's strange seeing them growing wild. All the plants along the road look so...big, and green, and...drapey. The further we travel the more foreign everything becomes.

I try to isolate exactly what's different about the people. It isn't just the way they look and dress; even around the rural area I've lived there were people of similar complexion. They closely resemble the migrant workers I've seen working the orchards in the summer. But not really. They're different. It isn't their clothes either, really. I've grown up in the same plain, unglamourous threads made thin and breathable by years of wear. Mine came from my grandmothers habitual garage-sale shopping. *Maybe these locals had compulsive grandmothers too?* There's something strikingly different though; and after awhile I figure it out. It's the way they *move*. They have more energy, but don't waste it–a kind of laid-back yet alert energy. The people in Ohio are always rushing around, but seem down-trodden at the same time, like they have to keep moving or else the huge weight of their debts and commitments will catch and break them.

At some point I realize how small my world has been, and how naive I am. Having lived all my life in northern Ohio, a big adventure to me is a wild run into Pennsylvania. I don't really know my own country. To me, West Virginia sounds like a foreign country. The Rocky Mountains sound like the other side of the world.

I glance at Specialist Adair. *This guy's pretty cool. Probably ought to quit sight seeing and take advantage of him.* "Are you with the unit I'm goin' to, Specialist?" I ask over the noise of the engine and rushing wind.

"Yeah, I work in the three-shop."

"The what?"

"S-3, part of Headquarters Company. You'll be going to one of the line companies."

"How *are* the line companies?"

"They're all right, if you like all that hoo-ah bullshit. I was on the line for awhile, but the three-shop is a cake assignment. Compared to the line."

"I love all that hoo-ah bullshit."

"Yeah, I know," he says with a big grin. "You're still new."

Yeah, that's me. The fuckin' new guy. The cherry. I couldn't possibly know anything.

We turn off the main drag and onto a well-used dirt road. I look behind me and the four other privates have their brown T-shirts pulled up over their faces. The road is dry and the Humvee is leaving a long, brown dust cloud. We've slowed down a little on the unimproved road and this makes conversation easier. The lack of constant wind suddenly kicks the temperature factor up a notch though. It has to be over 100 degrees now. As excited as I am to finally get to my new unit, the thought of stopping and losing *all* the breeze is enough to make my skin burn (not really, but my pale little arms *are* getting noticeably red.)

"So, Specialist. Why exactly are we down here anyway?"

He looks over at me and laughs. "Nobody told you guys before you left? That's wild."

I nod. *Yeah, it* has *been wild.*

He stops laughing. "Hey, listen man. What's your name? Where you from?"

"Jay Zimmerman. I'm from Ohio, Specialist."

"That's cool. I'm Steve. You ain't got to keep calling me 'Specialist' if there ain't anybody important around. Okay?"

I nod again. *Yes, Specialist.*

"I'm getting out soon, man. I'll be a short-timer whenever we get back to Bragg."

Uh-huh. Why are we in Panama?

He goes on, still not answering my now 24-hour-old question. "I don't care about all that petty Army crap. You'll know what I mean when you're short."

Well, I haven't been given any ammo yet, and this dude seems pretty calm. We can't be in too much danger.

"All I can think about is getting back to California. Taking a month or two off and kickin' back. Do some fishing."

This gets my attention. "You fish?!"

"Shit yeah!"

Outstanding! "Is there good fishing around Bragg?"

Steve raises his eyebrows and looks over at me. "You like to bass fish?"

I nod enthusiastically.

"Well, I never tell anybody where I fish." Steve grips the steering wheel tighter and gets a serious expression on his face. "But, when we get back, come hook up with me and I'll show you around. Because I'll be leaving soon anyway."

"That'll be cool...thanks." *Out-friggin'-standing!*

I look out at the passing countryside, thinking about fish and try to suppress a big grin. We're in a real jungle-looking area now. The last human sign we've passed was a grass-roofed hut about a half-hour before.

Yeah, I can handle a little bass fishing. . . .

"So, nobody told you why we're down here huh?"

I shake my head, still gazing up at the mass of foliage and dreaming of huge, southern largemouth.

"All right," Steve begins. "From what I know, the Navy and Coast Guard keep finding Cubans drifting around out in the Ocean. Trying to get to Florida in a rowboat or something, you know?"

"Yeah...?"

"Well, from what I hear, they were pulling 'em out of the water, or whatever, and sticking them in refugee camps somewhere in Florida. You ever see the movie *Scarface*?"

"Uh...no."

"Fuck, man! It's an American classic! With Al Pacino, you ain't seen it?"

"Uh...no, sorry."

"Anyway, they ran out of room and started putting them all here, in the Canal Zone. The locals aren't too happy about it, but we sorta own it." He looks over at me again. "I can't believe you've never seen *Scarface*."

I shrug my shoulders. "I heard some guys got killed."

"Yeah, that's why we got sent," Steve says. "A bunch of refugees started a riot and took over one of the camps, killed a few MP's."

"So, there's more than one camp?" I ask.

"Four of them. Each one has like twenty-five hundred Cubans. They're living in G.P. Mediums with about fifteen to twenty cots per tent. Which is about how we're set up too, except for the fences and concertina wire."

"No shit." I shake my head. "So what are we gonna do? Take back the camp?"

"Naw, that got done the night after the riot." Steve laughs and pounds the top of the steering wheel with the palm of his hand. "Yeah, from the story I heard it was real cool the way they did it. A Special Forces team busted in that night with pictures of all the killers and instigators. I guess they knew were they were sleeping too because all they did was pull the poles and collapse the tents. Then, get this." Steve looks at me to add emphasis to his story. "They beat all the lumps with clubs until they quit moving! I shit you not! Then they rolled the canvas back, little by little, and held a flashlight and picture up to each one 'til they found their guys!"

"Outstanding!" My heart is racing and my fists are clenched. "What did they do with the bad guys then?"

"Put 'em in another camp." Steve says. "That one's called Camp Five, the prison camp."

"No shit!?" *Wow, this is great!* "So, what are *we* gonna do?"

"Hell, I don't know." Steve motions up toward the sun. "Sit around, get tans and hope they riot again. Rumor has it they have one planned for Christmas eve."

"Really!?"

"Yeah, that's the rumor anyway." His smile disappears. "Everyone's stoked too. Personally, I don't think it's gonna happen."

"Just wait and see, huh?"

Steve nods in agreement as he slows down. We pull onto another paved road and pick up speed. I concentrate my attention on the large river paralleling the road. It's wide and seems deep. There are some almost unnaturally-sheer cliff faces along some areas of its bank. Then, when we pass a gigantic cargo ship, it dawns on me. *This is the Panama Canal, stupid!*

We stay on pavement for awhile and then turned back onto a dirt road. This one has patches of fresh gravel in the low areas and looks more heavily used, but better maintained.

"Almost there." Steve says loud enough for the guys in back to hear.

I have most of the important questions answered, and it feels good. I know the score, know my purpose. Now for the dumb questions.

"So, why ain't we allowed to wear our berets?"

Steve doesn't say anything right away. He cocks his head and thinks for a few seconds before answering. "Not one-hundred percent sure on that one. My guess is we don't want to be recognized."

"What do you mean 'recognized'? By who?"

Steve gives me a disbelieving glance. The same look most of my high school teachers gave me after grading my homework. "You remember we invaded this country five years ago, don't you?"

"Oh, yeah!" I feel stupid. "That whole thing with Noriega. I remember now."

He nods. "Yeah, there might still be some hard feelings. I guess we don't want any international incidents."

"That's cool. I can see it." I say. *Wow, that sounds neat, international incidents. I just want to lay low, don't wanna cause any* international incidents.

Another Humvee roars by going the other way. The soldiers in it give us hard looks. I cover my eyes as the dust cloud swamps us. I hear catcalls and turn around in my seat. Some of the soldiers are standing up with their hands to their faces, yelling back at us. They're too far away to be heard.

I look over at Steve and he's smiling. "What was that about?"

"Oh, look! We're here!" he says.

We stop in a vast, grassy clear-cut in the jungle. There are rows of big, green, Army-issue wall tents. The sides of the tents are rolled up, exposing tightly packed cots, cluttered with mosquito nets and lounging paratroopers. None of them seem busy. They all stop whatever it was they were doing and begin congregating at the openings of the hooches, checking out us new arrivals.

One older man is doing reps with a makeshift barbell–a metal rod with concrete filled coffee cans on either end. He drops the creation and it buries into the dirt at his feet. He reaches down, picks his soft cap off the ground, puts it on his head and saunters over to the vehicle. I notice rank on his cap–First Sergeant.

"Oooo, fresh meat!" he says.

Two Pantherville

I've lost track of all the hours and days spent sitting on this cot. Today I've been staying in the shade of the tent, but still sweating, peering through green mosquito netting at the same boring faces and stinking armpits. Since I've been here I've played more hands of poker and spades than ever before in my life. After our morning run and pushups everyone lays a towel out and works on their tan–or looks for some shade and a good spades partner. Our rowdy refugees have kept fairly quiet. The Christmas Eve riot never amounted to more than a good rumor, so the only breaks in monotony are the few hours of "stomp-and-drag" riot training, hand-to-hand training (which always ends in a squad-vs-squad brawl) or Spanish classes.

I took two years of Spanish in high school but didn't retain a thing. At the time I thought I was smarter than the teacher. I *knew* the class was just another check in the block for the public schooling system. They had to justify their employment somehow, so foreign language classes were shoved down our throats along with other nonessentials, such as grammar and writing. Now I gobble up every Spanish tidbit offered. Funny, isn't it, how things gain importance in one's life? Some of the damndest things suddenly become essential. Next thing you know I'll be wishing I payed attention in English class.

These past two months in Panama have been...interesting. The first few weeks were really bad. As soon as we arrived in camp the other new privates and I were made to stand in a five man formation for hours. We weren't allowed to put any of our gear down either, unless it was to do "T-Bones," "Mule Kicks" or pushups for one of the higher-ranking enlisted men who came by to entertain himself and fellow hooch mates. T-Bones are the worst by far because of the stupid song you're made to sing while doing them. The exercise is humiliating enough on its own–leaning back on your hands, ass about two inches off the ground and kicking out your legs. But privates must do their kicking along with the cadence of the song: "*T-bones are good for me.*" Everyone seems to think this is hilarious.

The group hazing concluded with a somewhat loud and disorganized auction, where the five of us new guys were divvied up, first into companies and then platoons. Once assigned to my platoon, I was handed over to a squad leader who was short a man in one of his two teams. And then, of course, the abuse picked right back up, only on a more personal and sustained level.

The hazing was easier to take in Basic Training; I was expecting it then, to some degree, but was not prepared for this never-ending crap. It has eased a little lately, but I'll be the cherry private for a long time. The other guys in the platoon don't care where I came from or what I may know; until I can prove myself here in the infantry, I ain't shit. And yes, there is a lot of experience-derived wisdom and military savvy bouncing around in the thick skulls of these men. I can learn a lot.

I've been trying to figure out all the different personalities in this tent. Some are relatively easy to peg, like Private Johnson who has one of the cots next to me. I knew he was a dweeb *days* before he pulled a Dungeons & Dragons magazine out of his duffle bag and removed all doubt.

I haven't made up my mind about my squad leader, Sgt. Brooks. He's a hard man to please, but that's what a good leader is supposed to be. He may be an ex-high school nerd buffed up from years in the Army with a few stripes and a Ranger Tab to command respect, or he could just as easily be a quiet jock from Nebraska, or somewhere, doing his duty as best he can. Either way, this much is clear: he can recite the Ranger Creed verbatim and knows the nomenclature of every type of small arm in the Army's arsenal–and may even be a decent shot with some of them–but, knows diddly squat about a 12 gauge shotgun. So, this leads me to believe wherever he came from and whatever he was in a past life, his dad certainly never took him hunting as a kid. This may sound like a moot point, but let me explain my concern. Since we aren't "at war" with the Cuban refugees–contrary to the beliefs of most of my tent mates–and are supposedly only here to maintain a peaceful environment in the *campamentos*, we have been disarmed. To replace all of our really neat rifles, grenade launchers and machine guns, we were issued two clear plastic shields (a large one to carry and a smaller helmet-mounted one to cover our face), a dozen flex-cuffs (these look like jumbo zip-ties and are used as disposable handcuffs) and one long black billy club that has been dubbed a CBG stick–to follow a long-standing military tradition of assigning acronyms to absolutely everything! (This stands for Cuban Be Good...if you're wondering.) The only firearms presently in our possession are old, pre-Viet Nam-era shotguns carried by the squad leaders only. You understand now?

When the armorer came around and issued each platoon their shotguns, I had to sit here on my cot watching a man–who can completely break down and then reassemble an M249, belt-fed, squad automatic weapon in less than sixty seconds–frantically grope a pump shotgun like an offensive lineman on the Cleveland Browns trying to pick up a fumbled football. It was almost too embarrassing to watch.

The rest of this tent and the other one also occupied by 1st Platoon, Alpha Company is full of some of the most wildly eccentric and vulgar nut cases of this century. Detailed personality profiles are meaningless at this point; they're all one big family of lunatics. Let me show you around, you'll see what I mean....

Hear that loud game of spades at the end of the tent? Take a look; the two older guys are Sergeant Brooks and Sergeant Barnes. They're winning, I'm sure, but you would never guess it by the hoots and hollers coming from Private First Class Roberts. Roberts is from Texas and likes to hunt and fish, but is a cocky son of a bitch. His pastime around here, other than playing cards and tanning, is sneaking up to a sleeping private, putting his bare ass real close to the oblivious face and spreading his butt cheeks, then urgently hollering the hapless guy's name. "Texas Tunnel Vision" he calls it.

PFC Roberts' partner, the stocky Mexican guy, is Specialist Haros, from Fresno, California. He is a cool guy and has a good sense of humor. If he smiles you'll see what I mean; he's missing a front tooth and it's enough to make you wet your cot. Story has it he left his fake tooth on a tray at Taco Bell two days before they deployed down here. Now he can't get a new one until we get back. Roberts *loves* to tell that story, especially drawing out the part about Taco Bell being the place where the tooth was lost.

Now, look over on the other end of the tent. That side is reserved for the more dangerously insane: our platoon sergeant and Specialist Guertz. We call the platoon sergeant "Secret Agent Man" because he apparently believes everyone's a spy and involved in some scandalous activity to bring him down. I seriously doubt anyone is conspiring against the man, but they sure are telling some good stories about him. One time, as the story goes, he was spotted running around downtown Fayetteville at night with his wife; both were armed and dressed in black fatigues. When questioned about it later, he said they were tracking runaway children. Makes you wonder, huh?

Guertz...well, just look at him sitting over there, staring at the end of his cot. The guy is wacked out of his mind. He never says much, but every now and then he snaps. It's wild; one minute we're all sitting around smoking and joking, the next thing you know Guertz is jumping up and down screaming off-the-wall orders at one of his privates. "POOP YOUR PANTS, PRIVATE WHITTY! POOP YOUR PANTS!" Everyone wants to laugh but is too afraid–even some of the sergeants.

I'm lucky to have a relatively sane team leader, unlike Private Whitty. Specialist Lowery has the other cot next to me; Private "Dragon Slayer" has the other. Lowery is a good leader and a great guy; he's been getting me squared away in short notice. He's a Native American–mostly Cherokee, I think–and knows his way around the tree line. He was in a recon unit before he came to the Eighty Deuce, so he has a lot to draw on.

We are way under strength, having only six men in our squad (as opposed to the ideal eleven) but have highly trained soldiers picking up the slack. Lowery is 3rd squad's Bravo team leader; Sergeant Bair is the Alpha team leader. Sergeant Bair is also high-speed, coming from the 10th Mountain Division. He was awarded the Silver Star with "V" devise (valor) for his actions in Somalia. I've not had the chance to get particulars, but we get along alright, so maybe one day I'll ask. Last night we pulled roving guard together and I was able to get him talking–a little, anyway. He says he's happily married, but his detached and somewhat sad look hint otherwise. He does know how to laugh, though, and that alone can carry someone far.

Not all the NCO's (Non-Commissioned Officers, i.e. sergeants) are as good natured as Sergeant Bair. The most obnoxious by far is Sergeant Conley, who enjoys tormenting me and any other hapless newbie who accidently wanders through his line of sight. He has wickedly vile breath and is very aware of it; he's notorious for locking a private up at parade rest and yelling long, windy sentences into his victim's face. "HECK OF A HOT TUB, HUH HELEN?" is one he's particularly fond of. I, as well as the other newer privates, go to great, ingenious lengths to avoid him. However, we are left helpless during morning and afternoon formations when we are forced to come out of hiding and stand in close proximity to Sergeant Conley. And he never squanders this opportunity to entertain the entire company at our expense. The companies' favorite performance is something called "Conley's Farm Animals" where we privates must assume the identity of a pre-assigned animal, complete with sound effects. I have the misfortune of being a duck and must waddle around reciting the line: "I'm Joe-Joe the duck and I'm all fucked up!" I don't even want to think about the long lasting psychological effect all of this is having on me.

The best way to avoid most of the abuse is to stay out of the way. Not too long ago I worked out a dandy routine. After PT (physical training) in the morning, or any of the other daily formations, I disappear into the jungle until chow time or the next formation. Lowery has no problem getting a hold of me if something unexpected comes up; he stands at the edge of the clearing, where a little stream sneaks out of the jungle, and whistles for me. I make sure to stay within earshot, and I always make it back before Sergeant Brooks becomes suspicious.

The stream is a tiny thing, small enough to step over in most places, but it actually cuts the camp in half. The engineers attached to our unit have nothing much to do, so every other week or so a new walk bridge gets built. These will become essential if we're still here in the peak of the wet season, but for now they only fend off boredom. They say this, the end of January, is the end of the dry season here and we should be prepared. We *have* been getting more rain; you can see the dark clouds trying to hide behind the green hills long before they slink between them and then pounce into our clearing with all the playful energy of a young cat. The clouds aren't big enough to block the sun, so at least once a day we have torrential downpours while the sun is still a blazin'.

Shortly after arriving and getting settled in, I noticed schools of minnows zipping around in the ankle-deep water of our camp creek. For years I've kept a short coiled leader and a few wet flies in my wallet, so I was well prepared. There are no sweethearts or credit cards tucked into those handy plastic sleeves, just a very basic fly fishing assortment!

At first, I tried dangling my smallest fly from one of the bridges, but the school hiding in its shadow couldn't find a mouth big enough to stretch over the bend of a #12 wet-fly hook. They did try, though. Yeah, they sure did try. After exploring the entire exposed length of the creek, with extra scrutiny under the bridges, I realized there were no wall-hangers in downtown Two Pantherville. (The black panther is our brigade's mascot; we are the second battalion in that brigade, hence the name of our camp.) So, naturally, this meant prospecting waters deeper into the jungle.

I tried the downstream side, figuring the water would get deeper, and it did, but the surrounding area was too mucky and swamp-like. The only other option was the upstream side. This turned out to be the hot spot. The channel stayed very narrow and shallow, but became almost three foot deep along certain undercuts. By then I'd made my fly rod: a five foot branch with a limber tip section that has similar characteristics of the old fiberglass rod of my dad's. I used two loops of como-wire for eyes–one at the very tip, the other halfway down. A length of 550-pound-test parachute riser cord suffices as the fly line, which is held in loose coils with my left hand. This rig works better than you might think. With a well-timed heave I can manage casts up to fifteen feet, which, coincidentally, isn't much less than what I can do under normal circumstances with a normal fly rod. The size of the creek itself, and the confined space along it, limits me to casts not much longer than my branch...er, rod, so the quality of my gear doesn't factor very heavily anyway.

My custom-made rod is stowed in the branches of a bush near my favorite stretch of creek. I don't dare pass by the entire battalion with what is obviously a device for fishing. With this many bored joes and such limited water, the first hint of good fishing would be enough to kill every finned animal from here to the canal.

I am sharing this creek with at least one other fisherman, though, but it's not Steve Adair; I haven't seen him around for a while. I have yet to meet this phantom fisher, but judging by the size of the boot tracks, he's a big guy. On the way to the mess tent one evening I saw a soldier glaring into the creek like only a fish junky would–he's the one, I'm sure. He is one of "Perky's Perverts," meaning he's in the 3rd Platoon of my company (named after their crazy platoon sergeant). I don't know his name or rank, but he's easy to spot in a crowd–the biggest son of a bitch I've ever seen.

There are no great riffles or sea-like pools in Two Panther Creek, only random pockets dug into the bank and partially hidden by the over-hanging jungle. The fish are not big or spooky; the only problem I've found is getting the fly to them through the mass of vegetation. The fish may be small, but they're fantastic! I didn't know what to expect when I brought the first one to the surface. These aren't normal, blue-collar creek chubs.

I have no idea what kind of fish these are–which is hard for me to admit–but I've noticed at least three different species. First, and most prevalent, are the bream-like fish. These are small, between three and four inches, have two white bars running from top to bottom with a black patch in between. The face is splashed with an iridescent blue like that of a pumpkinseed sunfish; there are spots of this coloring on the soft dorsal and anal fin, also.

Next are the "eel-cats." That may be the best way to describe them: a cross between an eel and a catfish. I catch these only when my fly has been on the bottom for a while. They come between five and six inches and are about as big around as a fat marking pen. With whiskers and a forked tail they are probably some sort of catfish, but they have an abnormally large number of fins.

Then come the "devil chubs," the only truly evil fish that exist, I believe.

I saw one of these monstrosities before I hooked one and was excited because it looked to be over twelve inches long–*far* bigger than anything yet landed. It was the lunker I'd been looking for! He was finning in shallow water on the far side of one of the more open pools.

I thought being so exposed would make him skittish and hard to hook, but I was wrong. He nosed up to the first fly I offered and promptly bit it off my line. I couldn't believe it! I set the hook and felt nothing. The fish turned and swam under the bank with my fly still lodged somewhere in his mouth.

The next day he was back, hanging out right where he was before, but was apparently not having anything to do with wet flies. I tried everything, even little gobs of tuna from my lunch–a tuna with noodles MRE (condensed and pre-packaged Meal Ready to Eat)–to no avail. Days went by and he was always there, and so was I, desperately scheming a way to catch him. After the first couple hours of trying to daintily coax another fly into his mouth I would put down my rod and just watch. He was an unassuming fish, almost shaped and colored like a sucker, but his movements were predatory. The way he would position himself in strategic places and remain motionless for a long time told me he was a hunter. I have seen pictures of Piranhas, and they look to be built more like a large panfish, not so sleek as he was. That left me with absolutely no idea what he might be.

One day as we hung out in the shade of the jungle canopy together I noticed him chasing a couple of small minnows around his pool. I'd observed this behavior on other occasions and had wished I had some streamers in my wallet survival kit. This time, though, I had an idea. If chewed on, the fluoride enhanced gum that comes in the MRE's could be molded onto one of my larger wet flies and would become a big white minnow!

After some rapid chewing and sticky artwork, I lobbed my carefully sculpted sculpin at the fish, gave it a couple suggestive jerks, and he attacked it. The ensuing struggle was hard fought but short, because I was using strong line and he didn't have much room to maneuver. I flipped him onto the bank next to me and hoped to get a good look at him so I could send a sketch home to the folks, but he was having none of it. He thrashed about like...well, a fish out of water. The entire time he maintained eye contact with me and snapped at my feet! I only *then* noticed his fine collection of really sharp-looking teeth. He never tried to get back into the creek; in fact, he appeared to have no greater desire than to latch his toothy mouth onto my ankle. This I found mildly disturbing. Finally the hook came out and, against his will, he rolled back into the water. I sat with my back pressed firmly against a tree as the leaves and dead branches began to settle around me, having been kicked up from my calm, almost nonchalant attempt to move farther up the bank.

The devil chub stopped at mid-pool and turned to glare at me, a tuft of grass protruding from one side of his mouth, a long stringy piece of gum stuck to a tooth on the other. I left my rod in the dirt and went back to camp for a safe game of spades, because, after that experience, even Sergeant Conley seemed tame.

* * *

"GO BIG OR GO HOME!" Shane Roberts yells at me from across the blue plastic milk crate we're using as a card table. Somehow I've gotten stuck with the crazy Texan as a spades partner.

"Do ya have to make so much bloody noise?" I mumble under my breath, still looking into my tightly held hand. "I can't think straight with you makin' all that racket."

Sergeant Barnes looks up from his cards and at his partner, Sergeant Brooks. "That ain't gonna ride," he says. "Trump it if you can."

"That's table talk!" Shane says.

Sergeant Barnes cocks his head and motions in my direction. "I figured since you were telling numbnuts over here to go big we were *allowing* table talk."

"I was just tellin' him to play to win," Shane says, skooching further back on his cot. "That ain't table talk."

"Yeah, uh huh." Sergeant Barnes looks back at his cards. "You owe me pushups after this hand."

"Roger that, Sergeant," Shane says, nodding his head. "You lose a game of spades and make *me* do pushups. That's cool, Sergeant."

"Yep, it's good to be king," Sergeant Barnes says. "Now, are you gonna play a card any time today, Private?"

He's talking to me. There's still only his card lying on the milk crate: the ace of diamonds. I don't have any of that suit, so I was going to trump it but can't decide whether to use one of my low spades, or my joker.

"COME ON, MAN! THROW A GODDAMN CARD ALREADY!" Shane hollers.

"I could have had my boots polished by now," grumbles Sergeant Brooks.

Shoot, what do I throw? Can't remember how to play this game. "Why can't we play poker, or something else?"

"Play a card!" they all say in unison.

Shit. I can't remember if the bigger joker has been played yet, but I throw my little joker. Sergeant Brooks quickly tossed out the big one. *Dammit!* Shane then follows suit with the jack of diamonds. Sergeant Barnes rakes in the trick with a smirk.

"Y'ALL SLOW *AND* STUPID, AIN'T YA?!" Shane belchs forth loud enough to turn heads in all the surrounding tents.

I roll my eyes and wait for Sergeant Brooks to lead. "Ain't you the one told me to throw big in the first place?"

Our platoon sergeant ducks in under the side of the tent and we all look up. He has a green, pocket-sized notebook in one hand and a metal canteen cup of coffee in the other. There had been a first sergeant's meeting and now the squad leaders are about to get "the poop." Sergeant Brooks and Sergeant Barnes are the two squad leaders assigned to this tent, so I'll get to overhear the information being passed down. I notice Sergeant Bair and Specialist Lowery have stopped what they're doing on the other side of the tent to listen in.

After a shaky-handed sip of his coffee, our platoon sergeant stares into his cup and makes a sour expression, then looks at us accusingly. We look back, trying not to crack a smile. He then flips open the notebook and reads aloud what was covered in his meeting with the first sergeant. It sounds like the same old crap: no one has heard anything about when we're going home, and the engineers are going to be spreading gravel between the tents before the rainy season –a bad sign, means we're going to be here a while longer. Also, the company commander wants to see more squad-level training going on instead of us sitting around, and the first sergeant "has the ass" because he saw an empty whisky bottle down inside one of the port-a-potties. Just why he was gazing down into the combined fecal matter of an entire battalion is a mystery to everyone, but regardless, alcohol is strictly off limits during this deployment. Lastly, there are some parachutes needing to be filled for a jump headquarters has arranged, and the platoon sergeant asks if either Sergeant Brooks or Sergeant Barnes has a new private they'd be willing to give up. They both turn and look at me.

"Hey, numbnuts. Guess what?"

* * *

A small collection of soldiers have begun to gather at the battalion headquarter's tent: a couple of donated privates, like myself, but mostly extremely gung-ho individuals. I stop in at the armorer's tent, am re-issued my M-16, and then join the crowd waiting for their ride to the airstrip. I mill around for a minute or two looking for a familiar face, then decide to inquire within about the whereabouts of my friend Steve Adair. A specialist sits behind a green, bamboo-cane desk held together by the same 550 cord I use as fly line. He tells me Steve was sent back to Fort Bragg in January to begin his out-processing from the Army. I hear our deuce-and-a-half pull up, so I thank the specialist and walk out of the tent. *Wow! Bet he's stoked about going home. Hope he's still at Bragg when we get back, so he can show me those fishing spots . . .* if *we ever get back.*

We arrive and are dumped off at a nondescript hanger sometime after noon. A pile of T-10 parachutes, reserves and canvas weapons cases are stacked on the smooth concrete floor. Everyone files by, grabs one of each and gets together with a buddy and begins what looks to be their own, many times repeated ritual of climbing into the harness. I don't have a buddy to help situate the parachute on my back and make sure the straps aren't twisted. As I look around in the shadow of the hanger I can see some of the older guys donning their gear by themselves. This is quite a bit less organized than what I've experienced in airborne school at Ft. Benning. There, we were under the watchful eye of the "black hat" instructors at all times and were checked and re-checked continuously before we boarded the airplane. Hours of pre-jump drills and practiced PLF's (parachute landing falls) preceded every jump. There isn't any of that pleasant reassurance today.

I try hard to remember exactly how everything goes together, catching glimpses of what the guys are doing next to me. *Okay Jay, don't panic. You know what to do. Done this before . . . done this before.* I unsnap everything, lay it out neatly and intertwine the shoulder straps of my load bearing equipment with those of the parachute harness. Then I put my right arm through and sling it onto my back. The kit bag has to go against my stomach before the groin straps come up between my legs–I remember that much–but there's a special way to fold it that fails me. I do my best to make mine look like everyone else's, but they're all already rigged and shuffling outside. *Come on, man. Let's go. Get this damn thing ready.* There's still a long strap hanging loose. I'm trying to hurry but my brain is threatening to freeze up on me. *What is this for?* I hold the strap up and look around. *What am I missing?* I'm now the only one in the hanger. *Shit, my reserve. That's right.* I quickly thread the strap through the back of the reserve parachute and snap it into place, then cinch it tight and slide the safety pin into one of the snaps. I put my rifle in its case, zip it, attach the quick-release assembly and snap it to the D-ring on my left side. I put my helmet on, spin around, don't see any loose gear anywhere near me, so I head outside and try to catch up.

Another strap comes loose as I near the airplane. The ramp is down and the last two soldiers in line are disappearing up the rear of the bird. The strap looks important; it has a fancy snap at the end with a long yellow tab. I don't know where it goes, but I snap it onto the nearest attachment ring and jog up the ramp.

One of the jumpmaster-qualified volunteers is getting everyone seated evenly along the folded down canvas seats. His job is easy because there are only two dozen of us and we're going to be jumping from only one of the two doors, plus, nobody's jumping with their rucksack. I wonder where he was when I needed him back in the hanger. He was supposed to have been inspecting us after we were rigged, but he doesn't seem all that experienced.

After sitting down I try to make eye contact with him. I don't want to ask for help and sound like a brand new cherry, but maybe if we got to talking he would notice something amiss and fix it. I can't believe I've forgotten so much about a parachute in such a short period of time.

He sees me looking at him and walks over and bends down to take the weight of the parachute off his shoulders. "You're gonna be my number one jumper," he says. "You ever jumped outta one of these?"

I see stripes sewn on his camouflaged helmet cover. "No, sergeant. I don't think so."

"Alrighty, no big deal." He looks up and raises his voice for everyone on board to hear. "Listen up! I'm your jumpmaster and safety all rolled into one. For anyone who hasn't jumped from a C-27. . . ." He pauses and pats the inside skin of the aircraft. "This old bird ain't equipped with anything to block the wind as you go out, so you're gonna have to exit the old fashioned way." This gets grins and nods from some of the jumpers. He continues: "When you come to the door, put both hands on the sides and give yourself a good push to get clear of the airplane." He smiles, looks behind him and nods at the flight crew, then turns back to us. "Okay, have a good jump! See ya on the drop zone!"

Ah, Hell. I'm dead for sure!

As the airplane rumbles out to the runway I look at my harness and try to compare it with that of the guy next to me. Something's different. He and everyone else have a thick yellow cord over their left shoulder–and I don't. My eyeballs are aching from peering out of my extreme peripheral vision, but finally I'm able to determine that it's actually the static line. I reach behind me and fumble around with the top of my parachute until the proper snap is located. I undo it and drape the thick yellow static line over my left shoulder. *Whew! Feels better now. Look about the same as everyone.* But there's still the dilemma of the mystery strap that came loose earlier. It has me so unsettled I hardly notice our takeoff.

This is definitely not like anything at airborne school. I can remember all the faces in the C-130 just before that first jump–or any of the five we had to execute to earn our wings–they were pale, wide-eyed and sweaty; and everyone had sat very straight. Not like this planeload of hard nose, steely-eyed paratroopers, most of whom have already fallen asleep. None of them seem all that nervous or concerned about the possibility of being dead shortly. *What would they do if my 'chute didn't open? Probably just kick some dirt into the hole I make on the drop zone. . . .*

We're in the air for slightly over an hour when the flight crew begins moving around and the jumpmaster tells everyone to wake up. The ones awake give sharp elbows to their sleeping comrades. No one needs to nudge me; I've barely blinked. After everyone's head is up and helmet on, we're given the hand and arm signal to stand and hook up. Once the last man gets off the long canvas seat, it's folded back into place and out of the way.

Everyone is hooking their static line to the thick metal centerline cable behind me; I can hear the clacking of the large metal snaps over the noise of the engine. *Shit, I'm not ready yet.* I take my own static line, snap it into place, and insert the wire safety pin. Then I notice another lanyard hanging loose from between my harness and weapon case. *Son of a bitch!* I don't care about sounding like a newbie anymore, but I can't get the jumpmaster's attention. *Don't panic!* I take a hold of the loose end; it's dark green and has no snap, just a big loop at the end. *What the hell is it for? Come on! Think, god dammit!*

I hear a loud whoosh, like a two-ton vacuum cleaner has been suddenly turned on inside the airplane. The jumpmaster has unlatched the jump door, slid it up on the rails and fixed it into position. As I look up he is bracing himself in the door and leaning out. Wind is distorting the skin on his face and pulling the fabric of his uniform tight against his arms. The men behind me are cheering and yanking down on their static lines.

I look back down at the green lanyard with the big loop. *Last chance, Jay. Where's it go?* I hold it out with my left hand and try to trace it back to its origins with my right.

The jumpmaster pulls himself back inside and begins awkwardly feeling around the edge of the door for any sharp edges that could sever a static line.

I can't find the end of the lanyard, so I yank on it in desperation. A button flies off of my left cargo pocket and out comes my neatly folded lowering line. *Oh yeah! No kidding!* I had put it in my pocket before leaving camp and had completely forgotten about it. At the other end is the mystery snap with the yellow tab–still hooked onto my harness.

The jumpmaster backs away from the door and motions me forward. *Aw, hell.* I move up, hand him my static line and turn toward the door. He puts a hand on the top of my parachute and yells at me over the roar of the engine and rushing wind. It sounds like he's telling me to wait for his command, but I'm not sure. I bend down, thread the green loop through the back of my weapons case and tie a knot. It isn't the proper technique, but it'll do.

Then I look out the open door. We're flying low and following the contours of the land. The tops of hills are almost higher than we are, and all of them appear alive, animated by the jungle. It all looks so *thick* and unpenetrable–a solid mass of vegetation looking up at the sun with millions of outstretched arms and open mouths.

We fly out past the coastline, past the narrow beach and the countless little islands with their steep, rocky cliffs. We're low enough for me to see large, white birds perched in the cliffs' crevasses. They look like pelicans.

Suddenly the pilot banks hard and I have to hold onto the sides of the door to keep from falling into the sea. The jumpmaster grabs the top of my parachute again and yells something inaudible. I look straight down into the seemingly motionless waves.

The airplane levels out and a second later the jumpmaster slaps the back of my parachute, yelling for me to go. *What? Over the water?* While my mind is questioning the logic, my body is following orders. I take a step forward and push off with both hands, but one hand slips off the edge of the door. The wind catches me head on and spins me back toward the side of the airplane. My head bounces twice as I skip along the outside, and then I'm free. My risers are badly twisted and the parachute hasn't opened. I'm upside down for a few seconds and looking past my boots at the long trail of olive-drab silk flapping madly in the wind. *OH, SHIT!* Then it catches air. The opening shock digs the harness straps into my groin and spins me around so my feet are toward the ground. I hit the quick-release assembly on my weapons case and watch it drop to the end of the lowering line. I slam into the earth.

Everything is black for a while and I can't breathe. Things slowly begin to come into focus; blades of grass, blurred around the edges. *What happened? Did I land already?* I try to raise my head but can't. Then the pain comes. *Aw. . .not my back!* I grit my teeth and try to take a deep breath. The pain in my back is excruciating, and it's quickly spreading to my neck and shoulders. *No. Uh, uh. I can't be paralyzed. Can I?*

I lay still in the knee-deep grass and continue to breathe. Something crawls onto my earlobe, jumps onto the side of my head and wanders up inside my helmet. I try to ignore it and listen to the waves. The ocean sounds very close, I can hear the waves turning over on the beach. I lie there and time my breathing with them and stare into the pale blue Panamanian sky.

A fellow paratrooper sails over my narrow line of sight. I hear him hit the ground not far from my position and then cut loose with a string of choice profanities. The slight breeze wiggles the grass that surrounds me. I don't hear any more from the other jumper. *Damn, he was coming down fast, too!*

A flock of brightly colored birds fly by. I can hear them cackling as they go over. They're staying in pairs even while in the larger flock. I count at least five pairs and wait for more. The pain has eased only slightly. *Okay, Jay. You can't lie out here forever. Let's try getting up again.*

First I make fists, then move my feet a little. *Whew! Good sign!* Lifting my head is too painful, so I roll onto my side, pushing myself into the sitting position and look around the drop zone.

There are two trucks parked in the shade near one side of the DZ. One has a large, white square with a red cross in it. I can see men climbing into the back of the other truck. *Must be our ride out of here.* I slowly and painfully stand up, get out of the harness, roll my parachute and put it all into the kit bag. The reserve parachute is then snapped onto the handles of the kit bag and slung onto my aching back. I retrieve my rifle, tuck the canvas weapons case under an arm and head toward the trucks.

I've only gone a few feet before coming upon the guy who had landed somewhere in the tall grass next to me. He's still in the harness and has his eyes closed. I kneel down beside him and am about to check for a pulse, when his eyes open and he looks up at me.

"Hey, man. You alive?" I ask.

He closes his eyes again and grimaces. "Barely," he says. "Damn, this ground is hard!"

"Yeah, I landed like a ton a bricks myself." My back and neck have settled into a throbbing ache, which is an improvement.

"Shit, dude," he says. "I love these fun jumps."

"You *sure* you're okay?"

He digs out a pack of Camel Lights and sits up. "Yeah, these daytime jumps kick ass. Ain't no follow-on mission to worry about. Nothin' but adrenaline, man." He lights his cigarette and looks at me. "You want a smoke?"

"No thanks."

"It takes the edge off the pain." He smiles. "Here," he says, holding out his cigarette. "You gotta enjoy this shit. Might be the last day jump you gonna make. They don't come along often."

I take it and he taps the bottom of the pack, making another fall out.

"Thanks, man," I say. Then I take a drag and walk toward the waiting trucks.

* * *

Back at camp we all go separate ways, trying to locate our platoons and find out what's going on. 1st platoon's tents are vacant. The sides are still rolled up and they appear to have been left in a hurry. All flack jackets, K-pots (kevlar helmets) and CBGs are missing. The riot shields all lay scattered, some of the face shields have been torn off so fast they're broken.

There are no more clues inside our tent, so I wander across Two Panther Creek and up to the mess tent. The cooks are still there and they give me a plate of chili macaroni and fill me in. They say sometime shortly before we got back five Cubans escaped from one of the camps, and all the line companies have been sent out to retain them. So far only two have been caught, but they later turned out to be natives out on a hunting trip. The local tribe–consisting of just twenty persons–has been hired to work in the kitchen. According to the cooks it was downright comical when the two hunters were dragged into camp and recognized by their chief. The squad of infantrymen tried to apologize and then quickly retreated back into the jungle.

I take my overly seasoned plate of food out to a table and sit down. A couple of other soldiers who were on the jump with me limp in to find grub but leave to eat it elsewhere. I sit alone and gaze out into the edge of our camp clearing. *Cool . . . tracking down some Cubans. How did I manage to miss out on all the fun?* I have been hoping, as has everyone, for another good riot to break loose, but this is even better. Now we get to go hunting!

As I'm washing down the last of my slightly toxic chili-mac with a two-quart canteen of water, one of the hired natives passes through. They don't *look* like the "Indians" I thought lived in the jungle. Hell, I figured they were all three-foot-tall, wore leopard-skin loincloths and shot poisonous darts at missionaries. When I was a kid I had wanted to be one; Dad had even made me a cool blowgun out of PVC pipe.

These guys in the mess tent wear jeans, T-shirts and old tennis shoes. Again, my naive, Midwestern imagination is let down. *Ah! But wait! What is that hanging from his neck!?* The native has stopped and sat down at the table beside me and has begun picking up food scraps. He looks to be about my age.

"Hey, cool necklace ya got there," I say. "What is it?" It appears to be a small antler. He gives me a puzzled look and goes back to doing whatever he's doing, so I get up and walk over. "Hey man, whatcha doin'?" I ask.

He looks up at me, grins and points down at his feet. Between the legs of the table run a foot-wide path of bare earth, which winds its way through the mess tent and back out into the gradually darkening jungle. The entire length of the trail is covered with thousands of ants, some coming, some going. He's dropping grape-sized bits of bread into the ant freeway and watching as they pick them up and head on their way. As they pass the tree line I loose sight of the trail, but can still make out the white pieces of bread as they weave their way around roots and tree branches. It seems fun, so I join in.

"So, you hunt deer, huh?" By now I've realized we aren't speaking the same language, so I add some gestures, pointing to his necklace and making antlers with my hands on top of my head.

He smiles, repeats the necklace and antler motions and nods.

Cool, me too! I nod, smile and point to my chest to say that I'm a deer hunter as well. *So, how did you take him? With a bow? A spear?* I make the appropriate gestures.

He snorts and looks at me quizzically, then makes a motion like he's holding up and aiming a rifle, complete with the eye squint and recoil.

Uh, yeah. . .naturally.

* * *

It's dark and I'm asleep before my platoon comes back. They're exhausted, hungry and drenched with sweat. I'm eager to hear their stories, but they don't have any. Specialist Lowery tells me the entire mission was bullshit. He says there was no organization at all: they had been rushed to the perimeter of the refugee camp and told to "go catch the escapees." He shakes his head as he tells me how stupid they all looked, crashing around in the jungle at night, not knowing where the other platoons were and not being able to see. They had not been issued their night-vision goggles or, even better, flashlights!

* * *

Early the next morning we're rousted from our cots and told that nine more Cubans have gotten out, "launched over the fence in port-a-potties" the report says. Some climbed into the crappers, others heaved the capsules over the fence.

This time things are better controlled. Each company is given responsibility for different sectors and then each platoon within that company is given a different grid coordinate and told to set up an ambush. Lowery agrees this is much better than the fiasco last night, but he thinks it's dumb to have a platoon-sized ambush, armed with billy clubs, when squad-sized elements could cover a much larger area and be more effective. I hear him comment–under his breath– how pathetically long it takes an elite military unit to adjust to the present situation. Sergeant Bair reminds him "Shit, man, they don't teach common sense at West Point."

We're trucked in as far as possible and from there we move into position. First platoon's ambush site is on the edge of a hill overlooking a narrow gully with treacherous terrain on either side, about two clicks' walk from the drop-off point. The company commander deems it one of the most likely avenues of departure from any of the camps. As it turns out, it isn't.

We lay motionless, waiting to pounce, well into the afternoon, but no one shows. Everyone's disappointed, but I, at least, am expecting it. Almost half my childhood seems to have been spent in tree stands or ground blinds, waiting for prey that never showed itself. Sometimes, though, I luck out and that's what makes the wait worthwhile. Plus, I get a front-row seat to the best show in town. And this time out was no exception. Instead of chipmunks and blue jays scolding me for trespassing, there are trees full of mocking monkeys and noisy parrots.

The monkeys are small, about the size of a house cat, only a lot skinnier and with a much longer tail. They have brownish fur, but I'm always looking up at them, so I can only tell for sure that they have white bellies. No one knows they're on top of us until they begin pelting us with sticks. Two, pencil-size twigs careen off the back of my helmet before I think to look up. And there they are, peeking down at us from limbs of the thick jungle canopy.

Sometime late in the afternoon we get word over the radio to meet at a pre-arranged rally point, so we pull out and link up with the rest of the company. The designated area is an intersection of two dirt roads, and as the platoons gradually begin filtering in and collapsing on the cool grass alongside the roads, we begin bumming cigarettes and telling stories about what we've seen–or were almost bitten by–while on ambush. Stories of run-ins with scorpions, spiders and a rogue fer-de-lance pit viper are enjoyed over the rock and roll emanating from somewhere off in the distance. A psychological operations unit is patrolling the roads in a Humvee equipped with a huge bullhorn, blaring promises of food and coffee to anyone who turns themselves in. These lies are intermingled with the best of The Rolling Stones and Credence Clearwater Revival. It's strange; I feel like I'm in a Viet Nam war movie complete with a good sound track.

Then the shit happens. The music sounds like it's getting closer, then it stops. A couple of seconds later a Humvee races around the corner and slides to a halt in front of us, a soldier leans out the side. "Four of 'em just ran across the road in front of us!" He points down the road. "Just back there!"

Everyone jumps up and tosses away his helmet, CBG and load-bearing equipment before racing down the road. A pissed-off pack of wolves. I hesitate for a second to locate my team leader. He and Sergeant Brooks are the only two who aren't going in the same direction as everyone else.

Lowery asks the man in the Humvee something, then they both turn and run into the jungle. I fall in close behind. Not far in we come to a faint game trail and follow it, running and jumping over anything in the way. We round a bend and I see a man standing in the trail. He looks at us like a frightened deer mesmerized by the bright light of a locomotive. He never has a chance to move; Sergeant Brooks lowers his shoulder and tackles him. I yank a flex-cuff from my cargo pocket and bind his wrists behind his back. Lowery stays close, providing security.

Sergeant Brooks pulls the Cuban man up into the kneeling position and whispers loudly into his ear. "*Donde estan sus amigos!?*" The man stares back at him, terrified. Sergeant Brooks shakes him violently by his shirt front. "Where are they, you piece of shit!?"

The commotion attracts many of the other soldiers who have scattered down the road and found nothing. They begin appearing out of thickets and crowding around us, tongues lolling and panting like hungry jackals circling a fresh kill.

As I stand behind our prisoner, I see that his body is shaking and blood flows freely from the bottoms of his bare feet. My adrenaline rush is gradually beginning to fade.

I slide one of our CBGs under the Cuban man's armpits. Sergeant Brooks gets a hold on the other end and we lift the man to his feet and march him back to the road. Our plan is to dump him into the Humvee, but the psychological operations guys think it better if we drag him back past the refugee camp he escaped from. They think it will be a good lesson for anyone else thinking about making a run for it.

We cover the mile or so back to the detainment area rather quickly. The Cuban man is not able to keep up. He has lost his shoes somewhere in the jungle, and the sharp spines of the black palm have obviously torn up his feet. As we walk he leaves a trail of bloody footprints in the dusty road. Sergeant Brooks and I lift the stick up an inch and carry him.

We slow down once we come to the refugee camp, deliberately taking the long way around the fence. The MP's in their guard towers peer down at us, hailing us with questions and congratulations. Other soldiers come out of tents and take photos of us as we parade by.

On the inside of the fence we receive a different kind of reception from the Cubans. Large, silent crowds form, casting angry glares at us through the tangle of concertina wire. I can feel their hatred. I look inside at them as we pass, feeling like shit, but still making eye contact and mentally baring my teeth.

* * *

The next morning we go hunting again, this time broken down as squads. Some are set in ambushes again, but others, like our squad, are given a large area of jungle to patrol. The thinking behind this is, for once, sound. The ambush squads are set in areas along major game trails, funneled areas and natural lines of drift. The patrolling squads can root through any likely hiding spots and, if nothing else, keep things moving toward the ambushes.

A deuce-and-a-half takes us to a new drop-off point, but we don't kick off right away. Sergeant Brooks takes us a few meters into the jungle and gathers us around a map. Sergeant Bair and Specialist Lowery point out different spots in our sector that look promising, then Sergeant Brooks plots the route we'll take. He even works in some of my unasked-for suggestions.

Then we get our crap together and move out, going slow and staying spread out. We're all becoming more familiar with our surroundings. After a while I get my old feeling of stealth back. It's like the second day of squirrel season back home in Ohio. No longer am I tripping around the woods like opening day, moving fast and making too much noise. I'm no longer a wandering stranger in a foreign jungle. I belong.

Several hours into the patrol we begin finding human sign, scuffed leaves and a freshly snapped branch that seem too clumsy, even for an "acoodamundy." We slow down even more and spread out, from a column into a wedge-shaped formation; alert, moving silently and thoroughly scanning the jungle just ahead before each step.

Sergeant Bair gives the hand-and-arm signal to halt as we near the edge of a small gully with a dried creek bed at the bottom. We all slowly kneel. Sergeant Bair goes to a knee also and is examining something. Lowery and Sergeant Brooks get up and move over to see what he has found. From where I'm kneeling I can't make out what it is right away, but then it comes into focus: a very primitive, well camouflaged lean-to. As I watch, Lowery holds up some palm branches for me to see, they've been matted down and used for a bed. He sets them down, moves over and takes a knee next to me.

"How fresh?" I ask softly.

Lowery shrugs his shoulders. "Looks like it was used this morning, but that doesn't–"

He stops in mid-sentence, leaning forward and staring straight ahead. I follow his gaze down into the dry creek bed. I don't see anything, just a thick tangle of exposed roots hanging over the cavern-like undercuts. Then I see movement and catch a glimpse of blue fabric. Lowery points the thumb-down, index-finger-extended hand signal for "enemy to the front." This gets the squad's attention.

Two Cuban men come into sight, making their way down the creek bed. The middle-aged one in the lead has an aluminum Louiseville Slugger baseball bat and the younger, twenty-something carries a blue backpack over one shoulder.

Sergeant Brooks stands up and steps toward them. They stop suddenly and look up at him. Lowery goes left and I go right, quickly closing the distance between us and them. They start to move again and Sergeant Brooks yells in Spanish for them to stop. The Cubans are still moving and looking up at him; they don't see Lowery or me until it's too late.

Lowery takes out the man with the ball bat and I go for the other one. He hears me coming and starts to turn toward me. I hit the back of his head with the palm of my hand and grab ahold of his tight curly hair, forcing him to the ground. Once he is face down in the dry rocks of the creek, I ram my knee into his crotch and spread his legs with my feet, so he can't roll over.

Lowery's having to be more brutal with his man. They lay struggling next to us for a second or two, then the Cuban stops moving. Lowery removes his arm from around the man's neck and looks over at me and grins.

The rest of the squad pulls security around us as we search through the two men's pockets. In the backpack I find a bright yellow

Fort Bragg Bass

Small flecks of ash drift from the end of my burning cigarette and land on the toe of one of my shiny black combat boots. I sit hunched over on the corner of my bed, looking at my rucksack lying on the floor. I have just finished rigging it for tomorrow's jump. The end of my lowering line is properly attached and the line itself is ironed, folded and taped to the metal frame of my ruck which is severely bent and disfigured from too many hard landings. Now I have to inspect my privates' gear to make sure they're rigged right.

I drag hard on the cigarette and smash it out into the red, plastic ashtray which sits on the chair next to the bed. *This job was easier before I took over Bravo team. Then it was just me I had to worry about.*

My right knee pops as I stand up, sending pain shooting up my leg. "Ah, hell!" I lean on my wall locker until the pain subsides. I reach into a pocket for my pack of smokes. *Dammit! I'm too young to be feeling like this! A twenty-one-year-old cripple.*

Someone knocks softly on the door of my barracks room and I stand up straight, wincing. I can tell it's a private by the way he knocked. I pull a fresh Camel Light out, tuck it into my lips and answer out of the corner of my mouth. "Yeah, whattaya want?"

"I have your mail, Specialist Zimmerman."

I had heard someone yelling "mail call" a few minutes before, followed by the sound of many boots running down the hallway. I knew without looking they were all privates–they're still new enough to be getting mail.

It's funny, the first year you're in you get at least one or two letters a day–family missing you, friends wondering what new, cool and exciting things you're doing. The second year slows down to maybe one or two a week. By the third year you just try to ignore mail call. Your old highschool buddies have lost your address, gotten married or forgotten about you–which is fine, because you can't relate with them anymore, anyway–and your family is still recovering from the last time you came home on leave, stumbling drunkenly off the airplane in your Class A's, slurring profanities and passing out in the car on the ride home.

I light the cigarette and open the door. Private Martinez hands me my mail. *Two letters! Wow!* "You all rigged up and ready to go?" I ask, knowing he is. He's my best private and I can count on him.

"Yes, Specialist."

"How about the rest of the team?"

"We're good to go, Specialist," he says and steps back to look down the hallway. "But Alpha team isn't going to be up for awhile."

"Sergeant Konkol still squaring away the new guy, huh?"

Martinez looks back at me and smiles. "Roger that, Specialist."

I flick ash into the hallway. "I'll be around to inspect the team's shit in a few, but in the meantime get all the cherries together to mop the hallway. Get those scuff marks out, too."

"Roger that, Specialist."

I start to close the door, stop, and look out as Martinez is turning to leave. "Hey, Marty."

He stops. "Yes, Specialist?"

"Thanks for the mail."

He smiles, nods and I close the door. *Damn good kid. Wish all privates came like him.* I limp over to my wall locker and open it. On the top shelf is an opaque, orange prescription pill bottle with a white child-proof lid. I take it down, pry the lid off and spill the contents into the palm of my hand. I have Motrin, and there are still a few codeine tablets left over from my last arm surgery. I pick out two of the eight-hundred milligram Motrins and dump the rest back in. The strong stuff is saved for *after* the jump.

I swallow the painkillers and sit back down on my bed. *Gear ready. Pretty sure I got everything.* We're jumping into Fort Polk, Louisiana, in the morning and going to be living in the woods there for almost a month. Nothing new, just part of the routine. No doubt we'll get rained on and be miserable, because that, too, is part of the routine.

I focus on how good that first warm meal and cold beer is going to taste when we get back here to Fort Bragg. I lean back and let the springs under the worn-out mattress take my weight. *Gonna miss you, bed.*

* * *

The door suddenly swings open and the biggest son of a bitch I've ever seen is standing there in camouflaged, cut-off BDU shorts and a Denver Bronco's T-shirt, holding two cans of Coors Light. I look up, it's Sergeant John Falton. I've been expecting this.

Keith Konkol squeezes into the room between the six-foot-eight, two-hundred-and-eighty-pound Elway fan and the door jamb. "Hey, Z," Keith points his thumb back over his shoulder. "There's somebody at the door. You want me to take care of him for ya?"

I add my now burned down cigarette to the growing butt collection in my ashtray and pull three new ones from my pack. Keith moves the ashtray from the chair to the floor and sits down. I hand him one of the Camels.

"Ah . . .you're the best Z!" He pulls out his Zippo, fires up and holds out the still burning lighter.

I light mine on Keith's flame and set the other one next to me on the bed.

John, realizing we're ignoring his dramatic entrance, walks in and lobs one of the beers at me. "When the hell are you two idiots getting off work?" He stops in the middle of the room and points to the cigarette lying next to me. "Gimme a smoke."

I crack the seal on my beer. It's cold and some foam comes to the top. "What do I look like? The PX?"

"I gave you a beer, dumb ass. Now give me a god damn cigarette!"

I toss him the smoke and he bums a light from Keith, then tells him that there is more beer down in his room. Keith leans over and taps his cigarette on the edge of the ashtray. "No, man. I can't."

John raises his voice. "Yeah, what the hell? When you guys gettin' off? Third platoon's off."

I laugh, take a swig from the can and wipe my face with the back of my hand. "Shit, Konk's gonna be here all bloody night."

John looks down at Keith. Keith shakes his head and exhales a lung-full of smoke. "Yeah, I have to stick around and make sure my new guy has his packing list. He's at the Main PX. Checked him and he's short two pair of socks and patches on an extra uniform."

John looks at me. "Are *you* off yet?"

"Yeah, pretty much. Just gotta inspect my guys."

"Packing list?" He looks impatient.

"Naw, I had them rig their rucks."

Keith gets up and stretches. "Well, been fun boys. Thanks for the smoke, Z."

"No worries. See ya bright and early tomorrow."

John steps aside and lets him leave, then flops down on the chair. "Hurry up and do what ya gotta so we can go fishing."

"Yeah, gimme a minute." I take another drag from my cigarette and notice him playing with an envelope tucked in his pocket. "Whatcha got there?"

"Oh, yeah." He sets his beer on the floor, takes the envelope out of his pocket and pulls from it a stack of photos. "Wanted to show you these pictures my old man sent."

I lean forward to get a better look. He's been telling me about all the great places to hunt and fish around his folks' place near Cripple Creek, Colorado, and now is obviously trying to entice me further. He really needn't bother, his stories have already done the trick.

"That's a good picture. Where is it?"

"Crystal Reservoir. It's on the way up to Pikes Peak." He turns to the next one. "This one's South Catamount, same area. If you come out I'll take you up there."

I catch a glimpse of the next picture in the stack and pull it out of his hands. It's a big rainbow trout lying in a bed of green grass. It *has* to be over eighteen inches. "Oh, sweet! Nice fish!"

"That one was caught out of the pond right down from the house." He flips through the stack, stops, pulls out a photo and hands it to me. "There's the pond. Walking distance from the house."

I take the four-by-six glossy and study it. The water is inviting. The far side of the pond looks like the steep side of a mountain. "So are these wild trout in here?"

John shrugs. “Well, I guess. Someone stocked it years and years ago.”

Man oh man. You lucky bastard.

He hands me another photo. “Here’s an elk just below the house. You can kinda see it.”

I can definitely see it. “You get a lot of elk by the house?”

“Oh, hell yeah! They’re all over the place!”

I got to get out there.

John spreads the photos out like a deck of cards, seeing a little of each. “Can’t wait to get back. Seven months and I’m home free.”

“You ain’t goin’ on block leave when we get back from Louisiana?”

John looks up from the photos. “Oh, yeah. Just sayin’. Seven more and I’m home for good.” He slips the stack of photos into the envelope and tucks them back into his pocket. “You should come with me on leave. Do some trout fishing.”

Ah, I’d love to. But. . . . “I ain’t been home in a while. Told my folks I’d be there.”

John nods, he understands. From the sound of things, he has the same kind of close relationship with his folks. We’re the only two who have been in for over three years (over five for him) and still get some mail. *Speaking of. . . .* “Shit! I got some mail, too! Where is it?” I stand up and feel my pockets with my one free hand, beer sloshing from the can in my other. Nothing but a pack of cigarettes. *Son of a bitch! Where’d I put ‘em?* I look around the room. “Dammit! I got two letters. I just had ‘em a second ago!”

John stands up and looks on the chair. “I ain’t seen ‘em. You check your pockets?”

“Yeah.” I throw my pillow onto the floor. Nothing underneath. “They were in my hand a second ago.” I pull my bed out from the wall and peer behind it. Nothing, not even dust. “I got two letters. One was from a chick, too.”

John opens my wall locker, trying to look like he’s concerned.

“They wouldn’t be in there. I just had them in my hand.”

He pulls the two envelopes down from the top shelf, next to the pill bottle, and throws them at me. “Here, dumb ass.”

I catch one and the other falls to the floor. I recognize Mom's handwriting and bend the envelope. No photos. I put it in my pocket to read tonight, and pick up the other one. "Yeah, check this out." I hold it up for him to see. "She's an old highschool friend of my sister's. Sends me a letter every now and again. Gonna see her on leave, maybe."

"You never told me you had a sister."

I tuck the letter in my pocket with the other one. "Yes I have. She's in college."

"Where at? Is she hot?"

"She's at the University of Cincinnati, for graphic design. Yeah, yeah. Smart, too, all right?" *And so is her friend.*

John laughs. "Well, what happened to you? Adopted?"

"Go get your rod," I say. "I'll meet you out by my truck in a minute."

* * *

The last time I checked there were thirteen legally fishable lakes within the boundary of Ft. Bragg–minus those on Camp Mackall. John and I are familiar with all of them, and we both have our favorites, but because the shore access is better, we decide to give Kiest Lake a try. Neither of us feel like fighting the lines for the one washer and dryer per platoon or like the idea of leaving wet and muddy shorts in our rooms until we come back from Louisiana– fishing at Wyatt or Lower McKellars means one or the other.

There's only one other vehicle by the lake, a newer, extended cab pickup, and its owner is fishing nearby. I park my rusty, blue pickup truck in the shade and we climb out and get our gear situated. We don only the essentials, I my vest, and John a large fly box with a strap worn over his shoulder. The other guy nods as we approach. He's reeling in for another cast, so I look to see what he's using. It's a bright orange and yellow crankbait, big enough to fillet if it were real.

"Hey, how's it goin'? John asks as we walk by him. "Doin' any good?"

The guy shakes his head. "Naw, they ain't movin'"

I stop and turn back. "Hey, man. Try somethin' a little more subtle. In this clear, shallow water they like those soft plastic jerkbaits, fished on top...."

He nods and goes back to lobbing his duel grappling hooks out into the water. I leave him to solve his own troubles. *Suit yourself, bud.*

John is already too far away for me to try and catch up. He's heading across the dam to the cove on the other side. There are submerged logs back there and I assume he's going to fish them. I head over the dam, too, but take my time, trying to spot fish holding tight to the bank.

Kiest Lake is typical of most lakes on Ft. Bragg. They were all created by damming small creeks, which can still be seen flowing into the lake at their "head" and then flowing out through the square cement drain poking up from the water near the dam or "tail." That's the way I refer to them, as if they were just a large pool in the course of the original stream. I've drawn a detailed map of each of the smaller lakes and many partial maps of the larger ones. At Kiest, every stump, submerged log and drop-off are accounted for.

Tons of stone and reinforced concrete make up the backbone of the dam, I'm sure, but the skin has been carefully disguised to make it appear more like an earthen dike. Tall grass and scrub oak grow between the water and the path along the top. I have a #10 Little Bastard dry fly on the end of my leader and try to cast it over the brush and down to the water. Getting my fly out there is the simple part, getting it back is more of a gamble. I have to roll cast over the little oak trees and as soon as the fly comes out of the water, jerk back the rod and hope for the best. The really amazing part is that this trick is actually working.

I finally spot a lone bass lurking in the shade under a clump of algae. He isn't a monster, but is the average twelve or so inches for the lake. My cast over all the tangled branches and overgrown weeds is a good one, and my fly settles a few inches away from the fish's hideout. The bass lunges for it, but stops. I pull on the fly line and the Little Bastard dry fly leaps out of the water, then I let go and it plops back onto the surface. Dappling for bass. My idea is to make the fly look like a dragonfly does when it's laying eggs on the surface of the water.

The trick pays off. I don't know if the bass actually believes he's eating a dragonfly or is just upset about his invaded privacy. Either way, I have a fish on. Now comes the part I haven't planned for: how to land him through all the mess between me and the water. As it turns out I don't have a chance to troubleshoot. When I set the hook the bass tries to head for deeper water, but can't. The leader gets thoroughly tangled in the scrub oak and after a short and splashy struggle, the fly shoots out of the fish's mouth and spins a half dozen times around the nearest branch like an Olympic gymnast on the high bar.

I break the fly off and find a place where I can actually cast properly. There's a spot about midway along the dam, near the overflow drain, that is clear enough of obstructions to allow room for a halfway-decent cast. I stop here and open one of my fly boxes. The only real choice I have is between one of my Yella Bellies and a newer streamer pattern I've recently been playing with. I go with the new guy, the Squirrel Tail.

It's getting darker and I can't see any fish in the water. I know they should be in the area, though, so I keep casting my fly out and retrieving it with fast, sporadic jerks. After a dozen or more casts I see the tell-tale wake of a good fish behind my fly, then the boil of water as he takes it. My line goes tight and I set the hook as firmly as I can without snapping the tippet. He jumps once before going with the stubborn, underwater route. In the end, I hold him up with a shaking hand for John to see. I receive a nod and a wave in return. It's a nice fish, easily fourteen inches.

I let the bass free and retire to the crest of the dam to watch John fish. The sun has already set and I can't make out his rod or fly line in the greying light. He has waded into the lake after all, boots and everything, like a large heron, standing poised and motionless in the calm water of the cove. I assume by his slow and deliberate line mending that he's fishing the submerged logs with a nymph. He likes fishing trout flies for bass, too, and neither of us are sure why.

Suddenly his right hand comes back, too fast to be picking up the line for just another cast. Then the calm black water in front of him comes alive with a splashing fish. I watch as he plays it, enjoying the fight almost as much as if it were me out there. I wave and nod when he lifts the fish out of the water and looks my way. *Damn fine fish.*

I watch John as he cranks his line in and wades to shore. Shortly, he joins me on the dam and we head back to the truck together. I comment on his sodden boots which made slurping noises and spit water from the cracked leather as he walks. He admits that, yes, he had gotten a bit carried away, but we both agree it was worth it.

The fisherman we passed earlier is putting his rod and tackle box into the back of his truck. As we walk by I notice a different but equally loud and obnoxious crankbait hooked to the first eye of his rod. Again, John asks if he had any luck.

"Naw," the guy says. "Must not be movin' tonight."

Working Nights

My eyes open and for a few seconds more I feel drowsy and comfortable; my mind and body are at ease. Then reality begins sinking in. I've been crammed deep into the guts of a C-141 along with over a hundred other troops. There are more planes in front and behind this one; the entire battalion is in the air. I might be able to tell you what state we're over if I could check the time, but I can't move the arm that my watch is on–it's too cramped. Alabama, maybe.

I know we've been in the air for awhile, because I'm numb from the waist down, which is somewhat pleasant–it means I can no longer feel the pain of the ninety-plus-pound rucksack digging into the tops of my legs. But my back and shoulders ache terribly. I try stretching my neck, but it does little good.

I conclude that I've slept through a rough flight once the smell of vomit reaches me. The weak stomach isn't hard to locate; it's the private seated across and down a bit from me. His reserve parachute and part of his rucksack are covered in a crust of hardened, red vomit. His head is hung, eyes open. A piece of dried noodle hangs from his chin. *Had the same MRE for dinner. . .spaghetti.*

It's dark inside the airplane, as well as outside, but in the dim light toward the back I can see a jumpmaster and some of the flight crew moving around. They must have just given the twenty-minute warning. I rest my head on my ruck, close my eyes again and try to get some more sleep.

The soldier next to me squirms, trying to adjust the weight of his parachute. I lift my head and open my eyes again, blinking away the sleep. One of the jump safeties is making his way down the center of the aircraft, perched on the metal rail separating the left and right-door jumpers. Occasionally he stops and yells down at us, alternating from left to right. I can't hear him. Soldiers are putting their helmets on, fastening their chin straps and tightening the parachute retention straps.

They're getting ready. By the time the safety is directly above me I've managed to worm my hand out from the jumbled mass of gear and body parts to remove my earplugs. He's yelling over the noise.

"...one pass, un-ass! We're gonna be over the DZ for fifty seconds! Gonna try for only one pass!" He moves further down the rail and turns to the other side. I can still make out some of what he is saying. "...good visibility...five knots...gusting to ten."

Yeah, right. Heard that line before. Means you can't see anything, and the winds holding steady at about fifteen.

I take both ear plugs out and put my helmet on.

The safety comes back down the rail. "...fifty seconds of green light. Don't rush the door! *Hand* me your static lines, don't throw 'em!"

He moves on down the rail, toward the rear of the aircraft. I nod off to sleep again.

"Outboard personnel, stand up!"

The jump commands have begun. *Time to go to work.*

The two rows of soldiers along the skin of the aircraft begin labored efforts to right themselves. I hold out my hand and the soldier directly in front of me gladly takes it, using my weight to pull himself up.

"Inboard personnel, stand up!"

I push myself up as far as I can and take the hand offered to me by the same man I helped. He heaves me to my feet. Now we're close enough for the brims of our helmets to hit if we turn our heads. I mouth the words "thank you." He nods.

The seats need to be folded up and out of the way, but we have too much equipment strapped to us to bend over and undo the legs. We're still almost too crowded to even lift an arm, let alone bend over to unfasten the legs from the floor–I can't even *see* the floor.

Once everyone is standing, or at least making the attempt, I can no longer hear the jump commands or see the hand and arm signals. I have to rely on what the men in front of me are doing. But I know what's coming anyway. I could do this drunk and blindfolded.

The sound of static lines being attached to the cable running directly overhead tells me that the "hook up" command has been given. The soldiers near me are attaching theirs. I do the same. *Doors should be coming open soon.*

I'm right. From the rear of the aircraft comes the sudden rush of noise as both doors are opened simultaneously. I yank down on my static line, over and over, and so does everyone else–venting adrenalin. A soldier somewhere behind me lets loose a long and rattled rebel yell. I bend over as much as I can, to take some of the weight off my shoulders, and breath deeply. *All right. Come on. Let's get out of this damn bird.*

The soldier to my front passes back the hand signal for "one minute." I pass it back myself and check my equipment for the last time. I pat the pull tab for my rucksack release and the reserve parachute handle. Everything looks in place.

I get the signal for "thirty seconds." *Okay! Here we go!*

The area above the door suddenly lights up. The green light has come on. The outboard row lurches forward. The private with his spaghetti sauce and hanging noodle goatee shuffle by, still wide-eyed. Then the last outboard soldier goes by, yelling "Last man! Last man!" We let him pass, then move over to the middle of the aisle and get ready.

The soldier in front of me takes a step. Then the airplane dips and we are sent tumbling forward, the green light quickly coming into view, then the safety, frantically trying to gain control of the flung static lines. The soldier I'm following disappears out through the roaring black hole of a doorway. I hold out my static line and try to slow my momentum, but can't. There's nothing to do but keep going, take the big step and let the night have me.

For a moment my eyes might as well be closed. I cannot see anything, only feelings– falling, turning. My chin is tucked and my knees are tight together, hands clutching the reserve parachute. I let loose, reach up, grasp the thick risers and pull down hard, ready to absorb the opening shock of my main parachute. It opens, and I hang, suspended somewhere above the earth, slowly oscillating.

Things begin to appear in the glow of the moon, but nothing of substance, only shadows. And the silk canopy above me–my wings. Alone in the quiet, comforting, yet peculiar void of space–no horizon, no earth, no solid ground to promise safety–just me. I'm floating in darkness, dangling before the giant white face in the sky.

I hear a sound like a large bird gliding overhead, wind in its feathers. The sound comes closer and for a second the dark silhouette of another paratrooper hovers before me. I can't see his face, but can hear him breathe. *Slip away, god dammit! I'm lower! I've got the right-of-way!* He vanishes without incident. I pull down on my left rear riser, slipping away, just in case.

Bad things sometimes happen up here. Once, in a high-altitude entanglement over a drop zone in Arkansas, another jumper drifted above me and I stole his air. His parachute collapsed and he rolled off of my chute before streaking by me. That's how the game of aerial leap frog always begins, two men, too close, way up in the sky. The other solider's canopy had then inflated below me and I watched helplessly as my own collapsed, like an air mattress on a campfire, and then came the terrifying seconds of free fall. Over and over, taking turns, hoping I wasn't going to be the first one to the ground. Knowing the odds were fifty-fifty, but not comforted by it. I lucked out that time, my parachute was the last to catch air. As I lay there on the ground, my mouth bleeding and my face buried in the dirt, I could hear the other guy cry out in agony. Broken legs, but alive.

Nope. Can't go home in a cast. No sir. Stay out my way!

I hear muffled thuds and grunts below me: other jumpers landing. I yank down on my rucksack release and watch as it disappears. Then the sharp jerk as it reaches the end of the lowering line. I find the tie-down, that keeps my weapons case tight to the harness, and untie it. My hand rests on the quick release assembly, ready to jettison it as well. I hesitate. Off in the distance, close to where the horizon should be, I see a bright white, drawn-out muzzle flash. A second later comes the report. It sounds like a burst from a fifty-caliber machine gun. More flashes of gunfire light up the darkness below me. *Chaos as usual.*

The soldiers stationed here at the Fort Polk training center are good at what they do, and have obviously been waiting for us on the drop zone. We're being shot at with blanks only, but that doesn't stop my body from pouring a twelve-ounce jolt of adrenalin into my system. I don't like the idea of being shot, with a make-believe bullet or otherwise. My pride is fertilized by my ability to survive. I have the heart of a hunter, the job of a worrier and, for a few seconds more, the wings of an owl. But these mice aren't acting all that meek.

The fire fight below dissuades me from letting go of my weapons case. I might need my weapon as soon as I land. Riding in any equipment greatly increases chances for injury, but we train as we fight, so I'll take the risk.

The ground is somewhere close, I'm sure, and coming fast. I pull the two front risers down to my chest, bend my knees slightly, keeping them and my feet together, and wait for impact. *Ahh . . . this is gonna hurt!*

I'm not aware of my feet touching, just the hard packed earth receiving the back of my head with all the loving caress the windshield of a speeding car offers a flying beetle. I've just been body slammed into Louisiana. My hands and feet feel numb and tingly. *Have to start breathing. Holy Christ and shit that hurts!*

A burst of machine gun fire reminds me what I'm here to do. Someone runs by, almost stepping on me, but not seeing me. He has an M-16 held at the ready and a radio hand mike against his ear. I lie still, can't tell whether he's a friendly or not. He leaves my field of vision, and a few seconds later I hear a three-round burst from an M-16 off in the direction he went.

All right, time to get into the fight.

I don't feel like much of an owl anymore. All I really feel like is curling up in the nearest stretcher and coming to terms with my most recent dose of concussion. But I unzip my weapons case anyway, pull out my M-4 (a carbine version of an M-16) and quietly chamber a round.

I unharness myself from the parachute, low crawl over to my rucksack and don my MILES halo and harness, my rifle has already been equipped with the MILES laser. These are a pain any way you look at it, but for war games it is the only way to distinguish between who has been shot and who hasn't. The halo is worn around your Kevlar helmet and the harness over your shoulders. Every time a blank round is fired from a laser-equipped weapon a beam is sent out and if it comes in contact with a soldier, the MILES gear he's wearing lets out a continuous, high-pitched whistle. This annoyance can only be turned off by taking a "key" out of the laser–thus inactivating it and preventing the hit soldier from "killing" anymore himself–and inserting it into the proper place in the harness. It sounds great in theory, but, as I've said before, more of a pain than good. It's borderline reliable in fair weather and not at all once it rains. Also, the slightest bump usually sends the laser askew. After the second day of fighting, or the first if you've jumped in, as we tend to, there's absolutely no point in aiming your rifle at all.

I stay prone behind my bulking rucksack. My night-vision goggles are mounted to the front of my helmet now. With their aid I have pushed back the parameters of the surrounding void. Through the tunnel vision of my goggles the world has become a dim green and eyestrainingly grainy place. I can faintly make out the nearest tree line, it should be the edge of the DZ were our company rally point is supposed to be. I double check my sense of direction with a compass, then peer back in the direction of the trees. *Yep, right in there somewhere.* There is no sign of the infrared company markings that were promised to be there in the operations order.

I don't need a beacon. It's better this way anyway: the opposition has night vision capabilities as well, so they would pick up and zero in on our company assembly area. I've studied the maps during the op-order and feel as though I know my way around, sort of. Right over there in the tree line is hilltop 105, or so named on the map, it's where I have to be.

The skirmish I apparently dropped in on seems to have dispersed. There's still some fighting going on, but nowhere near me at the moment. I check my surroundings one more time and then stand up, fasten the big, heavy, olive-drab monkey onto my back, adjust the shoulder straps and move out, stopping occasionally to rest my throbbing knee and to do a three-hundred-and-sixty-degree scan of the area.

During one of my security halts I spot a faint light emanating from a patch of tall weeds. I immediately crouch down and scan the weeds around the light, looking for more of the same. I saw the light move once already, there's definitely somebody in there. *Pen light maybe? Map check?* I flip up my night-vision goggles to see if the light is infrared or not. It's not, I can see it with my naked eye, small and red. It moves again and suddenly grows much brighter, then dims. I catch a whiff of tobacco smoke. *What the hell? A cigarette?*

I drop to the ground, quietly free myself from my mobile home of a rucksack and low crawl closer to the thick patch of weeds. Once I've moved close enough, I quietly flip the selector lever of my M-4 off safe. A challenge and password has been given out to everyone during the op-order, but using the challenge would automatically alert this stranger as to who I was and leave me at the disadvantage. I want the drop on him, not the other way around.

"Hey," I whisper as loudly and firmly as I can manage. "Who's there?"

"A dead guy," is the response I get.

It's Sergeant Konkol, I recognize the voice. "Keith! What the hell?" I put my M-4 back on safe and crawl into the patch of weeds.

"Z, is that you?!"

"Yeah, man. What happened?"

Keith takes the cigarette from his mouth. "Bastards were waiting for me to land."

"They still around?"

"No."

I sit up and lean against Keith's rucksack. He has his parachute already bundled into its kit bag, and is leaning on it.

"They almost got me too. Didn't even have time to bag my chute. Had to get the hell out of Dodge."

I see Keith has his helmet off, he's nodding. "Chill here for a bit, Z. Nothin' but a big mess out there anyway."

I flip up my night-vision goggles and look into the sky. "Moon's gettin' a bit of a ring around it. Think it's gonna rain on us?"

"Always does," Keith says, handing me the cigarette he's smoking.

I take it and drag hard, still looking up at the night sky. Distant gunfire poses the only imposition on the serenity. "I landed like a ton of bricks," I say.

"Same here, amigo."

Then we hear movement and cut short the complaining. Someone has walked up and stopped just outside of our two-man hideout. I cup the cigarette in the palm of my hand and flip down my night vision. I can see the soldier clearly, he's scanning the area through his own goggles. He doesn't know Keith and I are watching. I assume, from his similar uniform and large ruck, that he's a friendly. I adjust the focus onto the soldier's face. It's one of my guys, Private Martinez.

I take another long drag on Keith's cigarette and hand it back to him. "Well. Sorry, bro. Gotta go."

"Catch ya on the flip side, Z."

I stand up. "Hey, Marty. Don't shoot."

"Specialist Zimmerman?"

"Yeah, hold up. Let me grab my ruck."

I find my rucksack where I left it. Martinez holds my weapon as I heave the monstrous thing onto my back once again. He hands the M-4 back to me once I'm ready and we head out. After awhile we link up with a large group of other soldiers from our company, stragglers from all different platoons. Martinez and I fall into the rear of their wedge-shaped formation and follow them toward the prospective assembly area.

The formation is moving fast and not stopping. Not long after joining them the point man walks us into what sounds like an enemy squad. Martinez and I drop to the ground and shed our rucks at the sound of the first burst of automatic weapons gun fire. *Damn! Knew we wouldn't get of this DZ unscathed. Movin' too fast!*

As the firefight heats up Martinez crawls over to my side and we provide flank security. The soldiers in the lead of the formation have moved an M-60 gunner to the front and it sounds as though he has gained fire superiority. The darkness is filled with noise and bright flashes, other smaller caliber, belt-fed machine guns have joined in. I can't tell which muzzle flashes come from whom anymore.

Someone yells for a cease fire. After the last burst from the M-60 all I can hear is the ringing of my ears and the whistling of MILES equipment. *Somebody got wacked.*

The soldiers in the lead pick up and move forward, two at a time. The enemy has vacated. As Martinez and I move out we pass two men from second platoon sitting on their rucks, helmets flung to the ground and with little yellow MILES keys protruding from their harness. One soldier is digging into an MRE. Neither of them will have to heft the burden of their rucksack for almost a week and they will both get some sleep tonight too, luxuries we among the living won't experience. They don't seem all too pleased with themselves though;

this is not a game to anyone. It's training for war; one we may never be made to fight, but nevertheless, they would be dead.

The formation moves slower, for awhile, then picks up speed again. The primary mission is to secure the drop zone, or airfield, as quickly as possible, only then can the rest of the Army be air landed. This mission is only training though, so we don't have any support on the way, it's all on us.

Five-hundred meters from the edge of the drop zone we stop abruptly. I hear the challenge and password being exchanged, then we advance, moving into a small patrol base set up by what appears to be the remnants of Alpha company. Apparently a lot of us have been killed already.

The First Sergeant is at the center of the perimeter getting accountability of the company. Our formation files by and we get our names checked off on the First Sergeant's list before falling in with what's left of our organic squads. As my name is being checked off, I let the First Sergeant know that I ran into Sergeant Konkol. Once the drop zone has been secured, the location of a casualty collection point will be determined, and Keith, along with all the others, will be sent to the rear. There they will pick up trash around Fort Polk, or wash pots and pans in some chowhall until our company gets a request in for new troops.

Staff Sergeant Mario Miramontez, our squad leader, is pleased that Martinez and I made it to the assembly area. I tell him about Konkol's fate. That, according to Sergeant Miramontez, leaves us with only a five-man squad; apparently two others from 3rd squad have also been logged as "killed in action" on the roster.

Martinez and I have had our rucks off for only a moment when our platoon leader, Lieutenant Doyle, comes by with word that the company commander wants to have 1st platoon occupying Hilltop 105 first thing this coming morning. Lieutenant Doyle wants 3rd squad to secure the hill *now*, since we are all accounted for–either here, or dead– and hold it until the platoon gets to at least ninety percent.

I take a much-needed drink of water from one of the two one-quart canteens attached to the belt of my load-bearing equipment, next to my ammunition pouches, before taking my position as point man. The map and compass are rechecked and then I lead the squad toward Hilltop105.

There are a good two hours until sunrise; I have plenty of time to move under the cover of darkness. I take my time, moving cautiously. I'm sure the entire platoon won't stay out in the open of the drop zone once it gets light, no matter if they haven't got their ninety percent yet. All I have to do is take the hill, and keep it. If we sustain too many casualties getting there we won't have a chance in hell of taking it, let alone keeping it. *Watch there be a whole platoon dug in up there!*

We arrive unmarred, without making any contact at all with the enemy. The hill is an unassuming lump of terrain, not any different than the ones next to it, or the hundreds we crossed over on our way here. It's not very large either; spread out in a perimeter, our undermanned squad barely fits on it. None of us can understand what is so terribly important about occupying it. But all that is neither here nor there; we got here all right and now we own it–end of dilemma.

Sergeant Miramontez orders the squad to get some sleep, designating two men at a time to stay awake and provide security. Martinez is one of the two privates chosen to pull the first guard shift. I'm so jazzed up from walking point that I tell him to go ahead and get some rest, I'll take the first half hour. There's only going to be a brief hour for sleep anyway, and I want my men to be ready.

The squad is asleep quickly, laying prone with their weapons in hand, ready to disengage their dreams of home, or girlfriends, in an instant and fight–or so, as their team leader, I would like to believe. I want the privates in my team to be well trained and motivated and have the same benefit from me as I had from my old team leaders. I hope I'm a good leader.

Keith Konkol is a better team leader than I. He has been around longer, more experienced and better trained. I would feel more comfortable if he were with us, his men are now my responsibility. There are only three privates to worry about, so my job hasn't changed much, it was just nice to have Keith here to watch my back.

Our squad leader is a good man too. I've not worked with him for that long, but we seem to hit it off. He says he likes to fish and has heard that I was the one to talk to. I know his last duty station was in Hawaii, he has told me stories about catching trevally and barracuda. I hope he isn't going to be bored with a few pan-size largemouth. He might like the chain pickerel though; you know, remind him of baby barracuda, maybe.

Wonder what Konk's doing? Lucky dead bastard. Sure could use a smoke about now.

I'm tired. The last trickles of adrenaline have expired, or perspired–I don't know which. My eye lids have begun refusing any commands to stay open, no matter how threatening. If I blink too long I'll be asleep. *Got to stay awake. Can't. . .shut. . .eye bally thingies.*

. . .

I take another drink from my canteen, splashing a very minute amount of water onto my face. I also pull out a cigarette; not lighting it, but smelling it–I don't need to broadcast our presence. I contemplate putting some of the dry tobacco in my mouth, but Sergeant Miramontez has some chew, I remember. *Maybe I'll bum some. Wonder if he's awake?*

He is, as I bring him into focus with my night-vision goggles I can see that he is sitting up. He has the hand mike of his radio pressed to his ear, periodically whispering back to whomever it is awake on the other end. I crawl over to him.

"Hey, Sergeant. Let me get a little pinch of that chew ya got."

Sergeant Miramontez reaches into a pocket and brings out a hockey puck-size can and hands it to me. "Roger that, sir. We'll wave you in."

I look at him funny. *Huh?* Then I realize he's talking into the hand mike.

It's too dark to read the label on the can I was just handed, can't make it out through my night vision either. I take a pinch anyway. *God damn!* I spit it out.

Sergeant Miramontez chuckles. "Too much for you, Zim?"

"That shit's vile." I spit again, trying my best to be quiet. "What's the deal?" I ask, changing the subject. "The platoon comin' yet?"

"Yeah. They'll be here in about thirty minutes. Go around and wake everybody up."

"Roger that, Sergeant. They setting in up here, or are we gonna fall in with them as they go by?"

Sergeant Miramontez pats his shirt pockets. "What did you do with my can?"

"Here, you can keep it, Sergeant."

He takes it, pops the top off and stuffs a lip-full into his face. "Ah the el thee..." he stops, adjusts the wad of chew and continues. "All the Lt. said was for us to wave the first squad in. I don't think we'll be here long."

I crawl around and wake Martinez and the other two privates up and tell them the situation, then move back to my position in the perimeter behind my rucksack. The sky has begun to lighten, I can make out the silhouettes of pine trees around me. I remove my night vision from the front of my helmet and tuck the device into my shirtfront– it hangs, secured by a lanyard around my neck.

Good mornin' Louisiana!

I watch as the first rays of sunlight brighten my limited view of the drop zone and penetrate into the tree line. There's no sign of rain this morning, it could turn out to be a hot day. Have to refill my canteens. If we don't get a resupply we'll have to ration water. My guys already know that, but I'll remind them. I'll have to watch Martinez close too, he never complains; he could pass out without me even knowing he was feeling bad.

Three soldiers enter the tree line. I can see them silhouetted against the opening of the drop zone, the sun peeking up behind them. Sergeant Miramontez sees them as well. He rises up on both knees and waves to them. I hear him on the radio. "Okay, I see the lead element. Tell them to keep coming straight."

One of the privates sits up, stretches and begins digging into his rucksack. I squint into the morning sun, watching the shapes of the three soldiers moving slowly towards us. The point man stops, he has seen our signal. He motions the other two to stop and raises his rifle.

I grab a handful of pine straw and throw it at the sitting private. "GET DOWN!"

Too late. The soldier fires. The private's MILES whistles. I flip my M-4 off safe and touch off a few rounds in their direction. *Son of a bitch!*

Sergeant Miramontez is on the radio. "CEASE FIRE, GOD DAMMIT! IT'S US!"

One of the three soldiers takes cover behind a tree and continues firing at us, the other two run left.

Sergeant Miramontez is hit, I hear his gear whistling. "Fuckers!" He yells, throwing his helmet into the pine straw.

I follow the lead runner in my peep sight. As he passes the shadow of a tree I can see his uniform. He's not one of us. I touch off a three-round burst and the soldier stops running and takes off his helmet. *Gottcha!* I swing onto the other running soldier and empty my magazine. He stops and sits down. *Oh yeah!*

The soldier behind the tree is still shooting at us. I can't find him through my sight, the glare's too bad. I roll over. "Hey, Marty! You hit?"

"No, Specialist. But everyone else is."

Shit! I look over at Sergeant Miramontez. His helmet has slid down the hill. "Where's first platoon?"

He shrugs. He isn't allowed to talk once he's dead. *Dammit! I need his radio!*

I hear a long burst of machine gun fire. It wasn't the guy behind the tree, all he's carrying is an M-16, capable of only a three-round burst. I peer around my rucksack. 1st platoon is here, I see the lead squad entering the woods. They came from behind and got the last guy. *Out-friggin'-standing!*

I yell from behind my ruck. "HEY! WE'RE FRIENDLYS! DON'T SHOOT!"

* * *

Martinez and I are the sole survivors of 3rd squad, and as the platoon sets in a hasty perimeter around us, we conduct a thorough search of the enemy and their belongings. The first man I shot has a complete copy of the battalion op-order hidden in his rucksack. We ask him who he wacked out on the drop zone, but he's dead and won't talk to us. Whoever it was he killed, they must have been important.

I take Sergeant Miramontez's radio before he and the two privates are dragged off to a casualty collection point. Martinez and I fall in behind the platoon and listen in on the cursing and yelling of the squad leaders as they engage in firefights throughout the morning and afternoon.

By the end of the day we have been whittled down to less than forty percent, but our end of the drop zone and the buffer zone around it is almost secure. Our drastically under strength platoon sets in around the casualty collection point and waits for casualty evacuation and further orders.

Lieutenant Doyle orders me to take my team on a reconnaissance patrol around the perimeter. He says I can take my pick of other squads' privates to fill out my team, but I tell him I'm fine with only Private Martinez. Two men can move quieter than an entire fire team, and I trust Martinez.

We move patiently, stealthily. I enjoy being away from the platoon and on my own, feel safer and less burdened. I creep along for awhile and stop, then motion for Martinez to move up in the same way. It's exactly how Mom and I would hunt squirrel when I was young. I'm having fun.

We locate an enemy cache of five ten-gallon water jugs and three boxes of MREs. It's buried and covered with pine straw, but doesn't look quite natural enough. The day has turned into a scorcher and the platoon hasn't been re-supplied with water. All of my canteens are dry and some of the soldiers are severely dehydrated and close to becoming heat casualties. The water is a great find.

After Martinez and I refill all our canteens and drink enough out of the jugs themselves to make us sick, I call Lieutenant Doyle to report in. He wants me to come back to the platoon location immediately so I can lead a squad out to retrieve the cache and possibly set up an ambush overlooking the site.

We follow orders, but not without incident. On the way back to the platoon area Martinez and I run into some trouble. I am scanning my surroundings and am about to motion Martinez forward when I spot movement. It's a lone enemy soldier, a sniper. He's well camouflaged, the shredded burlap of his ghillie suit perfectly match the pine-straw carpet of the woods. I point him out to Martinez and then let the sniper walk into our hasty ambush. I don't trust my MILES laser enough for a long shot, so I wait until he is close before I shoot him.

* * *

That was day one. We stayed in Louisiana for almost a month, and as far as getting rained on and being miserably cold, we lucked out, it rained hard a couple of nights and that was it. But, there's never a comfortable medium is there? It was hot every day, the sun never could get enough of us. We swore we would never go outside during the daytime again, boycott the damn sun, maybe even court-martial it. Yeah, the heat was getting to us.

But we survived, and got to go home on leave for two weeks. The time passed far too quickly. Dad and I managed to squeeze in some fishing, which I greatly needed. We tried for smallmouth bass in the headwaters of the Huron River, and caught some too, all from the pool below a miniature dam the Army Corps of Engineers built back in the 1970's. It's one of only a few moderately deep holes in that part of the river, standing out from the long stretches of shallow, shale-bottomed runs–suitable solely for the less finicky carp and longnose gar that rile the otherwise clear water with their obstructive carousing. I curse at them every time for hindering my chances at smallmouth, while secretly hoping to snag one.

Trips like that with Dad are what I miss most. Homesickness was really tough in the early days of this enlistment and I would like to think I've gotten over it, but sometimes, I can still feel it. Usually it's bad for the first few days after I come back from leave, like now for example, but the worst flare-ups occur during hunting season. The nights get that nice chill, maybe even a frost, and the air has the smell of Fall. The smell of possibility, anticipation, luring you into the woods during the small hours of the morning. The cold making ghostly figures with your breath in the moonlight. The sounds. The stillness. All surrounding your red ears, numb fingers and nagging belief that anything can happen in autumn.

In my family it is deer hunting, not fly fishing, that defines our lives' routines and is taken as seriously as religion. Finger tabs and bowstrings are sacred items; the sharpening of broadheads and the hours of practice are ritualistic; the dinnertime stories of past hunts are a tradition. The unstringing of the bows at the close of season is always a somber time, punctuated by a lot of greatly exaggerated sighing; soothed only by the rehashing of our close, and often successful, encounters with deer, and, of course, the laying of next year's plans. I miss being a part of that, part of my family.

While I was home I got the chance to see one of my old highschool buddies, Steve Barnett. He joined the Army a year and some after I did and is now in the 1st Ranger Battalion down in Georgia. He was home for a weekend and it was good to talk to him. I wish we could get together more often. Neither of us have enough time to though, and we both know that too, but we still promise each other, over a handshake as we are parting, that we will definitely keep in better touch. I really wish we could.

I also had a date with a very pretty girl, though *she* didn't think it an actual date. She's small, and strong, and has beautiful brown hair. Her name's Valerie Taylor, and she's my sisters friend. We went to a late movie and then to Denny's for coffee–I couldn't think of anything more original. We didn't talk much, which was strange because we'd been writing letters back and forth for months. I guess I sounded a lot more fun in my letters than in real life. She told me, on the way to the movie, that she was attending education classes at Kent State University, to be a teacher. I said: "Oh, ain't that where all them hippies got whacked?" The conversation seemed fairly strained from that point on. Hell, I don't know anything about college. That was the first thing that came to mind.

Now I'm back at Bragg. I still work nights, miss family. Valerie doesn't write me letters anymore. But I have friends here, and they all speak my language.

River Rats

I've always been attracted to running water. This is not one of those passive attractions like some down and out moths have for their scuzzy porch-light hangouts, nor the uncontrollable weakness one of my barracks-mates has for really trashy women. No, this is a much more serious obsession, even though it does not involve endless nights of routinely subjecting one's self to something that will eventually either singe you silly or steal your car.

I don't know when my love affair began. Early on, I'm sure, because I found myself peering mischievously over guard rails, ignoring no-trespassing signs and ruining new tennis shoes since long before I was old enough to know what it was I was *supposed* to be doing with a stream once I had found it.

At first, the draw was the creek or river itself: the swift rapids and riffles that were so hard to cross when on my back pretending to be a fur trapper swept away by the wrath of some wildly untamed and uncharted potential trade route, or the mini waterfalls that always thoroughly thrashed said trappers' handcrafted rafts, thus providing the exhilarating and ass-gashing thrill of struggling frantically to shore over jagged rocks. But once the novelty of high adventure wore thin (the sun setting on wet clothes can do that for a kid) all the other intricate pieces of the river became equally intriguing: the masses of roughly polished stones, the gnarled driftwood and the green herons.

It wasn't long before I discovered the fish, too, and naturally set out to catch them, but I became an avid river angler only after I realized that the hook-and-line approach was actually more effective, although noticeably less dramatic, than the large-boulder-hurling technique. Before that I was just a scruffy kid standing neck deep in the nearest current, with pebbles in my pockets, moss stains on the seat of my pants and an inexhaustible supply of waterproof imagination. I will never be proud, or ignorant enough to forget my rather primitive fishing origins.

So, it was inevitable that I would be drawn, as if by some sort of pre-programmed genetic magnetism, to the Cape Fear River. I regularly force friends of mine along with me, and as they never resist and actually appear enthusiastic, I truly believe that they are submitting to some hydro-afflictive demons of their own.

The Cape Fear River is much larger than the Huron River back home. It picks up near the center of North Carolina (where the Haw River and the Deep River collide just west of Shearon Harris Reservoir) and flows past Fort Bragg and Fayetteville en route to Wilmington and its final destination and salty demise at the Atlantic coast. The part of the river that my fellow river rats and I are most familiar with is the stretch just outside the town of Erwin. This is what I like to think of as the middle of the river: the somewhat undistinguishable, and in this case the most volatile, stretch between the relatively tame and shallow upper reaches and the deeper, sluggish, mud-bottomed waters that mooch out to the sea.

A small island, about an acre, lies just below the Route 217 bridge where the road crosses the Cape Fear River shortly before going up the hill and into Erwin. "Our Island" serves as a staging area for the majority of our river adventures. Sometimes, this island *is* the adventure, or at least the act of getting there can become one if the river is up a notch or two.

One such island adventure almost ended in a fatal and watery grand finale. Although those with me at the time may remember it as a *mis*-adventure. By my standards, the two terms are easily interchangeable.

Shane Roberts, Keith Konkol and I had somehow managed to evade the Fayetteville police radar and found our way to Dave's Waffle House. This has always been designated as our pit stop for late-night, post-bar-hopping munchies and sobering up before throwing ourselves at the mercy of the Fort Bragg military police. We half-heartedly tried to bring the world into focus over a round of coffee and latest ration from Keith's pack of Camel Lights, which, because of an unanticipated shortage, had been turned into the communal pack.

Shane had already received his orders for Korea, and, although neither Keith nor I actually said it to one another, we knew that this meal was going to be the last time we would sit across from The Lunatic From

Texas and watch him dose a signature Dave's sirloin steak–over-cooked and as tender as vinyl upholstery–with half a bottle of catsup and creamy Italian salad dressing. Then he'd stir the concoction in with a greasy order of home fries. It was hard to sit still through it, especially if your body was already trying to reject that last shot of Jose' Quervo.

Sometime between the traditional banter over the culinary tendencies of Texans and the equally traditional rousting of wallets and pants pockets brought on by the arrival of the check, we decided to say our "catch ya laters" over one last fishing trip together. Our Island on the Cape Fear seemed the perfect place to throw such a going-away fishing trip/all-day excuse to be drunk.

The next afternoon–*not* early the next morning, as we had agreed to the night before–the three of us loaded as much beer into a cooler as could fit alongside the token bag of ice. We heaved the cooler into the back of my truck and then, almost as an afterthought, tossed in our fishing gear.

None of us had paid any attention to the fact that, although it was sunny then, most of the state had had almost six inches of rain in the past week. The significance of this suddenly became obvious as we crossed over the 217 bridge and got our first good look down into the roaring and mud-colored river, the banks of which were under several angry feet of water. This did not suffice as a deterrent, as it probably should have.

I pulled off the main road and parked in what had become our usual spot: a pair of ruts that at one time could have been called a dirt road. The three of us stayed in the cab of my pickup for awhile having a smoke, swatting deer flies and strategizing our next move. One of us (who that actually was has been a topic of several accusations since then) interjected the notion that Our Island could still be achieved, quite easily even, if we all held onto the cooler and entered the water well upriver. We would have to hold our rods up and kick out far enough to let the current wash us right up onto our lovely little island. By then we had enough beer in us to think this was a brilliant idea.

The plan actually seemed to be working, until we–clinging to the cooler full of beer, wallets and cigarettes–came bobbing around the last bend upriver from Our Island. We had correctly calculated the distance from shore that we had to be to hit the island. It was not all that far;

under normal conditions we only had to wade a thirty foot, waist-deep channel to get there. Under normal conditions the current was never a concern either. But the problem that day quickly became obvious: Our Island was no longer there!

We knew where it *should* have been by the trees protruding from the middle of the river like the masts of an old galleon after having had her big wooden ass blown off by buccaneers. We had no other choice but to grab the gnarled bowsprit as we were swept by.

Once the cooler, and any other odds and ends of our fishing gear that hadn't been lost yet, were tied off to an accessible tree, we tried our hands at fishing. We wedged beer cans in tree crotches, wrapped our legs around whatever was available and cast gobs of bloody chicken liver out as far was we could manage. I had only momentarily debated taking along my fly rod, but since catfish are the only fish that can be caught equally well while either sober or inebriated, I had left my *real* rod back at the barracks. And at this point in the trip I was congratulating myself for exhibiting such keen forethought, and as it turned out, that was the last time any one of us would be guilty of that.

We stayed on Our Island until the cooler had more crushed aluminum cans and empty chicken liver containers in it than actual live beers. Keith and I were pale and shriveled from the waist down from standing in the water for three or four hours. The last time I had relieved myself I had been reminded of the dead nightcrawlers I used to find in the puddles along my parents' driveway after a thunderstorm. Shane had occupied the only comfortable perch above water and was working on a good case of bark rash on the insides of his thighs. None of us had caught any fish, so the decision to leave was unanimous.

The plan had been to leave Our Island the same way in which we had arrived, but there was a slight problem. Well, in all actuality, the problem was quite large: the usually calm pocket water directly below Our Island had swollen into an endless stretch of violent plunge pools and what appeared to be *at least* class-three rapids further on down. This meant we would have to either wait two days for the river to go down some, or jump in at the head of Our Island and hope we could make it to the far bank before we were swept into the frothy maw of the Cape Fear.

We made a brave and drunken attempt. Shane and I had the handles of the cooler and I was in the lead (*must have been the drunkest*). Keith pulled up the rear with the rods held over his head. The current was wicked, but I made it to land with only a few short yards to spare. I clung to an exposed root, exhausted, triumphant and not a little anxious to be out of the water. It all must have looked like a lost editor's cut from an *Indiana Jones* movie. Now, all Harrison Ford had to do was summon the last of his cinematography enhanced manliness (not that I doubt his natural supply) and heave the cooler– er, treasure chest–to safety, along with his two comrades. But, as anyone who has made their living doing anything other than writing action sequences for Hollywood can tell you, real life is not quite so predictable. I was looking back at Shane's blue lips and bulging eyes and trying to catch my breath long enough to laugh–then the root I was holding onto broke free.

I lost sight of Shane, and everything else too, although I'm sure I felt him clawing at my shoulders at one point during our wild, water-gulping ride through the rapids. I did what I could to save myself: feet downriver, arms out, head up. Although, at the time, I figured those were only the feeble gestures of self-preservation that my loved ones would expect for their sakes. I really thought I was a goner, but I did manage to make it to the end of the rocky, foam-spitting hell with some air left in my lungs; and with enough energy to doggy paddle to shore, grovel about and spit sand and muddy water for a spell.

Everyone else eventually made it to shore too, even the cooler. Not happily, or in the same place, but more or less in one piece. We drove into Erwin for more cigarettes but passed on the beer. We were completely and unquestionably sober.

Shane Roberts left for Korea not long after that river trip. He has been gone awhile now, actually, and life is a tad less interesting. I might even go so far as to say we miss the crazy bastard. And I am glad he didn't buy it in the Cape Fear. Now, only if we're lucky will the rest of us be able to survive our tenure within earshot of the Siren-like song of the river. I suppose the safest bet is to stay well out of its way.

* * *

Keith Konkol is still trying to wake up and remember what it was he got talked into last night. He's standing over John Falton and me, holding a mug of fresh coffee and a half burned Camel Light in one hand and rubbing his eyes with the other. "So, *where* we gonna put in at?"

John orientates the map that we have spread out on the floor so Keith can get a look. "We're leaving your Jeep down here," he says, pointing in the general direction of Fayetteville. "Then we can put in off of 217." Now he is pointing up to where Our Island is.

"Yeah, we could," I say, turning the map toward me and smoothing it out more, even though it doesn't need to be. "*Or* we could put in up further. There's a bridge outside of Lillington."

John yanks the map back closer to him. "That's almost *twice* as far."

"I know," I say. "That way it'll be better. I don't wanna waste the rental fee for a *stupid* two-hour float trip."

Keith puts the coffee mug down on one of his new stereo speakers and flicks ash at the ashtray laying on the floor next to the map. "Whatever. Where do we got to go for the canoe?"

John brushes ash off of Fayetteville and looks up at Keith. "We already *got* the god damned canoe. I told you that last night."

Keith grins, flicks more ash down on the map and reaches for his coffee. "No kidding? I must have been drunker than I thought."

John directs his attention back to the thin blue line that symbolizes the Cape Fear River. I stop fighting over the map and sit up. My mind is already made up: we'll put in at Lillington. *That should be a good day trip.* I reach for my pack of cigarettes as John tries to estimate distance; the edge of the map where the scale should be is faded and wrinkled from the wet boots it was stored under.

"How far ya reckon?" I ask.

"Hell, I don't know," he says.

I look over at Keith, but he's leaning back in a chair, asleep. I wake him up while John folds the map. The three of us grab flannel shirts and spinning rods and head out to the vehicles. There's still our list of supplies to purchase: hooks, sinkers, bait, beer, ice and food. At the grocery store we make one pass down the main aisle with the cart and throw in whatever looks like it's something we could eat quickly and with limited fuss. We leave with potato chips, dill pickles, trail mix, beef jerky, hot dogs, a bag of apples, a loaf of bread, and maybe some other crap underneath all that. The morning is starting to warm up and we're in a hurry to get on our way.

Keith parks his Jeep outside of a bait shop/livery next to a bridge on the southeast side of Fayetteville. We choose here because it will be easy to spot as we cruise past; there's an old sunken barge just downriver from the bridge. It's large enough not to be missed, even if the trip takes longer than we think and we come in after dark. We all agree this is a great idea, so it must be flawless.

The on-post recreation center has a whole yard-full of red, fiberglass canoes, all your typical, overly-abused and ill-maintained rent-a-crafts. But, the one John and I picked out yesterday should work, there are no visible holes. My trailer-light hookups don't work though, so it's strapped on top of my truck. I don't have a rack up there, so it's a bit tricky. I think it should stay on all right, but the bow hangs down and obscures most of my windshield. I hope that isn't too much of a problem–we'll see.

The three of us cram ourselves into the cab of my truck and drive toward Lillington. My truck is small but has a bench seat, so we fit–barely. John takes up most of the room. I have to keep my shoulders sideways because we are so tightly packed, and my head is half out the window so I can see. Keith is riding in the middle and shifting gears when I press down on the clutch. Sometimes he's asleep, but the truck's jerking and my cursing wakes him up long enough for him to do his share of the driving.

John is not asleep. I think he is as excited about getting on the river as I am. He is a little irritable this morning though. He wanted to wake up earlier than we did, but we had too much to drink at the bars last night. A live band at the last place we stopped were playing some old Lynyrd Skynyrd and Jimi Hendrix songs. They were good, and got better as the night went on. That's the way I remember it, anyway.

The sun is getting higher and hotter, and I'm a bit impatient myself. I always misjudge how long it takes to coordinate a fishing trip, or any kind of trip for that matter, when there are other people going. I wind up forgetting things and speeding around town all morning trying to get it right. I need to remind myself that this isn't really a serious fishing trip; it is more of an exploratory float trip designed to be fun and let us forget, for a day at least, that we're soldiers: the over glamorized and underpaid indentured servants of the government. This trip is supposed to be refreshing.

I look at the dash for the time. *We should be in Lillington by ten. Hope everything fits in the canoe. We've got a lot of crap.*

John sees me checking the time and looks at the clock himself.

"You think we can be on the water by ten?" I ask.

"Probably a little after. Ten after, maybe."

"I forgot Lillington was this far away."

John nods. "Thirty miles from were we left the Jeep. I think."

"Lot of river for one trip."

"That's if it was straight." John looks at me and grins. "That river *ain't* straight. It'll be more like *forty* miles."

I look at John and smile back at him. "We ain't gonna make it tonight, are we?"

John's smile turns into something more like a grimace. He looks away and shakes his head.

I laugh. "Konk's gonna be pissed."

We both look at Keith. He's still asleep. "Fuck him," John says.

At 10:00 we sputter through Lillington and by 10:10 my truck is abandoned by the bridge, the windows down about an inch, and the last of our gear has been loaded into the canoe. We have two coolers: the biggest one, with the beer in it, is parked in the middle and Keith has claimed it as his seat. John says this makes Keith the "beer bitch" and is already yelling at him to pass over a cold one. The smaller cooler has our food stuffs kept cool with a few handfuls of ice lifted from the main cooler. Most of our fishing tackle is in a camouflaged assault pack we use to carry extra ammunition and mortar rounds in at work. Everything fits into the canoe and we appear to be ready to kick this thing off. I take the bow, John takes the stern. We push away from the bank with our paddles, wobble on the verge of tipping for a moment while we get organized, and then head downstream.

The river here is wide and there is only a moderate current. The Cape Fear has never been a very clear river down this far, but today she is at least calm and lazy, gliding along well within her banks. We start out by paddling hard because that's what we figure we are here to do, but not long after the bridge has safely disappeared behind the first bend, we agree to take it easy and do some catfish jerking and beer drinking. After all, we're not on an upper-body version of a forced road march. This is our time to chill out, get drunk, dehydrated and sunstroked–not exhausted.

The sun gets higher and the day turns middle-aged. Our shirts come off and our sunglasses go on. None of us was smart enough to bring sunblock, but now we don't really care. We have a half dozen eatable-size blue cats clipped to our stringer, and we have made a sizable dent in the contents of the beer cooler. Spirits are high and tongues are loose–bladders too maybe, if John's accusations are accurate.

We talk about work for awhile, about how the military's training priorities may be cockeyed, and about the stodgy civilians who don't have a clue. They're continually getting bent out of shape about the U.S. sending troops overseas. We are volunteers, after all, many times over. We volunteered to join the Army, then to became infantrymen, and airborne. It wouldn't break any of our hearts if tomorrow we were dropped over some hostile country without a clear end objective in mind. We're fighters, dammit, so civilians shouldn't be afraid to let us fight. Maybe they're just looking out for us, but it's like a police officer's mom telling him to stay home from work on Friday nights because *"It's dangerous out there!"* Besides, it would certainly break up the monotony of training year after year and only getting to test it out on the native after-hours population of Fayetteville.

That conversation is eventually ordered to a halt. We are here to escape the Army, not drag it down the river with us. And in the silence brought on by the lack of ranting and arguing, a wet, static noise is heard in the distance. It sounds like fast water. Paddles come out of the water and the three of us sit motionless, listening. The noise is getting louder. It is definitely getting closer, but I can't see any sign of disturbed water up ahead. It seems flat as far as I can see.

Keith dips his paddle back into the water and holds it there. We all look over at it to judge our speed. We are going faster now than when we were paddling. I turn slightly and look back at Keith. Both he and John have worried smiles.

"Can you see anything up there?" John asks.

I turn around and lean forward, straining my neck and squinting my eyes. "Not really. Maybe something about a hundred yards out." I turn back around. "Just a little line. That's all I can see."

"A what?" Keith asks, trying to see past me.

"A line. See?" I point downstream. *It's just a line. How else do you want me to describe it?*

The noise of rushing water is much closer now. I can make out the line in the river better. It appears to be the lead edge of a set of steep rapids, *or* the lip of a small waterfall. *Oh man!*

John digs his paddle into the current in a futile attempt to slow our progress. "It ain't a waterfall, is it?"

"I don't know. If it is, it's only a small one." I'm close enough now to see water spray spitting up from over the edge. Our speed has doubled, the current is sucking us forward. *Shit. We're too close now to back off.*

"Well, stand up," John urges. "Get a better look."

I laugh. That would be difficult enough sober.

"Hang onto your beers, men!" Keith shouts over the steadily rising noise. "We're goin' over!"

John is shaking his head, exasperated.

I swallow the last sun warmed swig from my can and I drop the empty to the bottom of the canoe. "Okay. Here we go."

I dig in my paddle, straightening us out. There is only about two seconds for me to decide the best route, but I can't see anything anyway.

"Which way are we going?!" John yells.

I don't know! "Straight ahead!"

I see the top of a large boulder over the lip of water. The main current wants to go to the right of it. I dig in hard on the port side, trying to push us into the current. "RIGHT! GO RIGHT!"

As the bow clears the lip I can see down. It is not exactly a straight drop, but I don't have time to be relieved. The current sucks us over the edge and I raise my paddle to push away from the boulder, but it does no good. The port side of the canoe is raked along the side of the rock and I lurch forward on impact. Keith's paddle somersaults past my head and I hear swearing; he has fallen off his cooler. The canoe stays momentarily pinned to the boulder, white water threatening to surge over the gunnel and swamp us, but the swift current catches the bow again and blows us through the shoot, depositing the three of us into the calm pool on the downstream side of the rapids.

Holy shitballs! That was great! I take my paddle out of the water and turn around. For a moment I see the backs of both Keith and John's heads. They, too, have turned to get a look at what we have just conquered. And we have all turned to look over our right shoulders, shifting all of our weight to one side. The canoe promptly rolls over.

I'm underwater for a second and can still hear the roaring of the rapids. Then I surface, spitting water, kicking my feet and still holding onto my paddle. The water is cold, and it comes as a shock. It's deep, too. I look around for signs of life. I locate Keith's bobbing head among all the other floating debris from our wreckage. "Hey, Keith!"

He spits out a mouthful of water and the wet, broken cigarette hanging from his bottom lip. "Z! You alive?"

"Yeah, but I think we tipped the canoe!"

John swims out from under the capsized craft holding two spinning rods and his baseball cap. He stops long enough to call Keith and me idiots, accusing us of tipping the canoe, then swims to shore with the gear he has salvaged. Keith and I right the canoe and throw in all the flotsam we can reach and then head to shore ourselves. We pass John as he swims back out to dive for more gear.

Once all three of us are on dry land we drain the canoe and take stock of what we still have. Luckily, John found the third spinning rod. Our fishing tackle had been in an assault pack that, also luckily, had been strapped over one of the wooden cross members of the canoe. Not as fortunate was our beer and food supply. Both coolers had been flung open, sending all of their contents down the river. We had corralled about ten or twelve beers before they had gotten away, so that wasn't an immediate emergency. Besides, the cans float, so if we get going shortly, we can chase down the rest of our stray flock.

The only items from our food supply saved from the river are a bag of apples and a loaf of bread, because they both float as well. Unfortunately, the bread is soggy and dripping little gobs of dough all over the bottom of the canoe as we're loading up. I tear a hole in the bottom of the plastic bag and feed it to the carp. We'll be fine, after all –we have a meal of fresh catfish to look forward to.

The last of the gear and garbage gets loaded and we shove off again. There is a long trail of silver Coors Light cans to police up, along with any other odds and ends that we can find.

"Hey. Check this out," Keith says, holding up the metal stringer attached to the port side of the canoe. It had held a half dozen or more catfish, but now it holds only the mangled head of one. We had forgotten to pull in the stringer before we hit the rapids. *Damn!*

We finish off the half case of beer in the cooler and alternate between the three of us on who gets the next floater we come to. I'm becoming steadily drunker and more sunburned. It has been discovered that our sunglasses and T-shirts were also lost to the river, so we no longer have protection from the big fiery ball in the sky. We can't catch another mess of catfish either, because our bait was lost. And, the later it gets the more reality sinks in: we won't be sleeping in the barracks tonight, or eating in the chow hall (John and I already had a hunch this would happen, but are not happy about the inevitable). And we're already sick of eating apples.

Keith has laid out his lighter and the sodden remnants from his pack of cigarettes on the lid of the beer cooler to dry out. But it's a futile effort; by now we are pickled enough to roll the canoe without the aid of rapids, although they certainly help. We've developed a routine: tip, drag, drain, gather and reload. We have it down pat.

"Now there's...a big...bobber," Keith drunkenly points out.

John and I follow his gaze. Yes indeed, a buoy the size and shape of a small football, half fluorescent orange, half white.

"Look!" Keith hollers. "There's somethin' on it!"

It *did* move, both John and I saw it. *No kidding. Gotta be a trotline marker.*

We had been seeing some limb lines hanging from branches and other trotlines too, but even the latter had been close to shore, not out in the middle of the river like this one. Whatever it was on the other end had obviously broken itself, and the float, free from the set line.

We paddle alongside the buoy and I reach down and grab a hold of the line underneath. There's something heavy attached to the other end. I feel the weight for a second, then it feels me and bolts. I hold on for a moment while the creature tows the canoe, then, as it turns sharply, I'm forced to let go or risk tipping again. The brightly colored float leaves my hands and disappears into the depths of the murky river. A few "Holy shit's!" and "You see that's?" are exchanged while we wait for the buoy to resurface, because sooner or later it *has* to resurface. Right?

It takes longer than any of us thought, but after almost fifteen minutes Keith spots the orange and white buoy. It has resurfaced over two hundred yards upstream. This time I have a better plan. As Keith and John paddle us closer, I dig through our assault pack and come out with my fillet knife. Once we are about twenty or thirty yards away they stop paddling and let me slide over the gunnel, shifting all of their weight to the opposite side until I am in the water. I'm hungry and drunk enough to do just about anything for something to eat other than another bruised Red Delicious.

I carefully breast stroke to within arm's reach of the buoy with the slender blade of the knife in my mouth. Once there I take the wooden handle in my right hand and grasp the line underneath the buoy with the other. I'm ready for a tussle, but nothing happens. I then slide the index finger of my knife hand down the line. It's a thick, cable-like length of monofilament, almost three feet long. At the other end I feel the smooth, cool skin of a large catfish. But only for a second, then it bolts again, towing me close behind clinging stubbornly to the buoy.

I'm underwater for less than a minute, but deep enough to feel pressure on my eardrums. I feel the fish tire and I pull myself closer, probing through the cold, wet darkness with my knife. Once the blade makes contact I thrust it forward into the fish. I try to kill it as quickly as possible.

A few moments later it takes both Keith and John to haul the dead blue catfish into the canoe. We may go to bed cold, wet, and sore from the sunburn, but not hungry.

* * *

We pass under the 217 bridge sometime late in the afternoon and beach the canoe on Our Island. John lays out to dry what gear of ours remains, and Keith and I pool what little cash we have on hand and jog the mile and a half into Erwin. Once in town we split up, he to the grocery store to get more beer and dry cigarettes; I to go after bait and ice. I find a bait shop and the man takes the damp bills I hand him. I'm not too worried about my purchases but am actually surprised to see Keith waiting for me back at the boat with a fresh case beside the cooler and blissfully toking away on a Camel Light. I guess "no shirt, no shoes, no service" doesn't apply if the patron looks crazy enough.

Once re-outfitted with the essentials, we slip on down the river, but darkness closes in on us before long and we find a comfortable place to crash–a sandy bank with plenty of visibly dry drift wood. We beach the canoe, hang our gear in the trees around the camp site and build a small fire. As the flames grow higher we fillet the catfish, gather another load of wood for the night and strip down, hanging our wet shorts by the fire to dry. Then we pull up the two coolers and a rotten log and commence drinking beer, bullshitting and rotating our apple and catfish shish kebab. John even props his spinning rod on a forked stick in hopes of adding some late-night, fishing excitement.

Sometime in the morning we wake up stiff, naked and with sand lodged soundly in places it shouldn't be. I'm curled in the fetal position with my feet in the cold black circle of ash that had been our fire. If anyone had drifted by between the time we passed out and before the fire burned down, well...they would have had one hell of a sight!

None of us has taken along a watch, and the morning sun is well hidden behind the damp haze, so we have to guess at the time. I'll say it's around 6 or 7 o'clock. We load our gear, pick up all the beer cans, bury the fire pit and begin the journey home.

The swift current peters out and the going becomes painstakingly labor intensive. At times we are overcome by hallucinations (usually involving logjams that looked exactly like half sunken barges) and frantic fits of paddling. Eventually (sometime late in the afternoon) we cruise past the real barge and haul out by Keith's Jeep. My back is aching so badly that I can't stand up straight, and my arms feel as if they've been caught and mauled under a combine.

On the way back from picking up my truck I have a small, half-baked revelation: even after all the torment I've received from various rivers since I was a kid, I still can not get enough of them. And, I may not be learning much from my kamikaze-like tribulations, but I *am* sure of one thing: the best adventures certainly can be miserable before they turn into good memories.

John seems to agree.

The Pisgah Pilgrim

It is dark and quiet in the tree line, but if I listen closely I can make out small sounds: rustling leaves, the metallic clink of a canteen cup. And snippets from a hushed, urgent conversation around a map, participants unseen. Only a tiny light from a red-lens flashlight, aimed intently at images of hills and valleys–bobbing, shifting, passing from one hand to another.

A Zippo is struck next to me. Keith Konkol's camouflaged face is illuminated briefly in a bright, wavering light. Then it goes out, and it seems much darker than it was just moments ago. I smell tobacco smoke in the clean night air, and it spurs me to rifle through pockets in search of my own pack of cigarettes.

I am relaxed, but the senses of urgency and foreboding around me are thick, consuming, hanging amongst the darkened underbrush with the swarms of mosquitos. I slap my neck and look half heartedly for my lighter. Nervous, muffled laughter rambles farther down our defensive perimeter–privates screwing off, gear being adjusted. Then silence. Complete silence.

I sense something change. I get goose bumps and my scalp tightens. Then I hear it. A faint, distant sound way off in the night– fast, rhythmic thumping. Heads rise and turn. Those asleep awaken. It is what we have been waiting for–the sound of birds...inbound.

Shattering the silence, five Black Hawks burst over the treetops, stacked close together and moving fluidly, a giant, mechanical dragons swooping down into the clearing beside us. The hot blast of wind from the rotors washes over our position. Static sparks form erratic halos above the machines as they touch down. I squint, keeping dirt and small stones from my eyes. With weapon in hand I stand up, swing my rucksack onto my shoulder and motion for my fire team to do the same.

Keith is up and moving with his team behind him, crouched and running toward the open doors. I follow, and feel the heat of the engine. Adrenalin. Rotors roaring overhead. I clamber aboard and position my rucksack at my feet. The men behind me pile in.

The flight crew is silhouetted by the faint green cockpit light. They are looking back at us. Thumbs up, good to go.

My world shifts sideways and the horizon jumps, then the ground falls away. The ride is fast, furious, the pilot staying at treetop level, massaging the earth's contours with the belly of his aircraft. He banks hard. I see the tail of the lead bird–close, then gone. I hold on. Hills, creeks, unnamed places rushing by, barely visible in the moonlight.

The helicopter drops suddenly, the nose flares up and the ground rushes at me. We hit hard and dismount. I take three quick steps, then drop to the ground. Ruck thrown out in front, weapon at the ready, finger on the trigger.

The birds are up, then gone. It is quiet again. Silence.

A cricket chirps. Another answers. The waist high marsh grass around me begins to rise, having been beaten down by the hot rotor blast. Soon I am engulfed. Cold dampness soaks my uniform. The drone of more mosquitos. My ears are ringing, but it is quiet.

Dark objects slowly begin to appear, rising from the grasses: men crouching, then standing. The soft crackling of a radio hand mike. Ruck straps being tightened. Hand-and-arm signals: *Follow me!*

* * *

This past week has been a long one. We prepped all weekend, which meant sitting through op-orders, checking packing lists, going through manifests and pre-jump drills, plus tying up countless other loose ends at squad, platoon and company levels. We jumped onto Sicily Drop Zone, the largest one here at Bragg, late Sunday night, actually early Monday morning–0030 hours. Half past midnight. We then patrolled for three straight days, hunting for an imaginary enemy. I managed some shut-eye whenever the opportunity presented itself–a couple of minutes during a security halt, a couple of hours, on and off, at a patrol base.

Things got more exciting on Wednesday night. Someone up at Brigade scrounged together a bunch of guys from another battalion as an opposition force for us and sent them out to MOUT site, the mock town parked out here in the middle of the Fort Bragg training area. Brigade also allocated some choppers, so our company air assaulted to within a mile of the objective and we hit it at dawn. The mission itself was good training and a little fun too, I suppose, but it was the same old shit, reheated. Tearing up another set of BDU's on the concertina wire (that's almost fifty bucks for the pants, shirt and patches) getting my weapon caked with mud (that will take hours to clean) and inhaling too many smoke grenades. Being trapped in a room or trench with one of those–even if it isn't tear gas–is enough to turn me off cigarettes. Well, for a day anyway.

It used to be more enjoyable. The whole "mission" thing; assaulting the objective at night, machine guns rippin' away, smoke everywhere, the high pitched whistling and then ground thumping explosions of the artillery simulators. It used to be such a rush. I had no problem convincing myself that it all was real. Now it's different. I look at everything as a chore. Not that it has ever been easy, but now, that is how I measure these things. How much is that torn uniform going to cost me? How long will it take to get my M-4 clean after crawling through that mud puddle? How mad should I get at my best private for falling asleep during a security halt? *I mean, hell, so did I!* The novelty of being paid to do what I used to do for fun as a kid has worn off. It's a lot of hard work.

I worry about a bunch of things, too. The same kind of crap I've lamented over before, like, how well prepared are my privates? What if something bad flares up somewhere and we get sent to extinguish the flames? Or add to the fire, or whatever. They might have to do this for real one day. Will they do alright? I'll be out of the Army soon, so it won't really be my problem any more. But have I given them all I have? I know Private Martinez will be fine, but what about the others? Am I so preoccupied with fishing and counting down the days until I'm out of here that I'm neglecting my responsibilities? Will I be to blame if my guys get hurt after I'm gone?

The chopper ride was great, though; I love them, always real and powerful. It wouldn't bother me if I never strapped on another parachute, but I believe I *will* miss the air assaults. And I will miss the comradery, too. My friends. Yeah...that'll be the hardest part.

John Falton is going to be heading home for good in a few months. Back to his beloved Rocky Mountains. He's getting awfully excited about being a short-timer. When I ask him what he's gonna do after he gets out all he says is, "Going fishing with the Old Man." Anything else is unimportant, trivial. I know exactly how he feels.

Last weekend while running around getting ready for the training exercise, John and I cut plans for an extended fishing trip. Alpha Company has a long weekend pass from today, Friday, through Monday. These four-days don't come along often, so everyone's taking advantage of it. Most of the guys are heading down to Myrtle Beach, South Carolina. They're hoping to score big with the summer-vacationing college-girl crowd. John and I were thinking more of the other direction: west. Not sure how far west, just as far as it takes to get to a mountain and a trout stream. All this catfish fishing and groping worms and bloody chicken livers of late has both of us feeling a little unclean and in need of the kind of cleansing only a cold trout stream can administer.

That was the plan anyway. John didn't get the bad news until today: he's been screwed with weekend detail, arms-room inventory. It's an all-day affair and scheduled for Saturday. I'd like to say I offered to stay back and bass fish on post with him when he was done checking serial numbers, but I didn't. I need this trip more than he does. He's heading home to one of the finer trout-fishing meccas of this country in a few months. I have to beat around here for almost another year.

I told him I'd bring back some photos.

* * *

My truck rocks gently, waking me, as a vehicle glides down the mountain road. A red glow of brake lights floods through my truck cap's tinted windows. I stretch and roll over on my cot. It is light enough for me to see outside, but the sun won't be up for another half hour or more. To sit up I must bow my bead under the low, fiberglass ceiling of my bedroom. My woobie, the same camouflaged poncho liner that keeps me warm at work, is wrapped around my shoulders. On top of my disorganized heap of fishing gear is the lighter and pack of Camel Lights I set there last night before sprawling out on the cot, exhausted, at 2 o'clock. I shake the soft pack and a cigarette falls out. I pick it out from the corrugated bed liner, put it in my mouth and light it. *Mmm . . . the best days always start out in the bed of a pickup!*

One lift on my truck cap is faulty and the other is missing, so I have to hold the hatch up as I gaze over the tailgate and try to focus on the complexities of my surrounding asylum. It is still cool, and this is good, and the dense fog–which refused to stand aside as my poor 2.3 liter engine labored up the winding mountain road last night–has lifted. The grass below me looks damp, as do the leaves on the hickory branches hanging over my truck. A few feet off the road I can see that the land quickly drops off, down the steep, ancient side of the Blue Ridge and into the inviting unknown.

I had gotten off Route 40 in Morganton for gas, a soda and a Slim Jim and hadn't been inclined to get back onto the Interstate. I knew I was at least at the edge of trout country, if not already well submerged, and what I needed more than fuel, caffeine or Tabasco-flavored cow's lips and assholes was a mountain road with a gravel pull-off where I could get some sleep.

The man I gave my money to said I could find all the trout fishing I could stand if I took State Route 181 up into the Pisgah National Forest. So I chewed my Slim Jim and drank my soda–to stay awake a little longer–and logged away the last thirty miles. And, when the fog was thick enough, the grade steep enough and my old truck driving painfully slow enough, I knew it was safe to stop for the night. I was, at last, in the mountains!

I climb over the tailgate, take my morning pee and get behind the steering wheel again. I'm thinking about the last time I saw a live trout. *Too long ago. Wonder if this is gonna be anything like Pennsylvania? Better even? Maybe?* Pennsylvania seems so long ago, Oil Creek and Vic's cabin so far behind me. *What has it been? Three years already?*

I check the map, but it doesn't really do me much good. I know I left the State Route a half hour or so before I pulled off to park and sleep. The map isn't the most detailed anyway, and the entire Pisgah

National Forest area is partially obscured under a permanently ingrained muddy boot print. Although I could easily be mistaken, I swear I'm somewhere in the northern part of Avery County, right in the gap between the half-moon of the heel and the rest of the blackish-brown tread marks. It shouldn't be all that far to the nearest trout waters.

My truck starts when I turn the key. This brings relief. There are always moments, when parked somewhere far from the familiar and in an aging vehicle, that the engine's faithfulness is tested. With each successful ignition, the bond between tired man and rusted machine is strengthened. This may account for all the old men who eventually drive the same, primer-coated monstrosity with the cracked windshield, until both are too worn down and have gone too many miles to move efficiently anymore.

I realize that I have placed myself soundly amidst what *has* to be excellent trout-fishing territory, but it is still hard for me to backtrack. I want to continue going forward, farther up the mountain, because, near the back of my over-militarized hunk of head cheese is the nagging notion that I must drive on. *Drive on! Drive on! Drive on!* I force myself to turn around anyway. Coasting down the mountain road will be harder on the brakes but easier on the engine. I owe her that. Besides, I'm after a trout stream, not the hazy summit of Grandfather Mountain, or any others listed on the multitude of signs boasting their road's destination to me as I passed by late last night.

The road levels out and I'm forced to either give the truck some gas or roll to an eventual stop. I have been playing with nothing but the brake and clutch pedals for going on fifteen minutes. It is comforting to have control over the vehicle again after straining so hard and for so long against the reins of gravity. I don't recognize this section of road, don't think I traveled this way last night. I've been trying to follow my fishing intuition more than anything else. My map is crumpled in a ball now and bouncing around behind the bench seat with the shotgun, loose shells and last night's empty soda bottle–its vague and inconsistent nature finally got the best of my temper. There is, still, my dowsing-rod-like fishing intuition to rely on.

I drive over a small bridge, look over, see water, and stomp down hard on the brakes. The truck fishtails off the road. *Trout stream! Hot damn!* I stumble out of the cab, tighten my sandals and then jog to the middle of the bridge. It is a small bridge, and a small stream, but it sure looks good! I run back to the truck, shut the door and scramble into the back for my fly rod and vest.

* * *

After several hours of closer examination the stream no longer holds the charm I originally attached to it. Pleasant enough, but not what I'm going to let myself be satisfied with. Too shallow, lacking really deep pools, and the water is clear and sluggish, hiding no secrets in black pockets or under fast, white riffles. I can see the shadows of every rock, if not the rocks themselves, and the slightest move, by either me or a fish, is broadcast vividly by a large plume of mud that lingers and spreads like the smoke from miniature, underwater explosions.

Yes, there are fish, small, about four or five inches long (yeah, real whoppers, I know). I've caught at least a half dozen of the strange chubs, along with a couple *normal* creek chubs, on a #12 Soggy Coon nymph left over from the last time I was on a trout stream. I have resorted to calling the little fish red-fringed chubs because they are all silver but have neat streaks of red in odd places. Besides, I find it too disturbing to land a fish, unhook it and watch it swim away–no matter the size–and think to myself, "Gee, wonder what that was?" I just can't do it. So until I get back to the truck and dig out my fish-identification book, they will be officially, and unarguably, known as "red-fringed chubs."

I make a few more casts into the deepest piece of water available and land another four-inch red-fringe. This is fun. It reminds me of fishing Chappel Creek as a kid. And I'm finding that if I squint right, the red band on the chub's gill cover is easily blurred, blending it in with the other dab of red at the base of the pectoral fin –vaguely, and with a van-load of imaginative assistance, like a...*like a cutthroat trout! They could be twelve-inch cutts! And I'm up in the Rockies! Yeah!*

I reel in my line and slog back upstream to the bridge and my truck, not being concerned with the trail of muck I leave in the water behind me. I'm done here. I shouldn't have to imagine trout anymore.

I don't always have to be the Walter Mitty of fly fishing. These are real mountains with real trout streams.

Once back to the bridge I lean my rod against the front of my truck–easily accessible if I decide to try a couple of quick casts before I leave and in plain view from the driver's side seat, so as not to be forgotten and left behind in a cloud of dust and flying gravel. I open two cans with the P-38 can opener on my key chain, one of peaches and another of pork and beans. After the beans are in the pan and the propane burner lit, I crawl into the front of the truck, wind down the windows and pop open the glove compartment. I think I remember putting my fish-identification book it there, and I'm right. I sit back, sip peach juice from the can and open the book.

I have the task of locating a four-inch minnow, with peculiar markings, lost (because I can't follow simple, written instructions, like those found within the first few pages) somewhere in a two-hundred-twenty-page collage consisting of six-hundred-sixty color photos and paintings of anything from Atlantic salmon, bucktooth parrotfish and blue whales, to tiny warpaint shiners that have a "vertical, red line behind eye" and dwell only in the clear mountain streams of the southern Appalachians. *Well, I'll be dammed! Warpaint shiner! Sounds a lot better than red-fringed chub. How did I fare, you ask? Oh, I caught a nice mess of mountain warpaint. And you?*

After solving the chub mystery, I continue flipping through the book, concentrating on the section about minnows, suckers, and shadlike fishes, because the three of these make up over half the fish I have caught in my lifetime, although I would never buy a T-shirt or bumper sticker that advertized that. I become entranced, lost in a world of brightly colored dace and drab, yet strangely shaped stickleback and wildly outrageous darters. I'm fantasizing about a creek that could grow two-pound rainbow darters when the first volcanic bean bombs erupt from my over-heated lunch. I turn off the burner, scrape the hard, blackened layer off the bottom with a fork and mix it in with the rest. I eat my peaches while I wait for the main course to cool.

After lunch the pan is wiped clean with a handful of dry leaves and tossed into the back of the truck along with the propane stove and the two empty tins. I take up my rod and limp back onto the bridge. My bad knee has stiffened noticeably, but the discomfort is easier to bear with the fly rod handy. There appears to be only one decent pool on the upstream side. It's shallow, but the bank is undercut on one side and the overhanging, root-entwined earth is throwing shadow over the deeper end. I notice the dark shape of a fish holding tight to the bank and only occasionally nosing out into sunlight long enough to inspect whatever insect activity is going on down in the mud.

This is enough excitement to let me completely forget about the ache in my knee. I sneak around the end of the bridge and into the woods on the opposite side of the pool to where the fish is. There is too much foliage along the stream to allow me to cast from beneath the trees, so I creep out into the water a ways. I'm staying crouched over while moving and once I am in position to attempt a cast, I take a knee–my good knee–and pull line from the reel. The cold water soaks the hem of my shorts, but it's turning into a hot day, so I don't have to worry about getting wet. All that needs worrying over is my back cast.

I make a sidearm cast, keeping the line low to the water and allowing the back cast to unroll upstream, safely away from the grabby blackberry bushes that clawed at my legs as I was trying to enter the stream. My cast isn't pretty or graceful, but I manage to lay the line down over an exposed rock out in midstream, reducing the chance of spooking the fish with a big splash. Five feet of leader, with the weighted nymph at the end, is all that drops into the pool. I watch as the fly sinks; it is only a few inches from the edge of shadow. When it settles to the bottom, I jerk my wrist once, giving the fly a lively twitch. The fish materializes from the shadow and eats it. I reflexively set the hook and almost jerk the ten-inch smallmouth bass clear out of the water. He recovers from my sucker punch quickly and gives a strong fight, even with aerobatics. I hold my breath every time the fish is airborne; not because I'm afraid of losing him, but for fear of him coming down headfirst onto one of the exposed rocks. He nearly hits one, leaving a splattering of water drops, dark in contrast on the smooth, water polished knob of dry stone.

I gain control of the bass, bring him into arms' reach and secure him by the bottom lip. As I am removing my fly from the corner of his mouth I'm also admiring his good looks, the subtle marvels of smallmouth: his exact, olive brown likeness to the mud-lined stream bottom and the bright red eye with deep black pupil–like a single mountain ash berry resting in the moss at the base of its parent tree. I think about keeping him to eat tonight, but instead I let him go and he darts back to his cool, shaded sanctuary along the far bank. The day is young and I am still full from lunch. He would not have been so fortunate later in the evening. Compassion, as well as pride and principle, can easily be overridden by hunger.

I am satisfied. I have done everything right: I found the fish, made the right cast, used the right fly, and successfully hooked and landed him. These are the wildflowers of life that should be appreciated and recognized with a quiet, reflective moment–but, I *am* mildly disheartened. I had hoped that the dark object at the shady end of the pool was a trout. And I do so badly want to find a trout.

I finally give in, abandoning the bohemian, non-directional approach to locating a decent trout stream. I decide instead to slip my humbled ass back into Morganton–the only town around here I know –and outfit myself with a real map, something that shows rivers and back roads as well as the main drags.

My intention is to head south, the way I came, but I can't find State Route 181 to take me back into Morganton, so I head south on a different road, U.S. Route 221. This gives me a smooth ride along a real dandy of a creek and on further down to Marion. I resist the urge to pull over and give the new water a try, since it's midday and hot enough now for the back of the truck seat to feel as though it's searing the sweat off my back. I need to take advantage of this down time and find myself a map, although I promise myself to give the creek a try when I'm through messing around in town.

I drive around downtown Marion for almost twenty minutes, stopping occasionally to check places on a hunch they carry maps– gas stations, bait shops, convenience stores–with no luck. They all sell some sort of map, but most are only slightly better than that which is wadded up behind the seat. I eventually find what I am looking for at a grocery store, of all places. I sit for a while in my truck, out in the scalding, frying pan of a parking lot trying to decide if the map is worth the almost twenty bucks I spent on it. It's a large DeLorme map book that advertizes, on its cover, topographical maps of the entire state of North Carolina. I have seen these monsters before, of other states, but have never checked them out. I'm reassured, after dripping forehead sweat on only two or three pages, that I spent my money well.

The first thing I notice is that the Pisgah National Forest is a lot larger. I've been under the impression it was small, because I've driven in and out of it several times in the past twelve hours. There is another, even larger National Forest farther west of here, the Nantahala. And the Smoky Mountains National Park is right over the state line, in Tennessee. I'm at the edge of more public trout waters than one sane, employed man could fish in a lifetime. I sort of knew that already, but it does feel nice to have all these thousands and thousands of green, contour-lined acres in front of me. Miles of mountains and trees stretch on for page after glorious page, laced with millions of thin blue veins, all bearing different but equally alluring names: Lost Cove Creek, Big Crabtree Creek, Blue Sea Creek. It's enough to salivate over for hours.

I came in along the North Fork Catawba River, not a creek after all (not that it makes a bit of difference either way). The map shows it flowing into Lake James, a body of water that, on paper, looks like a squashed salamander. The lake lies between here and Morganton, to the east–which is a relief because, after searching for what seemed like hours in vain, I was sure the entire town had vanished without a trace. I also see the main channel of the Catawba River on the south side of Lake James and trace its blue line with my finger down through about five other lakes and eventually into South Carolina.

The North Fork Catawba sounds as good as any. Besides, I have already had a look at it, I know where there is good access and I could see no other obvious fishing vehicles already parked along it. And, I actually found it *before* I had the aid of a map.

I pull the truck off of U.S. Route 221 and onto a back road shortly after the map shows me parallel to the river. It takes a couple minutes and a stop sign, but the place I come to is absolutely perfect. The river is even wider here than anywhere I could see from the road on the way into town. It is deep and clear and has a moderate current. I could wade across easily, but I think I can cover both boulder cluttered banks from one side.

After I have the truck parked at the base of a rather steep incline opposite the river, I haul out my rod and vest and eagerly find my way down to the water. I relax. No one else is here and the sun is still blazinging down in force, although definitely showing signs of easing off.

I still have time to mellow before the prime trout-fishing hours, so, with that in mind, I leave my rod against a tree, my vest in a pile beneath it and head back up to the truck for a pen, my journal and a cold beer from the cooler.

Back at the edge of the river, I find a large, flat-topped, kitchen-table-size boulder near where I had lain my rod and vest, and climb onto it. It is a dirty, reddish-brown granite, cool from the all-day shade cast over it. I cross my legs Indian style, set the open can of beer at my side, light a cigarette and thumb to the next blank page in my journal. I inhale a lungful of nicotine, tar and funny sounding additives and gaze out into the clean, clear water flowing effortlessly past my rock. I relax, contemplate and write:

> Sat. 26 July
>
> Made it up into the Pisgah Natl For. last night. Fished a crick somewere in Avery Co. this morn. Got a shitload a chubbs called "warpaint shiners." And a 10" smally on a #12 soggy coon. Am sittin on a big rock longside north fork of the Catawba River at presant. Gonna wait till it cools down some fore I try fishin. Real nice lookin river – think there are some trout in here. Will see though.

I cough, take another drag from my cigarette and look up again, into the river, into the dark green moss on the rocks three feet below the surface of the water. A limb overhangs the river from the other side. Under the limb, in the middle of the river, a large boulder lays half out of the water. On the downstream side of the mass of stone are the V-shaped lines marking the current changes. Beneath them is the seductive darkness of a deep pool.

I smoke two more cigarettes and finish my beer. What I've been eyeing is now covered by the same shadow covering me. I collect the mashed cigarette butts and drop them into the empty beer can and then set the can on top of my closed journal. It is time, I reckon, to fish.

Down from my rock, I grab my rod and put on my vest which carries all sorts of line, leaders, fly boxes, split shot and other assorted gadgets collected and stored in the one mobile, multi-pocketed junk drawer. Once situated, I climb back onto my perch. This puts me above the underbrush–to make casting less frustrating–yet back far enough from the pool for the fish not to easily see me. The first cast rolls out neatly upstream and across current but never gets a chance to drift into the pool because a creek chub smacks my Soggy Coon almost as soon as the nymph hits the water. I catch two of the little chub's brothers on consecutive casts, as well as an equally small green sunfish. Then the action stops. *What do I have to do? What's wrong here? There has* got *to be trout in this river!*

There are no insects hatching, that I am aware of, so I can't start from there. *So where* do *I start?* All I can do is try blind troubleshooting. First, some more line can be added to the end of my leader to allow a better drift. Say a foot and a half length of 7x tippet material in case the 6x was too thick for this clear water. Then I can tie on a smaller fly, maybe a different color, like a #14 Brown Bug; a simple, yet lively wet-fly pattern I dreamed up consisting of mainly pheasant tail fibers. Lastly, I pinch a piece of #4 split shot onto the leader, about ten inches above the fly. This is to ensure it gets to the bottom where the trout should be.

I drift the Brown Bug through the pool once and nothing happens. On the second cast the fly stops on the bottom and the end of my fly line starts to drag on the surface. I raise the rod tip to get free from the snag–but it's *not* a snag! I feel the heavy throb of a large trout and promptly fall off my rock. I keep a hold of my fly rod, but the spool is jarred loose from the reel and careens from boulder to boulder like a startled leopard frog, leaving a trail of pale yellow fly line behind it before finally splashing into the river. I lie in a crumpled heap, wedged firmly but uncomfortably amidst an assortment of extremely hard, watermelon-size boulders, but I am thinking about only one thing. And it is *not* the agonizing pain in my bad knee.

I try to take in the slack line while still on my back, but it's too late. Nothing but a tiny piece of lead and a lonely wet fly at the end of my leader. *Dammit!* I pull myself up and look around for the spool. I follow the line to the water, but the spool is deep, out of sight, so I have to wind in by hand one-hundred-fifty yards of fly line and backing before I can get my bruised and bleeding hands on the spool-turned-mad-runaway-yo-yo. Then I spend a solid half hour untangling the inevitable knots before winding all the line *back* onto the spool. If I had any patience left, this would be trying on it.

I finally get everything wound up and put back together, but after all the commotion, there isn't much use in fishing this particular pool anymore, so I explore on upstream. There are some good runs of fairly deep water with enough boulder structure to break up the current. More fish are in the river too. Before it gets dark I tally a few more creek chubs, a baby smallmouth bass (meaning it is even *smaller* than ten inches) and two for real, by god, rainbow trout! I catch them both within ten minutes of each other just as the sun is dipping below the other side of the Smoky Mountains. They scrap and jump while I hold my rod tight and try to stay upright. After the second one is landed I go back for my journal and empty beer can and call it a day–a darn successful one at that! The one I keep is nine inches. I gut it and turn it loose in the bubbling hot corn oil.

It tastes good. No...it tastes exquisite; brown skinned, lightly salted perfection. But, as I snuggle warm and satisfied in my woobie alongside a now familiar stretch of strange river, it is the memory of that mysterious weight of the Big One that I dream of.

* * *

I wake up to the grey half-light of a dreary morning and the sound of raindrops parading around noisily above me on the truck cap. I reach for my cigarettes and lighter and squint out at the grime that only yesterday was a gravel road. The puddles are the same cloudy grey as the sky. I light my cigarette, roll onto my back and close my eyes. *Rain, rain, rain. Did I bring a raincoat? Maybe I have one behind the seat. Or should I go back to sleep?*

I lie awake, watching my smoke. Some lingers in faint, thinning wisps above me, the rest dissipates or gets sucked out through one of the barely opened windows. The rain has slowed to a drizzle, hissing through the leaves and branches, no longer pounding on my truck cap. The weather could not be better for trout fishing; I know this, so there are no excuses left.

My raincoat is nowhere under my pile of fishing gear beside the cot. It's not behind the seat, either. By the time I have gear strewn all over the cab of the truck and spewing out onto the wet ground, the rain has ceased. A slight breeze has picked up too, but not bad. I throw the now muddy tire iron back onto the front seat next to the jumper cables, pair of smoke grenades, empty soda bottle and all the other odds and ends I have just dug out from behind the seat. I hesitate, pick up one of the grenades and check the pin. It's safely bent. *Mmm. . .wonder how these got in here?* I check the pin of the other one and then drop them both back behind the seat and close the door.

I fetch my rod, don my vest and tighten my sandals–it's time for round two. I light another cigarette and try to walk casually back down to the riffle and batch of pocket water which I had taken the two rainbows from last night. As I stand along the river, smoking and eyeing the water–pretending to be relaxed and reading the water –a small rainbow trout leaps from the fast water and falls back in without making a splash or noise louder than the rushing water. I finger my cigarette and try to appear calm; my heart is about to blow a valve.

There aren't any masses of emerging insects–*So, what was he after?* I study the water in earnest this time. A tiny bug flies over my head from the direction of the river and I try to catch it but miss. I follow behind it, making jumps at it when it falters, but it appears to sense that something large and earthbound is after it and quickly gains altitude. I give up the chase and walk back to the edge of the river, but can't see any more leaping fish or flying insects. No trout rising either. *Well? What now? Do I try to imitate whatever kind of bug that was? Or stick with what worked last night?*

In the spirit of pretending I know what I'm doing, I remove my wet fly and split shot and replace them with a #16 dry fly of roughly the same, opaque grey as the original. I'm not even sure that it was a mayfly; I couldn't tell, but that's what my wound, feathery creation is supposed to be.

I drift the fly over the riffles several dozen times and nothing happens. I move down and fish the deeper run, and then on to the shallow pocket water behind the herd of cooler-size boulders. Still nothing. I switch back to the #14 Brown Bug wet fly with a pinch of lead, and I take a small chub out from behind a rock.

By now I have gotten to within sight of the big boulder at midstream, the one with the deep pool behind it. The home of the Big One that got away. I stop casting and wade over to it, being careful to keep my head and shoulders ducked low. As I crouch behind and upstream from the massive rock, I clip off four inches of tippet and retie the improved clinch knot, in case the leader has any nicks or burrs too small for me to feel. I pull more line from the reel and dump a short roll cast into the current beside me, letting the fly drift naturally out of sight and into the depths of the pool.

On my first drift I catch a tubby creek chub that croaks at me when I am unhooking him. The next several drifts come up empty. Then, at the tail end of one, as I am beginning to raise my rod to pick up the line, the Big One takes my fly. I set the hook and stand up straight. The rod bends and jerks as the fish shakes his head. The world seems to stop and wait for the outcome. How strong *is* 2 pound, 7x tippet, really? There is no place for error. I give him line when he asks for it, but still make him work for it. *Should I be more aggressive? Or just hang on?* Then he jumps–two feet into the air! A nice, fat rainbow. Big, too. *Oh, man!*

He makes another spectacular leap and several more hard runs, pulling me nervously downriver. I am sorely lacking a net, but I and the tippet hold up.

The trout tires and I make several heart-pounding failed attempts to lead him to shallow water before I am, at last, successful. He is easily the largest trout I have ever landed. With violently shaking hands, I yank my disposable camera from my vest, lay my rod in the water next to the fish and snap a photo–for John. Then I measure him.

Sixteen solid inches.

* * *

"So, which one of these *is* he?" John Falton asks, holding the lid of my cooler open and looking down at the three large trout heads peering up at him through the ice.

"Ah, the Big One still lives. These are all stockers," I say. "And they're another story all together."

I had gotten in late, surprised to see light coming from the crack under John's door. He wasn't at a bar. He had decided to stay back, save some money and watch *Jeremiah Johnson* on the television. He let me and my cooler in, anxious to know about the fishing, and just in time for me to see Robert Redford finally win peace with Joaquin Martinez and the Crow. I tell him my story only after the last chorus is sung and the tape has ended.

I am feeling mighty proud of myself for catching that big rainbow. It may not be considered a monster by some more experienced trout fishermen, but that photo is going to get framed. I have a spot on my barracks-room wall already picked out.

After the Big One, I fished a few pools farther downstream and then left the river. I explored a smaller creek a little north of where I had spent the night that was good for another ten-inch rainbow trout. From there, I drove up to the South Toe River. Beautiful river. Landed some very small, but very pretty, native rainbows there.

I fished a long time at the South Toe, had it all to myself and it was nice. But at the best pool I came across a bunch of people having a party. A family thing with kids, dogs, grills and everything. The pool undoubtedly holds some of the best fish in the area, but at the time, it also held someone's noisy litter of popsicle-stained kids kicking around on inflatable rafts.

On my way back to the North Fork Catawba, after spending another night (and lazy morning) in the back of my truck, I passed a sign advertizing "Elliott's Trout Pond." I was curious and naive enough to turn back and check it out. The old man in charge, Elliott himself I presumed, told me the deal. He had a pond full of trout that I could catch, for a price. I was ready to thank the man and be on my way, but, as he continued to explain, I got to thinking. One did not have to "pay to fish" he said in a roundabout way, only to *catch* the fish. $2.75 a pound. He had a bucket hooked to a scale next to the folding lawn chair he sat in to be sure no one was letting any fish go. You *had* to keep what you caught.

Foolishly, I walked to the edge of his pond, and had a look. I was already there, so I might as well have a look. Right? Well, there were more damn trout than I'd ever seen in my life, all swimming around like trout-pellet time at the hatchery. Oh, and I looked close, too. Mesmerized. Like a cat watching a busy bird feeder through the kitchen window. Under the swarms of ten to twelve-inch tame rainbows were the shadows of a couple real horses. Hogs. Alligators. Whatever–really big trout. It wasn't fair; it was entrapment. I walked zombie-like back to my truck to get my fly rod and check the level of ice in my beer cooler.

Elliot took a seat in his lawn chair.

I rigged my rod with an extra long leader and the lightest tippet material I had with me, some 8x, one-pound, monofilament spider web. My idea was to cast a dry fly–so as to see which fish had taken it–break off any small fish and wait until the monsters got lured to the surface thinking a hatch was on.

I lost a dozen flies to a dozen trout and gave up the idea. Instead I fished a weighted fly, getting it down to where I could see the big ones. I went through all of my Brown Bugs and most of my Soggy Coons, all to small trout, but I did manage to hook one of the bruisers. He broke me off without trying very hard. But I did bring in three decent fish that I couldn't force myself to lose. Five pounds worth, to feed the guys in the barracks. I know because I had to pay $13.75. I didn't measure or photograph any of them. That way I can disregard them, maybe even forget all about them and what I let myself degenerate to. I guess I can kid myself, say I only did it for my friends.

After the last one, a good two-pounder, I switched back to a dry fly with the hook snapped off at the bend with plyers. I missed strike after strike for an hour. I felt silly, and Elliot probably thought I was the worst damn fisherman he had ever seen, but it was entertaining in a sick, compulsive sort of way.

When I was done playing in Elliot's pond–the rainbow trout whore house–I drove to the North Fork Catawba, where I had originally intended to go. It was getting late and I had to be heading back to Fort Bragg soon. But I didn't go to the river to fish this time. I went just to sit on my big, flat-topped boulder and contemplate and watch the cold mountain water glide effortlessly by.

This always makes everything else in life feel so much easier.

Freedom and Rocky Mountain Trout

Boulder Creek is low and clear. From my vantage point on the wooden walk bridge behind the Millennium Hotel, I can see almost every detail of the creek's rocky bottom. Behind me, on the other side of the bridge, is a deep pool. I suspect that's where most of the fish are sulking now, avoiding the mid-day August sun.

I'd been lured down the concrete steps of the fish-viewing alcove built into the stream bank. The signs suggested an excellent view into the hidden world of a Boulder Creek pool, but the round glass windows were too covered in green lichen and black creek gunk to see much of anything. I couldn't even make out the dead insects trapped between the two layers of thick Plexiglas–not clearly enough to identify them, anyway. I peered through, or tried to, and then stood aside so as not to be in the way of the two ancient gentlemen on the bench behind me. They're still there, staring at the circular view up the ass end of an algae colony. Better than watching their wife's panties twirl around down at the Laundromat, I guess.

There's enough shade on the creek to block some of the sunlight, so I'm hoping to spot a trout feeding in the shallow run upstream from the pool. My sister said there are trout, that's why she brought me down here. And at first glance I knew she was right. Now I'd just like to spot one.

I see a fishlike movement in the eddy behind one of the larger rocks. I cup my hands around my eyes and peer closer. *Yep! A trout!* "Eve, over here," I point with the burning end of my cigarette.

"Where?" She asks, sliding closer to where I stand against the metal handrail, cupping her own hands around her eyes.

"Right behind...well, just this side of that biggest boil of water."

"I don't see it."

I peer harder. "I can't either, right now. Keep watchin'."

And then, as if orchestrated, the fat brown trout drifts into view, eats an invisible insect on the surface and then settles back down to the loose gravel behind his rock.

I drop my hands and turn to my sister. "You saw that, I hope."

She's still staring intently down into the water, her face still hidden behind her hands.

"Please tell me you saw that." My hands are shaking slightly, sprinkling the bridge with cigarette ash, and my heart rate has increased significantly–my usual neurotic reaction to trout within eyesight.

Eve turns and brushes her shoulder-length honey brown hair out of her eyes and nods. "Uh, yeah. There's two of them down there. I think."

We both have another look. "Yeah," she says. "A little bit in front of that one that came to the top." She points. "Look."

I am looking–and seeing. Sure enough. Two nice browns! *Man, can't believe it's been over a year since I've seen one! I knew it! Should've brought my fly rod!*

"I told you," Eve says. "You should have brought your fly rod."

Yeah, yeah. "There wasn't room in either car. With all your stuff in there."

She laughs.

"I didn't want to take up space." I give her the crinkled forehead, arched eyebrow and cocked head look that means I know what I'm talking about, but she doesn't seem to be buying it. "I didn't think there would be enough time to fish, either," I add.

Now she's smiling. "They sell rods down at McGuckin's, you know."

Well, now. I could find a use for a new rod.

She keeps on. "They have a little (she makes a hand motion as if casting) fly shop thing in the back of the hardware store."

Yeah. . . .

"We can have a look on the way back to the apartment," she says, still smiling. "It's on the way."

"Yeah, I suppose," I say, mashing my cigarette out on the hand rail and pocketing the butt. "It couldn't hurt to look."

* * *

This trip out to Colorado was a spur of the moment thing–for me anyway. I came along for the ride and to help my sister search for an apartment. Though she really doesn't need any help, it just sounds better than saying that I'm "tagging along." She has worked here in Boulder before, some co-op stint between semesters down at Cincinnati, so she knows her way around town. And now that she has graduated and everything, she's taking a permanent position as an environmental graphic designer at CommArts Inc., the same place she co-oped with. That all sounds pretty cool to me. I'm mightily impressed, and bragging to anyone who will listen.

She and her guy friend, Donnie, had both their cars packed and were ready to leave the coming morning. I was sitting outside at my parents' place with Donnie, killing mosquitos and smoking cigarettes, and it came up in conversation: Why don't I come along? I've no job, no commitments. I've been out of the Army for a month now and doing nothing but staying holed up in the folks' cabin, spending much of the day as intoxicated as possible. So I, the ever-ready opportunist, leaped at the offer. I could help drive, help look for the apartment, and leave with Donnie after Eve was settled in. He was going to be looking around for potential work, and, if he found some, come back once his last jobs were complete in Ohio (he does concrete footers, subcontract stuff).

Hell, it was a chance to finally get to the Rockies; I was all for it. Besides, since my discharge from the Army, my life has been showing the beginning stages of serious stagnation.

The last year in the Army is a blur (a very *long* blur) but a tad on the wild side. John Falton got out about five months before I did, and Keith Konkol got orders from 2nd Ranger Battalion: he was getting ready to be reassigned out to Washington state about the time I was heading home. And some of the time was spent in Germany. Nothing too outrageous, just a bit of training with the German paratroopers, the 314th Fallschirmjager Battalion. We stayed with them and a group of Belgian commandoes at a *casern* outside of Oldenburg. It was a blast. They were a high speed, hard drinking bunch of Krauts. Good soldiers, too. I remember our units general consensus being along the lines of: "Damn glad our countries get along. Wouldn't want to have to fight these bastards." I believe they were thinking the same sort of thing.

I can't remember most of the training. I do recall being dropped out of one of their helicopters though. They didn't have a predesignated drop zone, so we floated down into a wheat field somewhere along the French border. The farmer was super upset, but none of us understood what he was yelling. We packed our parachutes and looked for our ride out, trying to ignore him. What else could we do?

During the last month back at Bragg I was given permission to live off post with a guy from the platoon, Sergeant Conrad Sedja. I was a short timer and couldn't handle the barracks life anymore, and he and his wife Jessica didn't seem to mind. However, I did overhear more than one late-night argument concerning my negative influence on his alcohol consumption.

Conrad and I did quite a lot of fishing together at that time, mostly bass fishing in Lower McKellars lake. We caught some really nice fish. The rod and gun club had a bar right there next to the lake, too. I believe we may have spent our time equally on the water and on the stool.

But now, here I am–at last– right at the base of the foothills of the great *Rocky Mountains*, a trout fisherman's dream come, oh, so very true. And what? I don't have my fly rod with me? What *was* I thinking? Well, like I was trying to tell my sister, there was way too much of her crap crammed into both of the cars–an Escort and a Camaro. I was surprised there was enough room for me and my two changes of clothes.

Some other things haven't worked out neatly either (funny how life can scuttle plans and foul up intentions). Eve found an apartment without too much trouble, but Donnie never could find anyone needing a footer guy. I think my sister got exasperated with him, or impatient–something. I don't think she realizes how different their chosen lines of work are; no concrete company or subcontractor is going to take on someone who doesn't even live in the same state yet. I wouldn't think, anyway. All he can do, as far as I can see, is make the move out here and do what he can, start from scratch. But he's fairly established down in Middletown, Ohio, and I think he's a bit hesitant to leave that. I don't know the particulars and I didn't ask. All I know for sure is that he's not here anymore, he drove the two days home. His relationship with my sister is on shaky ground.

I passed on the ride back with Donnie. I'm not done here yet. Eve and I could use some time to get to know each other again, it *has* been awhile. The folks called today, said they'll drive out in a week to check out their daughter's new place and bring what she forgot or couldn't fit. They'll be my ride home, if I feel that way inclined.

I've given John Falton a call, too. After we caught up on the latest whatcha-been-doin' BS and he congratulated me on my recent escape from the talon-like grip of the military, I asked him if he was busy this weekend and if maybe we could get some fishing in. There was silence on the line. A good four seconds worth. He had no idea I was calling from within the same state.

He's driving up to get me after he gets off of work today.

* * *

John leaves his pickup truck running in the middle of Euclid Avenue and gets out. He has seen me standing on the sidewalk with my day bag and shiny new rod case. I meet him out on the street in front of his truck.

"Well, no shit!" he says.

I look him over. "I'll be damned!"

A car slows down, having to drive into the other lane to avoid rear-ending John's truck. The driver glares at us. We pay little attention.

"What's that scruff on your face?" he asks, waving his gigantic index finger in the direction of my chin.

I scratch at my new mustache and goatee. "My freedom beard." I see he has one too.

"Well, no shit," he says again. "Good to see you, Jay."

We shake hands. *Yeah, you too, my friend.* "Alrighty then." I toss my bag and rod case into the back of the truck. "Let's do some fishin'!"

* * *

We run into the tail end of the rush-hour traffic going through Denver, but once we're clear of the city the conversation is able to regain some of its original intensity. I have to catch him up on who has gotten out of Alpha Company, so far, and who is still in. I tell him about Keith going to 2nd Ranger Battalion. We agree that that is probably a better place for him. We start up with more Army talk, but then both stop and look at each other.

"Screw it! We're out!" we say almost in unison.

We bump along in silence, glad to be free. Enjoying it. Savoring it. And appreciating old company.

After awhile John glances over at me again. "You still driving that 'ol blue heap?"

I nod. "Yeah, she's seen better days."

"Good," John says. "I left some stuff back behind your seat."

"Left some stuff?" I look at him pointedly, waiting for more information. "What *kind* of stuff?"

"Some pyro."

Pyrotechnics? So that's where they came from. "Yeah, I got your smoke grenades."

"Any chance I can get 'em back?"

"Sure. I woulda brought 'em out if I knew they were yours. Can't send 'em in the mail you know."

John digs in his pocket for his tin of Copenhagen. "No rush," he says. "Whenever."

I hand him the Snapple Ice Tea bottle that's half full of a dark brown saliva syrup and rolling around at my feet.

"Thanks," he says, taking the bottle and wedging it firmly between his legs. "There's a couple smoke grenades...and some other stuff."

Other stuff? Oh, Christ! "Yep. No problem. I'll get 'em to ya."

I ponder for a few seconds over the odds of my being blown into neat little sandwich-size pieces next time I catch a pothole wrong, then I open the plastic fly box I bought in Boulder and hold it out for John to see. "I picked up a bunch of new flies. Cost a packet."

John looks in and nods.

"I got a new rod too," I say, thumbing back to the long silver tube lying in the bed of the pickup. "Five-weight Cortland."

John holds the bottle to his mouth, spits into it and then sets it back between his legs. "What happened to your other rod?"

"Still got it. Needed a new one anyway, figured I might as well look for one out here." *See? That's the way I planned it.*

I finger a couple of the compartments of the fly box; I have a diverse assortment of streamers, drys and some beadhead nymphs ranging anywhere from barely-castable bulky to where's-the-eye-on-this-damn-thing petite. I'd been sucked in by the great selection of interesting fly patterns at McGuckin's. I'd felt like a homeless, hungry trout standing over the buffet counter at an extravagant underwater diner. But after parting with the wad of cash it took to get a new rod, reel (with weight-forward line and backing) a half-dozen tapered leaders and a non-resident fishing license, twenty more dollars for flies came out of my numb wallet almost without pain. Though I did feel dumb for not bringing along at least *one* of my own fly boxes from home–it wouldn't have taken up that much space. I feel ill-equipped, too, without the few patterns I've developed and grown to trust and rely on–like going into combat with someone else's rifle, or sneaking back to my tree stand with a bow I've never drawn. They could shoot straight, or fool trout just fine, *but I don't know that!*

Our first stop is John's mother's ice-cream shop so that he can introduce us. She's a very warm person, and an incredibly interesting lady–tall, blue eyes and a lingering German accent. And she gives us free ice-cream. John and I take our dripping waffle cones over to a table and try, at first, an organized frontal assault on the triple-stacked towers of real ice-cream; with quick, lizard-like flanking maneuvers on the dribbles. But this soon gives way to uncontrolled gluttony. We're thirteen years old all over again, or at least until the last bit of waffle cone is inhaled, then it's nothing but absolute seriousness. After all, we are two grown men who happen to have highly important matters to attend to, weighty incumbencies, an entire pond full of very nice-sized and lure-hungry obligations!

We say our thanks, get our hugs and then are on our dutiful way.

The house is as he described it: up a long and winding gravel road, surrounded by aspen trees and within sight of Pikes Peak (on the less populated side of Pikes Peak, not the Colorado Springs side). We stop at the house briefly, only long enough for John to grab his fly rod and fishing vest. The sun is threatening to set on us, so we drive the short way down the backside of the mountain along the dry rills and washouts that look like miniature canyons at the edge of the road. And over the loose, clay red gravel that crunches under the coasting tires. The pond is about as I've imagined as well, and right where John has always said it was: within walking distance of his parents' house. I've been hearing him tell me that for as long as I've known him, goading me for a reaction, or enticing me, I don't remember which.

The pond is a good size, a bit bigger and with more room to cast than the one I grew up within walking distance of, although it's not nearly as cozy or as fertile looking as my Orchard Pond. (Cattails always add a sense of something good to a body of water: coziness, and even liveliness, maybe.) The tough spot here, after thorough scrutiny, looks like it'll be on the far bank, because it's the steep side of a hill. And right along the water–the best looking water, of course –is a lot of thick brush. The two options I can see are either to squeeze in alongside the brush and take chances with roll casts and sidearm casts, or climb up to one of the big slabs of granite on the hillside and cast *over* all the mess and hope nothing actually takes the fly, because there would be no way to land it.

I'm trying to evaluate the pond and strategize my exact moves while stringing my new rod. And farting around with the leader that needs to be tied on, too. I'm watching the water for rises, and not seeing any. John has himself ready to go before I've even gotten to the part where I stare stupidly into the fly box.

"They'll hit spoons or streamers," John says. "Anything that looks like a minnow." He slams the driver's side door and walks toward the pond.

I glace his way. "What are these? Rainbows?"

"Yep," he says and tugs line out from his fly reel. "Give me a second, I'll show you one."

Yeah, I'll bet. I look down at my fly assortment. *Well, locals know best.*

I pinch the red yarn tail of a #8 beadhead Woolly Worm and lift it from its compartment. I've heard these things are popular, but have never tied one before. *Simple, really. Black chenille with grizzled hackle. . . .*

"There he is!"

I look up from my improved clinch knot and see John's bent rod. Then the splashing of a decent-size rainbow trout out on the surface of the pond. *Nice! Outstanding!*

Up until now I have, surprisingly, been able to maintain my calm.

John kneels at the edge and I can just see his head and shoulders behind the tall grass, then he holds the fish up for me to see. My guess is about a pound. Good fish for a first cast.

I bite the tag end off the knot, spit it out and nod. "Nice one."

He lets the fish go and pulls a string of pondweed from his fly. It looks like a #8 Royal Coachman streamer, another well fished pattern. My hands are beginning to shake. *Nothin' fancy. Just fish it like it's a scared little bait fish.*

I walk to the edge of the pond and get a better look at the water. All along the edge, just below the surface, are tangled masses of pondweed. They extend out maybe ten feet and peter out. There are smaller patches of the weed scattered about randomly in deeper water. There's plenty of open water though, and it's clear and appears to be fairly deep. But it's still, nothing's moving.

John casts again. I watch his line and leader unroll onto the water, then his steady retrieve. Nothing takes. He picks the line up, false casts twice and lays it back down. And again with the steady retrieve.

Okay. He's fishing shallow. I'll try deeper.

I pick a likely looking spot: the edge of one of the migrating patches of pondweed that I figure is within my range. Enough line gets stripped from the reel to allow for the cast, then I air out the line with a few false casts. I keep the line in motion for almost a minute, getting the feel for the shorter, lighter rod. *And, wow, the new line!* It responds so nicely! Before this, I've made do with the one fly rod: an eight-and-a-half-foot Browning, with a temperamental little Martin reel that cost under twenty bucks. If I remember correctly, the entire setup–rod, reel and the cheapest, flat, bright yellow (now pale yellow) fly line I could find, or afford–didn't go much over seventy dollars.

When I'm done playing, I drop the rod tip and lay my new, ultra buoyant fly line down onto the water. The Woolly Worm plops in the general direction of where I'm aiming. *Casts good. I guess.* I let the fly sink maybe three feet, then begin a slow, pulsating retrieve. Nothing takes it. And I have to pull off strings of pondweed. I try another cast to the same location, let it sink and do a slower retrieve. Again, nothing. John is trying different retrieves, too. He looks in my direction. "That's the way this pond is sometimes," he says. "Catch the easy ones right off the bat." He looks away, concentrating on his current retrieve. "We'll have luck with drys here in a bit though," he adds more softly. Reassurance for us both I think.

Yeah, that's good. But there ought to be some easy ones on my side of the pond too–dammit!

I cast again, this time to the other side of the underwater weed patch, and watch the leader slowly disappear with the sinking fly. I begin the retrieve once there is only a couple feet of monofilament still visible above the water. Then there's a sudden large flash of white down where I know my fly is, and at the same time the end of my fly line comes to an abrupt halt. And I set the hook into a heavy fish.

Hang on, ya'll!

* * *

After the initial pair of rainbows, there's a lull that lasts until dusk. But shortly after the sun has set, John and I notice the rise forms of feeding trout dotting the water near the far bank. Both of us switch to dry flies. For me, at first, it's a #12 Yellow Humpy; then a #14 Grizzly Wulff; and finally–with success–a #16 Adams. We stalk rising trout well past dusk and into complete darkness. The last rainbow I hook is after a cast, not to the rise, but to the *sound* of the rise. I cast and–hoping my leader isn't in a gnarl–wait for the subtle pop-splash and then lift the rod. I can't believe it actually works!

We never do figure out exactly what the trout are feeding on – our knowledge of entomology not being all too hip–but it's something very small, I know that much. But a size-16 dry fly is small enough to fool them once the light is bad, so I guess that's that. We land a half dozen rainbows apiece, none smaller than fourteen inches and none larger than sixteen. All but two smaller ones are released, and they're breakfast.

In the cab of his pickup, on the short ride up to the house, John says that he has fed me the pond as an appetizer, only to whet my appetite. He promises me more trout and more variety. And in the next few days he is true to his word. I'm in an almost constant state of bliss.

One day we borrow a fourteen-foot boat with an outboard motor–from John Falton Sr.–and take it out to Skagway Reservoir. Nothing outstanding is taking place on the reservoir itself, but after we've given up and hoisted the boat back onto the trailer, we try West Beaver Creek. There are a couple of nice holes just below and within sight of the noisy overflow over the Skagway dam. It's in this water that I catch three trout species in the same helping–brook trout, rainbow trout and brown trout. None are all that big, but the brookies are almost too beautiful to be real, the bows leap like they're suddenly scared to be in the water, and the one stubborn and lonely brown fights harder than a smallmouth bass twice his size. *It's fantastic*! All are taken on the one fly: a #14 Hares Ear Soft Hackle. A fly of delicious buggy simplicity, something I'd be forever proud of creating on my own vise.

The following day we drive out to Pikes Peak and fish two of the three large reservoirs on the way up, the Catamount twins. We fish South Catamount first and do a fine job. The twelve-inch Snake River cutthroat are taking any silly thing we throw at them. When John detects my growing casualness, he quickly whisks me over to North Catamount. There I fish to–or try to fish to–what seems to be a hundred thousand trout rising at one time, something I've never seen before. And I can't fool a single one. John does though. He holds it out of the water for a second before releasing it and I see that it is exactly the same as the ones we were educating right next door.

I can see now that to be more consistently successful I'll need to start reserving compartments in one of my fly boxes for small flies, midge imitations. And *not* the #16's and #18's I've considered "the small ones" before.

At the end of each day we have a fling with the pond. It's a nice place to come back to, always good for a fish or two to boost self-esteem. After the all-afternoon affair with North Catamount I'm especially in need of some easy-trout morale boosting.

John tries to finagle some more time off from his job as a bouncer down at Bronco Billy's Casino in Cripple Creek, but he has already been granted a week off for the coming elk season. I refuse to let him cancel that on my account. So, at the end of the last day, the Faltons invite Eve down from Boulder. The five of us have dinner together–generous helpings of home brew, seasoned with lively conversation. At one point in the ruckus I bring up the idea of Alaska. John and I have hashed that one over before, back when we were still in the Army, but neither one of us has brought it up since. The plan, at one time, had been for the two of us to liquidate, consolidate and beat feet for the Last Frontier. But now things have changed, life and reality being what they are and doing the things they do. John says he has his name on a waiting list for a position with the prison-security gig out in Sterling. He says it's a good job and he has high hopes. I think there might be a girl that has caught his eye, too, and that certainly can't help matters any.

After all is eaten and done, we say our "so long"s and down the mountain go Eve and I in her little Escort. On with our lives.

* * *

Mom and Dad arrive in Boulder a few days later with the rest of Eve's belongings. Mom is eager to see the apartment and Dad is itching to do some trout fishing. They will take me back to Ohio when they leave.

The first day is spent in town, but the following two are spent at higher altitudes. The four of us drive up into the Rocky Mountain National Park in search of some high-country trout. As we roll through the town of Lyons, I have a strange sense of *deja vu*, like I've been here before. Or maybe just read something about the place a while back. Something about the St. Vrain River. Or maybe not. We're through town and on our way before I can make any sense of it.

We wind up fishing one of the branches of the St. Vrain. In a stretch nearest the road there are trout which we catch easily on size-12 and 14 weighted nymphs. Greenback cutthroat mainly, small and pretty with a barely-noticeable orange cutthroat mark. The signs posted along the stream say they're part of a reintroduction program. Apparently they, as a species, were here originally, before the crazed stocking of anything that could be kept alive in a bucket for more than a few hours became popular.

The higher and farther away from any roads we get, the fishing becomes more rewarding. The pocket water gets smaller, but definitely more rugged. But they're worth the walk and extra effort. The greenbacks up at higher elevations are absolutely magnificent. Some of the most beautiful living things I've ever seen.

Dad and I keep on going farther and farther upstream, both excited about what bright and colorful new gem lies hidden in the next pocket or pool. Each fish, although a member of the same species, is entirely unique.

The highest we achieve is a little lake at 10,000 feet. After going into raptures over the descriptions of the previous fish, I don't know how I can do justice to the beauty of these high-lake cutts. The tinge of emerald over their back, with bold, closely-patterned black spots that thin out toward the head, splattered over a field of a vivid yellow–like a rich watercolor wash. And the bright crimson on the gill covers and down the belly make me think I've accidently killed the first one with a hook deep in the gills, but my #14 Brassie is hanging visibly from his jaw and there's no blood dripping from his tail as I hold him up. That's just the way he's made.

I release him and he darts away, out into the cool center of the lake, under the giant reflection of mountains. I hope he'll make the most of his freedom.

Mind Sludge

The air smells clean and cool and is a pleasure to breathe. There was a heavy frost on the ground and over the tent this morning, and this evening I'll be able to see my breath again, then I'll be allowed to call the air *crisp*, as I would like to. And the portable weather radio (referred to as "god" in our deer camp) has promised the folks and me more cold in the days to come.

The oak and hickory leaves are dry and crunchy on the gravel road. It's still and peaceful as I walk, fully camouflaged and with my recurve bow at my side–except the distant, muffled *tock tock tock* of a scolding chipmunk and the occasional shrill cry of a blue jay. I'm avoiding the dead leaves whenever possible. It seems that during the times I most need to be quiet, the leaves are always the loudest under foot. That's fine. Once I stop moving the noisy leaves will be working to my advantage.

This is southeast Ohio, Vinton County, in the fall–some of the best land this state has to offer a guy like me. The northeastern part of the state may have been a prime candidate for that kind of praise until all those people squatted along the banks of the Cuyahoga River, simultaneously grunted and gave birth to another steaming pile of concrete, asphalt and high-rises.

I don't like cities.Any city. They're all the same to me: Cleveland, Columbus, Cincinnati...Denver. Too noisy, too busy and too damn many people.

But there's not a soul anywhere near my tree stand. I'm going to sit there, not making a sound or a sudden movement, until dark. For now I'm a deer hunter. Today that's my job. It's a good job. I know I'll be rewarded with solitude and maybe, if I'm lucky, I'll even see a deer. And there's always the off chance that, while on stand and alone with the woods and my mind, I'll unravel the other, more tangled, parts of my life.

But I'm not counting on it.

The gravel road continues on in a generally predictable route following the top of the ridge. I veer from it, heading downhill on an old jeep-turned-four-wheeler trail. The trail is a pair of easily followed ruts for most of the length which I must follow back to my stand, but at times it becomes less noticeable and obviously less used. There are fallen trees over it in places. Some have been chainsawed to open the trail, but others, which appear to have fallen this spring or summer, have not been manhandled yet. At all times it is fully carpeted with fallen leaves, so I'm forced to walk very slowly to maintain quiet. I don't want to announce to the woods that I'm a clumsy trespasser, an outsider. Instead I want the woods to absorb me, accept me and allow me to act out the role I'm here to play.

I come to the place in the trail that I've marked with a rotting log, propped as inconspicuously as possible, in the low crotch of a coppiced maple. I cut into the woods at this point and move as slowly and quietly as I can to my stand.

My tree stand is a small, portable contraption I have chained about fifteen feet up in a large beech tree. The folks and I have eight of these set up in the vicinity of our tent, which is pitched along one of the many gravel roads that meander through the Wayne National Forest. I set this particular stand only yesterday. None of us have been seeing any deer, so some of the stands have been moved around, including this one. It's overlooking a deer trail that, if the shredded saplings and multiple scrapes are any indication, is being frequented by a nice buck. Not that I'm after antlers–I'm primarily out to put meat in camp–but fresh buck sign does vamp up the list of possibilities for this evening, and that's definitely part of the attraction.

I lean my recurve against the tree and tie one bow limb to the length of surplus 550 parachute cord that hangs down from my stand –this is my bow rope. I then climb to my stand using strategically placed, strap-on tree steps, as well as a sturdy limb or two. Walking stealthily is basically straightforward when compared to the attempts I make to climb quietly. Imagine, if you will, a mime dressed in five layers of thick clothing and straddling an imaginary ladder on stage. Now, in your mind, dress this fool in camo, put a quiver full of razor-sharp arrows on his back and give him a bum knee. I don't know what kind of scenario your imagination can concoct with that, but it's a perfect Three Stooges episode if I ever imagined one.

Once in the stand I hoist up my bow, then remove my quiver from my back and hang it on a branch beside me. I reposition the clusters of oak boughs that have been wire-tied around the stand for added concealment. I've chosen oak because the leaves are big and close together, and if the boughs are cut in the preseason–while scouting–the leaves will dry and stay on the branch all winter. (And, although whitetail are smart and wily, they don't know that oak leaves aren't supposed to grow on beech trees.) Next, the shooting lanes are checked, and they're good. I have a clear, ten-yard shot down to the deer trail at two different spots. This way, in theory anyway, I can get a perfect quartering-away shot no matter which direction any deer may come.

I slip on my finger tab and situate myself. I feel ready. I pinpoint a bright yellow tulip poplar leaf on the trail and slowly rehearse, coming to full draw and then letting down.

Yes. Everything feels right.

* * *

During the first hour on stand–before my mind and body have been melded into the smooth grey bark behind me–my thoughts are as scattered and flighty as the chickadees and titmice that take turns bouncing around on the end of my arrow. Most prevalent of these obtrusive thoughts is the desire for a cigarette. But even if I hadn't recently sworn off them for good, the smell of tobacco smoke would eliminate all the elements of stealth which I've tried so hard to achieve. Still, one sure would taste good right now.

At a bar back in Fayetteville, Keith Konkol and I promised each other that we would quit cigarettes as soon as we got out of the Army. I guess we figured it would be a cinch after all the stress and hassle were gone. We always talked about the real world–the one outside the Army–as if it were the place where everything came easy; the land of no worries, easy money and lots of beautiful women. With all that working for us we wouldn't need nicotine, let alone the case of beer and bottle of Irish whiskey we would sometimes polish off together before leaving the barracks at night. I don't know how he's going to fare once he gets out, but for me...well, this "real world" ain't all we trumped it up to be.

While I was still in, I always thought that after four years in the airborne I wouldn't even notice the trivial amounts of stress and hardship of a civilian life. I'm finding, though, that those years have had the complete opposite effect on me. I have absolutely zero tolerance for stress or even the slightest amount of bullshit. So, there's no point in me looking for employment. I wouldn't last a week.

There is still some time for me to figure things out. I'm not in any dire financial straights yet because of the nice bankroll I managed to build up while I was still working for Uncle Sam (surprisingly enough, most of it during the time I was a private and not making beans). More importantly, my folks have offered me sanctuary in their home–a blessing which I'll never take for granted.

My folks understand. I know that my dad has had experience in my situation. (Or is *predicament* the proper word for this?) Neither one of them ever harp or nag at me, they're nothing but good humor and encouragement...even after I wrapped the front end of my pickup truck around an ash tree along their driveway–a result of too much time and money wasted in the beer tent at the Milan Melon Festival.

The next morning I had to take a sledge hammer to the front bumper, wire one headlight back into its socket and permanently bend the passenger's side door into the closed position. Unbelievably the old thing still runs. And luckily, the incident served as an in-my-face wake-up call. It taught me that I'm not invincible and if I continue on that reckless path, it'll be a considerably short one. There was some deep thinking to do and a few conclusions to be jumped to in the days that followed. And the obvious prevailed, as I should have known it would: my only chance of surviving my discharge was to submerse myself as deeply as possible into the hard but honest arms of wilderness, and as far away from the confusing facades and false security and pretenses of the "real world."

Or maybe it's all me. Maybe my problems are a result of my own far out expectations and their subsequent disillusions. I'm a bit of a dreamer and an idealist, which may be the root of my problems, and many of my dreams are radically different from the run-of-the-mill

Midwesterner's. I don't slow down to admire the gigantic new houses going up in what used to be a farmer's field–I see it as gluttony. I don't consider a new road or parking lot to be progress – I see them as the heart-breaking destruction of the natural world that is the immediate outcome of our overpopulation. And lastly, and most incisively, the merit of my existence will have absolutely *nothing* to do with how many children, vehicles or television channels I have.

These people to my left and right are about to get swallowed by the ghastliness of urban sprawl and they don't give a damn. Maybe it's because their entire lives are spent indoors, so why should they care? Down the throat of the beast they waddle, with double chins and blissfully ignorant smiles bulging from their faces.

It's because of my apparent disdain for the ignorance and over-consumption of the masses that I've always had a hard time mingling with them, their shortsighted and often naive beliefs, or any other aspect of their *created* norm. And now–since spending a few years in an environment and community so unlike anything that my civilian peers have been molded by–these antisocial tendencies are greatly and obviously accentuated. I don't know whether my lack of comprehension of, or empathy for, my contemporaries is a sign that *I* am out of touch, or that the bulk of the world is out of touch. There is, I'm sure, strong evidence to support either possibility.

* * *

After the first tormenting hour, I gradually expel the mind sludge and slip into the tree-stand calm that is the chief opiate addicting us bowhunters. It's only after this sense of calm has been reached that the heart-pounding adrenaline rush that comes with seeing a deer can be fully enjoyed.

At times like this, I feel most alive. Whether I'm crouched at the base of a tree, cradling my squirrel rifle, or perched high in the tree's limbs, waiting attentively for the slightest noise from the world below. This is the revelation of being truly awake after farting around in a half-conscious, self-important daze for far too long. But at the same time that I feel all of my senses becoming more acute, I swear my metabolism is actually slowing down. My breathing slows, and as it gets later in the evening, I can begin to hear my heart beat–its pace almost matching my breathing, falling in with the tempo of the woods.

On this day no deer are seen or heard. But, at one point in the evening I am fooled into a stationary frenzy by the sound of a ruffed grouse tiptoeing around behind me. The delicate foot falls in the leaves are exaggerated by the otherwise utter quietness.

The sun sets and the full November moon casts its pale light down from the cloudless sky. I can see my breath and the faint glittering of frost beginning to form on the branches around me. The hairs in my nostrils seem to have frozen. There's a barred owl hooting in the distance, its call echoing lonely through the rolling hills. I climb down from the tree carefully yet clumsily. My hands are too numb to properly grip the metal tree steps and my body is shaking violently, my teeth clattering about uncontrollably in my mouth. The brisk walk back to camp will warm me.

I'm cleansed. From were I stride down this gravel, moonlit road, everything feels as it should be. I remind myself of how lucky I am to have my health, and to have been born in a place where, although it may be expected of me, I don't have to conform. I'm a free man, with nothing but my own lack of ambition standing in the way.

As I near camp, I can see the glowing lantern light from under the dining fly. There is a shadow fussing around in front of the light–Mom heating supper. I hear the rattling of a spoon inside a metal can. The smell of brewing coffee. The sound of voices. And the soft hum of the lantern.

Road Trip

The blustery winds and warm rains of spring are brewing, but behind this veneer are cold nights and the lingering threat of a final, violent offensive from winter. The few red-winged blackbirds are always a promising sight. Mom's crocus are popping up around the house too, and the treetops are speckled with the reds and pinks of breaking buds. Margaret Phillips, up at the Berlin Township public library, is nervous about the peach trees blossoming too soon in her orchard–a sudden frost could do them in. It's much too early, though, for even the more restless or ambitious farmers to begin turning their soil. A tractor could be lost forever out in this slop.

And so could I, if I'm not careful.

I cross the road and walk back to Chappel Creek, following the high ground through our neighbor's field. This is not the direct route back to the creek, but the dry route. Besides, as with any high ground near a permanent water source, there is always the chance of finding treasure.

I have, and no doubt will always have, a lingering boyhood fascination with hidden treasure. At an early age this manifested itself with sudden fits of random hole digging and later provoked dreams of becoming rich with the aid of a metal detector. Nothing ever did come of those endeavors; apparently no pirates ever buried their loot in our blueberry patch, and the only riches my new metal detector ever turned up were rusty square nails and spent rifle cartridges. But I can still remember the resolve with which I swore, as I held up my beeping and buzzing birthday present, that our family's days of penny pinching were at last over. But, as it turned out, Dad has not been able to quit his job in the pressroom.

My quest for treasure did provide hours of enjoyment away from the rigors of tracking down my next squirrel or creek chub (which, I might add, I did quite dutifully). Eventually–low and behold–I did stumble upon real treasure. Finding that first flint arrowhead was enough excitement to forever keep me peering into and poking at any patch of disturbed ground I stumbled over–plowed fields, construction sites, even woodchuck holes.

So today, while I'm toting along my fly rod and the hopes of tricking a few of the creek chubs that have forgotten the lessons I forced on them when I was a kid, my eyes are relentlessly scouring the patches of exposed field. The matted down soy bean stubble, remains of last fall's harvest, are covering most of the mud, but I do manage to kick up a pocketful of flint chips and an inch-long tip broken off of what could have been a gorgeously long spearhead. I pocket this as well, considering myself lucky to have found anything at all.

I cross the field and swing my legs over the top strand of sagging barbed-wire fence that separates the field from the pasture and halfheartedly discourages the surly community of cows from migrating at will. As I stand at the edge of Chappel Creek, one of the many watering holes of my youth, I keep one watchful eye on the temperamental locals, and the other on the muddy, cattle sewer of a pool I may be about to fish.

In a humorous essay, *How To Fish A Crick*, Patrick McManus ironed out the confusion over creeks and cricks. He accurately pointed out that a crick is *not* a creek mispronounced, and eloquently explained the differences between the two. He described creeks as being pristine, and went on to explain that if the two were people, and not bodies of moving water, "creeks would smoke pipes; cricks, chew and spit." Most notably, and what I'm recalling now, is the passage where Mr. McManus explains that the presence of only one determined cow can turn even the cleanest, most pristine creek into a crick in only a matter of hours. Well, Patrick–and anyone else interested in cartographical accuracy–Chappel Creek is a bold-faced misnomer. It is a full-fledged crick, and has been for as long as I've been alive.

The cows chew their cud and eyeball me as I move cautiously down the fence line to the far corner of the pasture. At a pool under the shade of a leaning box elder, the water is less disturbed. It's downstream from the marauding herd of beef, but miraculously most of the filth has settled in a long expanse of shallow, rocky-bottomed water I call Crawfish Run. It's where I used to sneak Mom's deep fryer basket from the kitchen to come down here to catch smallmouth bass bait.

At the head of the pool facing downcrick, I tie on a #14 beadhead Black Bird. This may not be the ideal place to stand and fish a pool, but because of the overhanging limbs it's the only way to ensure I don't hang a winter's worth of fly tying out of reach of both myself and the fish. And besides, who am I kidding? Chubs don't give a damn about presentation, drag-free drifts, or whether or not the clump of feathers at the end of the leader resembles anything living– or that ever was living, for that matter. This is why I come here: not for the challenge, but to dream, to pretend and, of course, to contemplate.

But today, I've actually come to say goodbye.

In a week or two I'm going to leave Ohio, the Midwest and the entire lower forty-eight. I'm going to pack a duffle bag and rod case into my new four-wheel-drive pickup and drive as far north as it takes me to feel like I fit in. All I'm waiting for now is a favorable weather report.

This makes no sense! This section of creek is chock-full of the most gullible group of creek chubs and rock bass that ever swam, but I've not had a single strike in over a dozen casts. *What gives?* I came down to say my goodbyes to an old friend and am getting the cold shoulder! I stop casting and hook my fly into the keeper ring. There's no explanation for this. None that I can come up with, anyway. *What happened to all my chubs? Have they been poisoned? What could kill a chub?* I crouch down and study the water closely, something I haven't done on Chappel Creek in years. I already *know* this water.

A large fish rolls near the bottom of the pool and then disappears. *A carp! Son of a bitch!* A pair of the large fish nose their way into the riffle at my feet and then turn back into the pool and out of sight. *Damn carp up here spawnin' and spookin' all my chubs.* One of the fish enters the shallow riffle again, hovering for a moment and then turning away. *Them ain't carp. Wrong shape. Some of the biggest suckers I've ever seen!*

I shuffle into the riffle and bend down closer. Three of the bruisers enter the current this time. One is much larger than the other two, but the smaller ones look to be at least twenty inches. And they're definitely not suckers. I try to get a good look before they turn and vanish again. The last fish got close enough for me to see an adipose fin. And I think I saw spots on the tail too.

STEELHEAD!

I've heard people–mainly older locals–say that some of the creeks around here have had small runs of steelhead in the years past. There have been some fresh reports of the big coastal rainbows coming up to spawn, but these rumors are always sketchy and at least third or fourth hand. "Yeah, a friend of my cousin used to go after steelhead in Old Woman Creek," or "A guy at work said he knew someone whose brother caught a couple out toward Cleveland last winter." Just the right kind of fish gossip to make you jealous, or cause you a touch of pneumonia from wading around Old Woman Creek all through the months of February and March.

Yes, these are steelhead. No doubt about it.

I bite off the #14 Black Bird and dig frantically around in my fly box. *What do I use for steelhead?* My hands are shaking so badly all my closely arranged flies blend into one big fuzzy blur. Through the chaos of my brain, somehow a dab of useful information surfaces: *orange*. It's not much, just a color, but it's something. I've seen a lot of steelhead flies that have their fur or feathers died orange to simulate dislodged roe, or just as an attractor pattern, I don't know.

I don't own any orange flies, so I go with the next best thing: yellow and red. I tie a #8 Bloody Yolk to my leader (a streamer pattern that has the same color scheme as a fertilized chicken egg in a frying pan). I miss the eye of the hook three times with the end of the monofilament tippet before I can begin the knot.

As I'm getting my new fly ready, the steelhead are still making sporadic appearances in the shallow riffle at my feet, which isn't helping my already frazzled nerves. I get situated, add a tiny bit of split shot to the line–as well as a half dozen to the edge of the stream –and make a cast. The fish aren't in sight, so my cast is out into the middle of the pool where I last saw them. The fly sinks and I retrieve it slowly. Nothing. Now is when I need a good drift.

On the second cast one of the steelhead takes my fly. It's on for only a second, so I'm not able to determine if it is one of the twenty-inchers, or the *real* big one–not that it matters. *Okay. Pricked one of 'em. I got what they want. Two of 'em still don't know what's goin' on.*

I retrieve my line and try to regain my composure. *Settle down, Jay.*

One of the smaller steelhead moves up, alone, into the clear current. I roll cast to the head of the riffle and watch the little dab of yellow feather drift down to the fish. I see the steelhead move toward the fly. The yellow disappears. I set the hook. The fish turns sideways in the current and races for the pool, bending my lightweight rod and taking all the slack line piled at my feet. He makes several powerful runs and rolls on the surface twice. But I'm lucky and don't mess up, and I bring him in. I remove the fly from his jaw and hold him up, milt dripping down my forearm and off my elbow.

* * *

". . . and so that's all I did. He hit the first time I drifted it past him. Couldn't believe it."

Dad nods, eyeing Mom and then the last of the baked steelhead.

"Go ahead," she says. "I'm full."

At this point I've told and retold the story more than a dozen times it seems. The fight gets longer and more drawn out with each telling. And now that the evidence has been consumed, the fish itself has the potential to grow to reach unlimited proportions.

Mom savors the last sliver of morel mushroom and sets her fork down. "That meal was heavenly," she says with her chin up and eyes closed.

Dad eats the last of the trout. I lean back in my chair, scratching my untrimmed goatee and finishing my beer. *Yep, good grub.*

I set my empty mug on the table and glace toward Dad. "Think it'll be worth lookin' for more mushrooms?"

Dad wipes his beard with a paper towel. "Might find a few, but I'd wait 'till after another warm rain."

Mom gets up from the table with her plate and silverware. "The paper called for more rain tonight." She reaches across the table for my plate. "But they said it was going to get colder tomorrow."

"Knew this weather wouldn't last," Dad says, looking out the window. "I've seen snow clear into May." His facial expression changes from relaxed and reminiscent to a brow-creased scowl. "Who in the *hell's* this?"

I follow his glare out the window. Mom leaves the dirty plates on a kitchen counter and comes over to the window. A small white car is moving slowly down the driveway. I catch glimpses of it through the trees, slowing to a crawl at times in areas I know have potholes.

"Ain't nobody I know," I say, rising from my chair and heading to the bookcase for the 12-gauge shotgun kept behind it. *Bloody people. Privacy don't mean nothin' to 'em.* I check to see if the shotgun is loaded–it is. Both barrels have double ought buckshot. But I don't want to kill anyone, so I remove them and drop in two high-brass #6s from the half-empty box of shotgun shells snugged between a book on beekeeping and Jim Corbett's *Man Eaters of Kumaon.* I just want a couple loud bangs and some BBs whizzing through tree branches.

I head for the front door, glancing out the window one last time. What I see makes me hesitate. An attractive young woman has gotten out of the vehicle. She swings the car door shut, pauses for a moment–as if thinking she has forgotten something–then turns and walks toward the house empty-handed.

Well, she ain't sellin' nothin'.

"Hold on!" Mom exclaims. "It's Val!"

Huh? I approach the window for a better look. *I'll be damned.*

I exchange the shells in the shotgun and hide it in its place behind the bookcase. *Valerie Taylor. No kidding.* We'd exchanged letters for awhile when I was still in the Army, but our failed attempt at a date when I was home on leave was the last time I'd heard from her. And that was a couple of years ago.

By the time I make it over to the door, Mom already has it open.

"Hello there, stranger!"

I see Valerie smile and hear her say hello. Mom gives her a hug. I have no illusions; it's my mother she is here to see, but I slide in and give her a one-armed hug of my own. She seems as surprised by this as I am.

"Hey, Valerie. Been awhile." Her shoulder is digging into my sternum– to keep me at bay, I suppose–so I let go and try to cover both of our embarrassment with shallow conversation. "So, how ya been?"

"Oh, come on," Mom says. "Let her in the house."

Mom isn't helping.

"I'm good," Valerie says, making eye contact for the first time. She's more at ease now that I'm at a safer distance. *What was I thinking? What a moron!*

"Uh..." I stammer momentarily. *Shit. Keep talking.* Valerie's still looking at me, waiting for me to finish. "So...Eve said you just got out of school. All graduated and everything, huh?"

"You're just in time for dessert," Mom says from the kitchen. "I'm trying to use up the last of the frozen rhubarb before I get inundated again."

Valerie nods. "Yes. I talked to your sister a few days ago. But, no, I still have two weeks of student teaching to finish before I'm done."

Oh, yeah. That's right. I think I knew that. "Oh. Almost done then, huh?"

She nods again, still looking at me. I'm looking back at her; at her brown eyes and shortly cut brown hair. I can feel my face beginning to turn red.

"So, uh...where were you at?"

Her look turns quizzical. *What'd I say?*

"My alma mater?"

"Uh, yeah." *Dumb ass! Don't say another damn word!*

"Kent. I'm going to school at Kent State."

"Oh, right. Kent State." *I knew that. That's where all those hippies got wacked.*

Valerie smiles.

"Ain't that where all them..." *GOD DAMMIT MAN! SHUT THE HELL UP!*

She's still smiling.

"Uh, that's where...um, somebody I knew went to school."

"Really? Who?"

She seems genuinely interested. *Shit.* "Who?" I ask. "Oh..." I look down at my feet. "Aw hell, I can't remember. It could have been you, actually."

Her smile is looking more strained.

"Well, come on in. Don't let me keep ya from dessert."

Jay, you are the number one, biggest dipshit that has ever lived. Now go sit down and shut up!

Valerie edges past me and into the kitchen with Mom. I hit the refrigerator for a beer and head to the livingroom to flop on the couch. Dad has pulled the usual vanishing act he reserves for when we have company. I ought to go join him, quit while I'm not too far behind. But, dammit, all I want is to get one string of words out without making myself out to be a complete ass.

I drink my beer and eavesdrop on the conversation Valerie is having with my mother. Mom has asked her how she is doing with her student teaching, and has commented on how difficult it must be for a petite young woman to command respect in the classroom. Valerie has denied that there is a problem, saying her lack of organizational skills are getting in her way more than her size or age. I continue to lounge on the couch, frantically thinking up an intelligent question to ask. My beer is about gone.

The conversation moves from the kitchen out into the living-room, so I stop eavesdropping and begin pretending to be a part of it. Actually I haven't made an utterance. No wise maxim or inquisition on the world of high school education has crossed my mind.

Mom gives me a bowl of rhubarb crisp with warm pudding and she and Valerie sit down on the other couch with their dessert. Valerie's rendition of how she broke up a classroom fight between two unruly eleventh-graders is interrupted long enough for Mom to ask me where Dad went. I shrug my shoulders and finish my beer. Valerie continues her story. I fumble around in my mind for something to add.

"So, who won?"

Valerie stops again and they both look at me, eyebrows raised.

"What?" Mom asks.

"The fight. Which one of the kids won the fight?"

"I did," Valerie says.

"Oh."

I put my face back into my bowl of rhubarb crisp, continuing to mentally reprimand myself for being a knob, and the chat goes on without any of my brilliant contributions. I stop listening and scrape the bottom of my bowl. When the last of the pudding is gone I get off the couch and take my dirty bowl to the kitchen. Valerie is done with hers too, so I pick it up on my way. She looks up at me, startled, and thanks me. I nod and don't look back at her or say anything. In the kitchen I congratulate myself. It's better to keep your mouth shut and be thought an idiot than to open your mouth and remove all doubt. That's the old saying Dad sometimes offers as advice (paraphrased many different ways to fit the occasion, of course). I recite this a few times while grabbing a fresh mug and another beer.

I wander over to the dinner table, sit down and flip through a *Wild Ohio* magazine Dad must have been looking at before he vanished into thin air. Valerie sits down in the chair across from me. *Huh?* I look up at her, then out to the livingroom. Mom is gone.

"Ma leave ya stranded?" I ask.

"Yeah, she went to look for your dad," she says. "His dessert is getting cold."

"Uh-huh," I say intelligently.

"Eve said you were all done with the Army. How long have you been out?"

"Yeah, I'm done. But it's not done with me yet," I say, patting my right knee and reaching for my mug. I take a swallow and wipe the foam from my scraggly mustache. "Been almost a year. Got out last summer."

"Your mom mentioned that you were driving up to Alaska in a week or two."

I nod, sipping more of my beer.

"Do you have room for a passenger?" she asks.

Huh? I nearly spit a mouthful of Miller High Life all over the kitchen table. "Yeah, sure. Why? You wanna come?"

May 17th – Day 1

Originally I'd planned to be well on my way by the end of April, but, as you well know, the unexpected has a tendency to be just that. But I was flexible, so I could adjust. Valerie still had two weeks of student teaching to wrap up, then she had to move all her things back home. All the while I kept expecting a telephone call saying she changed her mind, or decided on a shorter and more reliable graduation road trip. I suppose I didn't really give a damn either way. I figured a ride of this caliber with a basic stranger could end many different ways. Great friends being one side of the spectrum of possibilities, murder on the other. It may just turn out all right, I thought. She could hold the map, maybe take a turn at the wheel now and then, and I could work out some of the conversational glitches I have with talking to women. The worst that could be in store? Maybe a few hours of interrogation in a po-dunk police station and a missing person report for one of us to fill out.

The first day went smoothly. I had the truck packed the night before and made it over to Valerie's parents' place by seven in the morning. I'd met them briefly before, back when Valerie, my sister and I were still in school. Her dad seemed cool with the whole thing, but, as he was giving his daughter a hug goodbye I heard him say, "Now remember, this is a working vacation." This threw me. First, I'd never once described the coming trip to be anything even remotely resembling a vacation. I told her that we wouldn't be roughing it necessarily, but to me "roughing it" meant muddy fox holes for weeks on end with nothing to eat but condensed corned beef hash. And secondly, at that early point in the trip I was still under the impression that Valerie was along solely for the drive and that she would be getting on an airplane in Anchorage or someplace to go home and continue on with her more normal life.

Her stepmother was a tad skeptical at first, but after I told her that I wasn't taking full responsibility for her stepdaughter, she was downright opposed to the whole idea. Hell, I thought, Valerie's an adult, a year my senior even. Besides, it was her idea to come along, not mine.

So we got all of Valerie's bags loaded, she said her goodbyes and we hit the road by nine. We made good time and put in a solid 700 miles. As it turned out, Valerie did most of the driving. She said she would rather hold the wheel than the map, and I wasn't looking forward to the Chicago traffic, so I didn't complain.

We didn't talk much; a lot of, "Okay, stay in this lane," or, "What exit do we want?" That kind of necessary navigational stuff.

At about nine in the evening we pitched my tent at the A-J Acres campground in Clearwater, Minnesota–ten miles or so from St. Cloud. I fired up the lantern and set it on a nearby picnic table. We brushed our teeth, tossed our pillows and sleeping bags into the pup tent, and I tried to walk off the bad roast beef sandwich I'd eaten somewhere outside of Minneapolis.

On my way back into our temporary abode, I stopped just outside the circle of lantern light and watched Valerie. She was at the picnic table writing in her journal. I watched her for awhile; she would pause, gaze into the darkness of the campground around her for a spell, then turn back to her writing. I watched and admired her slender fingers and pretty hands.

I coughed and grunted so she would know that I was back, then I walked into the light and sat down across from her.

She looked up from her writing and asked, "Are you feeling any better?"

"Yep," I answered. "Nothin' a good shit can't cure."

She arched her eyebrows and returned her attention to the journal.

Damn. And I was doing so well, too.

I swatted at one of the moths racking up combat sorties around the lantern and tried again. "Ya writin' a book there or what?"

"No." She didn't look up.

"I keep a journal too," I said. "I already wrote in mine." And I had. Jotted down what time we had left, when we had stopped and what city we were near–as a reference.

"Sheesh, this is just the first day," I went on. "What has happened so far that could be worth all them words?"

"The sunset," she said. Again, not looking up. "It was gorgeous. A strip of magenta separating the orange and the blue–truly amazing. Didn't you notice?"

I hadn't.

May 18th/19th – Days 2&3

The first night went eventlessly well–which is what is supposed to happen in the confines of small tent with an attractive yet platonic traveling partner. I spent a large portion of the night awake, in fear of waking up to the sound of horrified screaming, and to find that I'd rolled over next to Valerie's sleeping bag. I imagined a mob of barrel-chested truckers taking turns standing on the back of my head and hearing Valerie's voice trailing off as she climbed into the cab of a rig headed back to Ohio: "Really, I don't know what I was thinking. I knew his sister very well...thought I could trust him...."

Valerie seemed more at ease with the sleeping arrangement than I was, as she fell asleep almost immediately. *I* was able only after skootching as far to my side of the tent as possible and strategically placing my wallet and keys between us (to wake me up if I rolled on them, thus eliminating any chance of engaging in a trucker death match and being forever branded as The Pup Tent Rapist).

We both had a smooth, laid back morning. Got up at 9:00 (no need to rush), packed up the tent and got back on to the road. My only plan as far as a travel schedule was to spend the second night in Canada. Which almost didn't happen, along with the rest of the road trip, because we stumbled into Tower City, North Dakota, and I became convinced that my search for a new home was over. I felt like I could spend the rest of my life there and be perfectly content. We'd pulled in for gas and Valerie asked me to find a post office because she needed to send out a few bills and buy some postcard stamps. I drove around town for a bit–on streets that had Yield signs at the corners instead of Stop signs, the first hint that this was my kind of place–but could not locate the post office. Valerie finally insisted that I ask for directions, which, grudgingly, I did. A boy with a dog on a chain stood at parade rest, like he was a new recruit, called me "sir" and pointed us in the right direction. "Do you know where the bar is?" he said. "Well, the post office is the brown building right across from it." It was at that moment I fell in love with the place. "The Bar"–connotation leaning toward it being the *only* bar–used as a landmark by all, even by ten-year-olds.

We arrived at the border crossing into Saskatchewan shortly before the sun set. Canadian Customs inspected the truck and had us park and come inside for some paperwork and questioning. I fessed to having a shotgun, but it had already been registered with US Customs before we left, and it was in a locked case, so we weren't drawn and quartered. The female agent asked us how long we planned to stay. Just passing through we said. What were we going to be doing in Alaska? Vacationing? No...moving. That's still legal, right? (Stern look.) Moving, huh? Are you two sweethearts?

Fucking Customs. Give them a toy gun and a uniform and they think they're John Wayne. Put a loaded rucksack on their back and an M-60 to carry and they'd probably fall down on their smug, neatly pressed asses. These crackpots apparently believe they're going to *personally* win the war on drugs by opening the lid of my truck toolbox. If smugglers were dumb enough to keep the three kilos of cocain *on the bloody top,* then maybe, but I doubt very many of them are. Oh, and the line of questioning was really grueling, too. I almost cracked under the relentless pressure.

"So, where are you headed?" Aaaug! You got me! I was planning a shooting spree up in Saskatoon! Aaaah!

I ranted on and on to Val about how badly I resented any kind of authority figure, especially those with badges and attitudes. I was so revved up that I never stopped to pitch the tent. Valerie never said a word all night, she kept a steady gaze out the passenger side window and let me vent. I was bent out of shape and not exactly sure what it was that set me off. It wasn't really the Customs ordeal itself that did it–that only took half an hour and was basically painless. Although, somewhere in the back of my mind I kept hearing that "sweethearts" question they asked us. Valerie answered it very quickly and adamantly. "NO! He is just the younger brother of one of my close friends." I mean, it's not that far fetched, is it?

We got two hours of sleep behind a gas station–heads on pillows against the steering wheel and dashboard–and I spent most of the next morning trying to convince myself that I didn't have a massive crush on my road companion. The elaborate mind games with myself were all in vain. During a pit stop in Calgary, Valerie softly complained of a neck ache, so I gave her a very quick neck and shoulder rub...while watching her reflection in the glass of the refrigerator door (pretending to be contemplating over a sports drink or a soda). I justified this incident by telling myself that it was her turn to drive and I needed her to be fully functioning, but afterward, as I stood in front of the mirror of the men's room practicing Lamaze style breathing techniques to calm down, I realized that I was going to be in some serious trouble.

Before I left the men's room, and after I had myself together, I made a verbal agreement with my reflection: I would do absolutely nothing to jeopardize the partnership Valerie and I had. We were trapped in the cab of the same truck together and were both a long way from any friends or family. We needed to depend and rely on each other. There would be no room for any silly shit. *Jay, keep your grubby hands off the girl's neck!*

I desperately needed something to keep my mind on the scenery *outside* the cab, and when we pulled out of Calgary I was granted just that. The great Rocky Mountains loomed up in front of us, the white peeks mingling with the low hanging clouds, making the distinction between land and sky breathtakingly obscure.

We agreed to take our time driving through Banff National Park, as we were making good time and Valerie didn't want to forego the opportunity to use up a few rolls of film. She would alternate between color and black and white, taking multiple photos of any scenery or cloud formations that attracted her attention. I would drive as fast as possible, but at all times ready to lay on the brakes and either back up or pull off the road. A few times we parked and hiked. It was fun, I even started getting into the photography thing too, although I was more interested in getting close-ups of the elk and mule deer than finding an artistic angle on the water droplets in the pine boughs along the trail. I'd always thought of cameras only as tools to help record the memory of fish I'd caught or deer I'd shot. Valerie, on the other hand, was obviously after a bit more.

We passed a campground near Jasper while it was still early, but decided to call it a day anyway. It was situated among the edge of a pine forest and looked to be a good spot to end a very relaxing day. There was a small stream just big enough to jump over trickling right through the middle with a light haze and a herd of semi-tame elk meandering around between camp sites.

After the tent was set up I unearthed my portable propane stove and heated a can of chicken. I cubed a few potatoes, too, trying to appear fancy and chef-like, but they just stuck to the bottom of the frying pan and made smoke. Valerie choked down the too-salty, over-dry chicken, thanked me, grabbed her towel and overnight bag and headed for the showers. I stayed back to keep a watch over our stuff and when Valerie came back I took my towel and bar of soap and got a shower myself.

On the way back to the tent I slowed down to soak in my surroundings–the stream, the trees, the silhouette of elk through the fog, the faint sound of a drum being tapped on by one of the hippies camped near us. It made me feel alive and awake.

I had a smile on my face when I got back and Valerie looked at me suspiciously.

"You didn't beat up the hippies did you?" she asked, with more than a touch of sarcasm in her voice.

May 20th – Day 4

The lackadaisical mood which we let ourselves slip into the day before carried over to the morning. We didn't crawl out of our bags and break camp right away. Instead, we stayed in the tent talking and didn't get on the road again until 11:00. I was trying my hand at sounding more positive and uplifting. Maybe, I thought, with a little effort Valerie might stop perceiving me as a crass, insensitive prick. I'd never cared before. If I insulted someone, or hurt their feelings... well, that was their own fault for having thin skin. I was getting the hang of not sounding like an arrogant jackass.

Once we got going we drove until almost midnight and stopped at the Sportsman's Lodge, a motel in Pink Mountain, British Columbia. The light was on, but there was no one at the front desk, so we took a key from the peg board–as a sign said to–and flopped our road weary selves down onto the mattresses. We had cranked another day's worth onto the odometer, and Valerie had gone through another few rolls of film–photos of mountain peaks, beautiful rivers, herds of caribou, and a couple shots of a black bear gnawing on roadkill as her young cubs goofed around behind her. The wildlife shots, I might add, were mine.

Alas, we were officially on the Alaska Highway. I lay in my strange bed and the thought of that kept me awake and alert. *"Goin' to Alaska!"* I whispered over and over to myself.

May 21st – Day 5

It felt as though we'd slept in again because it had been light out for hours, but it wasn't until we were packed up and ready to get going that we discovered how early it still was. The days were getting substantially longer the further north we got. The cheerful woman behind the counter–whom I payed $50 Canadian for the room–took the key, gave me the time and wished us happy travels.

The day started out pleasant enough, but quickly began to unravel. First there was the broken windshield. A logging truck kicked up a stone that left a golf-ball-size hole in the windshield and showered Valerie–who was unlucky enough to be driving at the time –with broken glass. She took it well, and so did I, which was actually more surprising. I got out and duct-taped the hole while she shook the shards out from her sweater and brushed off the seat. Then came the bear mauling. Well, actually, I didn't stick around long enough for him to maul me, but by rights he probably should have, as he should any dumb ass who pulls the stunt I tried.

I had spotted two grizzlies about thirty yards off the highway with their heads down, feeding on more roadkill I assumed, and I stopped to get a couple photos of them. The smaller one ran off into the woods as soon as I stopped, but the other–larger one–stayed put. But he wouldn't look up at me. I wanted a good shot of his big brown mug, so, like a tourist after the Darwin Award, I got out, got closer and even kicked some loose gravel at him. Well, I got what I wanted. He definitely looked up–about three strides into his charge.

I don't know how blurry the shots will be because I was moving pretty fast, and so, actually, was the bear. And that's fine, at least I beat him to the truck with enough time to shut the door and peel out before he could chew any paint off the tail gait, or enlarge the hole in the windshield.

"Did you just see that?" I asked breathlessly after I had safely reached 65 mph.

Valerie looked up from the book she had been reading and marked the place with her thumb. "The bears?" she asked tiredly. "Did you get a good picture?"

Through all this, the busted windshield, the bear attack (or, more accurately, the dumb ass attack) I kept up the gentleman-like facade. I even began to think it had stuck, but it all ended once we stopped for the night and I regressed to my former self. It was at a gas station in the Yukon Territory. The signs advertized the cheapest gas for miles (it was the only gas, or even *building*, for miles) as well as tent camping between the gas pumps and the river that paralleled the partially gravel highway. After we had the tent in place I strolled back up to the gas station to buy Valerie and myself some soda to drink with our canned tuna dinner. On the way back I found her, much to my chagrin, helping another fella put up his tent. I walked by without so much as a nod in their direction. As I sat in the cab of the truck eating my tuna and crackers I couldn't help stewing and watching the two of them chatting it up like they were old friends. Craig was from Wyoming. He was a journalism major and on his way up to Seward for a summer cannery job. I know all this because Valerie came back and filled me in. I gave my best disinterested smile and nod, said something charming like: "This tuna tastes like shit" and stomped back up to the gas station for a pack of cigarettes.

They didn't sell American brand cigarettes, so I settled for a pack of what the guy said was the Camel Light equivalent. And they also tasted like shit. I smoked one as I sat beside the river and scribbled in my journal (at 11:00 p.m. birds were chirping and it was still light enough to write). Then I threw the pack away in disgust. Disgust over my nicotine weakness and silly jealousies. I wasn't even supposed to like her....

May 22nd/23rd – Days 6 & 7

The rest of the trip went well, apart from the speeding ticket and frightening bulge in the front right tire. We made it to Alaska by 6:30, stopped in Tok–for a hunk of halibut and some salmon chowder–and eventually camped just outside Delta Junction. The mosquitoes were miserable, but we were both in extremely high spirits. We had made it!

I used the restaurant telephone in Tok to get a hold of a family I knew living north of Fairbanks–the Koegle's. They're old friends of my folks and, after I explained my situation, they agreed to take us in until we got ourselves straightened out. So, on the afternoon of the 23rd, six days, four hours and 4,126 miles later, our road trip was over.

I introduced Valerie to Jack and Allyson, and to their daughter, Maegan and son, Adam. Both of whom have mutated into teenagers since the last time we chummed around together. Allyson and Maegan kidnaped Valerie and took her to help out with the fieldday being held at the elementary school where Allyson teaches. Adam, on the other hand, had his own plans for me. He took me for a bone-jarring ride on his four-wheeler down to the Chena River where he commenced to fish circles around me. The water was too cold for me to wet wade out far enough to reach the main cannel. But I did manage to pluck a fourteen-inch arctic grayling out from along a grass-lined undercut. Adam caught and released four fish, a couple that looked a pound better than my only one.

That evening, back at the Koegle place, I was able to meet up with Valerie again. She told me about the sack race and I told her about my grayling. It felt good to be near her again. She said she had felt odd when we went our separate ways, her to the school and me down to the river. She said that she had begun to feel safe and comfortable around me. I smiled and gave her a hug. And...she returned it.

Blue fox

Halibut Hotel

Valerie and I stayed with Jack and Allyson in Alaska for almost a week. After we rested up, worked the kinks out and stopped seeing a yellow median every time we closed our eyes, it was time to move on. I had picked Jack's brain for everything I could and listened to his stories–helpful or just plain entertaining. Although a carpenter by trade now, he has dabbled in both guided hunting and commercial fishing. It was that–his stint as a longliner down in Petersburg–that really grabbed my attention. I had that sort of thing in mind when I decided to come here.

We left after dinner on May 27th and, with bellies full of caribou burger and renewed wanderlust, drove the five-hundred odd miles along the Nenana River; through the Alaska Range; passed the Talkeetna Mountains; in and out of Anchorage; and on to the coastal city of Seward. We arrived on the morning of the 28th and purchased our reserved ferry ticket to Kodiak Island. The ship would be shoving off later in the evening. Before we left, Jack had read from a newspaper of a shortage of deck hands on the island, and that brief, and possibly outdated, blurb appeared to be the best lead I could expect.

We pointed bald eagles out to each other, browsed the local library and, at the end of the day, enjoyed a wonderful meal of stuffed salmon, clam chowder, crab-stuffed mushrooms and smoked-salmon Caesar salad in a restaurant overlooking the harbor on the cold waters of Resurrection Bay. We lingered at our table long after the meal and through at least one pot of coffee, watching the eagles perched in the rigging of the fishing boats and talking about what Kodiak might be like and if we would manage to find work–anxious chatter while we were trying to relax.

When the time came we policed up our things, checked our ticket one last time and then drove down to the water. The ferry was waiting and the line of vehicles–mainly Jeeps and pickups–had already begun inching forward. I have been on ferries before, across the Illinois River once and over to Kelly's Island on Lake Erie to go deer hunting, and in both instances the ferry was small, with a ramp at the stern and the bow. In those smaller ferries they could accommodate a few cars, a herd of cyclists and that's about it. But, as we rolled up onto the stern of the *Tustumena*–a 296-foot *ocean*-going vessel–I knew it wasn't going to be a cross-river jaunt or a twenty minute zip over to deer camp. This was the Alaska Marine Highway, a whole different league.

The *Tustumena* crew motioned us onto a platform and then lowered us, truck and all, into the hold. More crew directed us off the platform and got us and the other oncoming vehicles packed in as tightly as possible. Valerie and I bagged up our toiletries, rain jackets and change of clothes and headed topside as the truck was chained down and blocks wedged behind the tires. I had spent the extra money for a berth for the same reason I treated the two of us to a fancy supper, because I had no idea what I was getting us into and I wanted to at least go into the unknown and unexpected–and potentially unpleasant–with a full stomach and a decent night's sleep. Of course, the full stomach would have ruined the night's sleep if either of us were prone to sea sickness.

The rooms were very small, as you would expect, but suitable. There were bunk beds, a sink, mirror and just enough room for two close friends to get around each other. Which made it fortunate that Valerie and I were becoming more at ease with one another. We secured our room, stashed our belongings and went out on deck as the ferry cast off from the mainland, to lean on the railing and watch the seagulls chasing our wake.

As we moved further out into Resurrection Bay, the wind picked up and Valerie got chilled. She put the hood up on her rain jacket, but eventually retreated to the cabin. I stayed out much longer, captured by the ocean and the ever changing Alaskan coastline– distant pyramidal giants looming ominously through the gray half-light.

Finally, I too grew cold and returned to the warmth of the cabin and the promising comfort of my bunk. But before I left the railing I took a last long breath of the salty air and nodded to the waves and the mountains as I would to a stranger whom I respected for his immensity. I felt as though this new world knew who I was and had plans of its own for me.

I had to remind myself that I was fearless.

* * *

The *Tustumena* nudged alongside the Kodiak ferry dock at 2:00 p.m. on the 29th of May. The trip had taken fourteen hours, slightly longer than scheduled, because of a storm whipping up the Gulf of Alaska. I had been woken at one point in the night by the increased pitching and yawing of my bunk. I rummaged around for my long-sleeved flannel shirt and then stood with my face pressed against the tiny porthole, bracing myself to keep from staggering with the sway. Something metallic and heavy was clanging somewhere above us, striking steadily on about a five-count rhythm, the only sound apart from the low vibrating hum from the engine room. There was enough visibility to see out the porthole, but it was late and we were well into the Gulf. Although I couldn't hear it, I could tell the winds outside were bad and the swells were enormous–huge, rolling hills of water silently rising and falling, lifting and pulling at the hunk of iron and steel forging steadily on through the night. The mountains were no longer on the horizon; they had been replaced with a thick, black band of nothingness. I watched the ocean and felt cold.

The weather cleared and the seas settled down the closer we came to the islands. There were charts unrolled and posted on an information board outside our room and Valerie and I studied them in the morning. It showed masses of islands. We gazed up at the charts and saw Kodiak and Afognak, and I read aloud some names of the many others: Spruce Island...Marmot Island...Whale Island. Others I just rolled around in my mouth quietly because I couldn't pronounce them. There must be a hundred more, all woven in amongst the bays and peninsulas. It was fantastic, and overwhelming. My anxiety had faded into restless excitement. I was stoked. Pumped up. Ready to go.

And I nearly shrieked with glee when I got my first close-up glimpse of the Kodiak shoreline. The desolate stretches of pebble beaches. The foamy breakers flushing out the dark stone niches and hollows of the steep, weather carved cliffs; towering, deep green spruce above them. The brown hills of early spring further inland, hardened patches of snow at their higher points. All wrapped in a damp, ghostly mist.

I had deliberately avoided forming any notions about what Kodiak would be like, but the introduction I got as we rolled down the ramp and onto Center Street was quite different from the impression framed by the small porthole of the ferry. It was sort of...disappointingly civilized. But, because it is forced to be a compact town, it has a certain sense of coziness and independence, giving it more charm than a small Midwestern town.

Valerie and I tried to absorb our immediate surroundings as quickly as possible, like the first time in a strange bar when the front door slams shut and all the patrons stop talking, turn on their stools and look at you. But it felt like a warm and welcoming place, a busy little sea port tucked almost precariously between snow-capped mountains and the equally frigid ocean. To our left was *The Star of Kodiak*, a ship that appeared to be permanently dry docked (I later learned that it was brought to the island to use as a cannery after all the other canneries, as well as most of the town, got flattened by the 1964 tsunami). To our right were the blue, onion-like domes of a Russian Orthodox Church. On down Center Street were the usual assembly of shops, banks and restaurants found on Center Streets anywhere–as well as the sidewalks full of bustling people.

Our first line of business was to buy a newspaper (which was easy enough to locate) then, to find a campground (which wasn't). Eventually we did find a place to camp, but only after making sense of the small and insanely confusing road map which we were given on the *Tustumena*. It was at the end of a gravel road, an ideal place: secluded, close to the coast (which, really, is redundant) and, best of all, right on the Buskin River–a clear, swift river that is small enough to wade or cast across, but with a definite big-league personality. I fished it for an hour the first evening and caught a whole mess of nothing, and it became immediately obvious that I was either in way over my head or playing an entirely new ball game. Although fishless on my first attempt, I knew I had the time and stubbornness to learn any new water. Time for that later, first we had to find a place to live.

We spent two nights in the campground. During the day we browsed the most recent *Kodiak Daily Mirror*–I stealing the page with Hank Pennington's outdoor column and Valerie concentrating on the classifieds and trying to line up an apartment over the campground payphone. In the early evenings, I would stalk the Buskin River looking unsuccessfully for some of the fish life that I had read about. I came across only one other fisherman: a soft, heavy-set man in his late forties who was on an Alaskan vacation with his wife. He told me he had caught a small Dolly Varden char the day before, but had heard that other guys were getting into some red salmon.

At night Valerie and I drove into town to enjoy the festival that was already in full swing, which explained all the people bustling about when we first arrived. It was the kind of annual festival that most towns put on, and I believe they say a lot about the character of a place–or lack thereof. Take, for example, the towns I grew up in and around: Huron's *Water* Fest, Milan's *Melon* Fest, and Berlin Heights with it's *Basket* Fest.

But *this* was the Kodiak *Crab* Festival!

And, apart from the plywood-sided booths selling crab legs in place of cotton candy, it was just like any other. So, we ended up going back to our tent, and Valerie taught me how to play cribbage.

We eventually move into an apartment on the third floor of a three story building with one bedroom and an open loft. It's in town and overlooks Lily Lake, which is really just a narrow pond. There is a big bay window in both the bedroom and livingroom and I can sit on the couch (bought from the previous tenant) and watch the float planes take off.

The previous tenant was in the middle of packing the last of his belongings into the back of his truck when we moved in. I bought a lot of it from him: a mattress, vacuum cleaner, a full set of silverware and a cupboard full of coffee mugs. He had said he was getting back together with his wife so wouldn't be needing them anymore.

So, here we are, with a solid roof over our heads, warm running water and an inside toilet. I feel like royalty. Our things are all unloaded and the refrigerator actually has food in it now. Thank you, Safeway. We have been on the island for over a week now and are beginning to feel settled. Valerie has the real bedroom and I have arranged all of my fishing gear and other things in plastic totes in the loft. A carpet and sliding-door closet up there makes me a comfortable bedroom once my sleeping bag is rolled out. Our livingroom is looking good, too. I have set out two folding camp chairs by the couch and cleaned off the lid of my cooler to double as a coffee table.

Valerie got a job right away at the Budget Rent-A-Car booth inside the airport. It's not a high-paying gig, renting cars to tourists and salmon bums, but it will do for her half of the rent and groceries. And it's pretty cool for an airport, not the hellish labyrinth of gates and corridors swarming with vile perfumes and nervous body odor that make for the usual airport nightmare. The parking lot is the size of those beside an average high school or supermarket. One main room, one gate. All the other things that belong in an airport are there as well: rows of interconnecting chairs, the baggage check-in, a baggage-claim carousel and two car rental booths. All are neatly placed around the centerpiece: the glass-enclosed, full-body mounts of a black-tailed deer about to be ravished by a brown bear. There's somehow room amid all this for a coffee cart, which is run by a young married woman about Valerie's age. She has a crib behind the cart and often brings her eight-month-old daughter to work, and feels safe with that–it's *that* kind of airport.

My employment opportunities were looking a great deal more dismal. I beat the docks of St. Paul Harbor in the rain for a week, as well as St. Herman Harbor across the bridge on Near Island. There were some skippers who were short a deck hand or two, but they weren't interested in hiring me. They clearly pegged me as a "mainlander," or worse yet, a "lower-forty-eighter" before I got within ten yards of their boat.

But my luck kicked in yesterday. I realized the last of my Army bankroll was gone, so I drove down to the water, parked outside Tyson Seafood and prepared myself for a last ditch effort–a cannery job. As I sat there in the cab of my pickup with the engine and windshield wipers on, I looked out at all the tied-off fishing vessels in St. Paul Harbor and cursed myself. Then I cut the engine, leaving the wipers stranded in mid swipe, and strode defiantly back through the rain and down to the slick, shifting docks. I would try one last time before surrendering myself to the cannery.

Most of the boats were in, but because of the steady rain no crews were working on any of their decks, though some cabin lights were on. I hadn't gone far down the docks when I passed a man in his mid fifties with a graying moustache headed in the other direction. He wore faded blue jeans and had his hands jammed deep in his pockets.

The collar of his thick wool jacket was turned up and a baseball cap was pulled down tight over his head, its bill almost completely hiding his face. I could tell he was a fisherman from his simple, durable clothes and the brown, rubber knee boots folded down even with the hem of his pant legs. I asked if he knew of anyone needing another deck hand (the same question I'd been asking on those docks for a week).

He said that *he* was, "But hey, there are lots of guys around looking for work. "And besides," he added, "I'm not even set up to go out yet."

I nodded, used to hearing different approaches to saying, "No, I want someone with experience." But he continued, explaining that he considered himself semi-retired and that he was looking for someone who didn't mind if they didn't make much money. He said he was sure I could do better on one of the other boats–the price for red salmon was still up. This gave me hope. Not hope of eventually making a fortune with red salmon, but of talking this skipper into taking me on as a hand. Judging by his comments, he mustn't have recognized me as a greenhorn, or, in the Alaskan lingo, a cheechako. My rain-soaked flannel and three-week old beard must have been a sufficient cover.

There I was, standing in the rain out on St. Paul Harbor, doing my best to impress upon Charles Lewis Jr., the skipper of the *Bluefox* –the 38-foot wooden seiner which we were standing beside–that I was not out to make a packet. I'd scrub decks, gut cod or anything else that could help pay for the outrageous rent, groceries and maybe a bit of fly-tying material over at Cy's Sporting Goods.

Chuck was interested in the last bit, the mention of fly-tying material. He asked how long I had been fly fishing. I said, "Oh, a while." Then he wanted to know if I had been having any luck. I replied: "Oh...nothin' spectacular." (i.e. "I ain't seen a fish in weeks.") We stood together in the rain and talked fly patterns and tactics for a good twenty minutes and then he said he had to go pick up his longline reel and mount it to his boat. I told him I'd come along to help, even though he said he wouldn't be able to pay me for my time.

We drove out to where he had the reel stored and loaded it onto his flatbed pickup and then drove back. Somehow we managed to winch it aboard. Imagine a baitcasting reel about the size of a 55-gallon steel drum that holds over ten-thousand feet of braided line thick enough to rappel with, and then you would be seeing what the two of us were struggling with.

Once the reel was mounted, the bin boards in place–to keep fish from sliding off the deck–and the baiting table firmly bolted in behind the reel, Chuck declared it time to quit working. "After all," he said, "I'm supposed to be retired." I had the feeling that he said this sort of thing a lot. He was laid back to the extent that I couldn't picture him ever being in a hurry to work and I knew he wasn't exaggerating when he said he'd been living and working on Alaskan waters for the majority of his life. His manner and appearance reminded me of a Jimmy Buffet who had to bust his ass for a living instead of singing songs and drinking margaritas...or singing songs *about* drinking margaritas. Not that I see anything wrong with any of that.

We talked both commercial fishing and sport fishing while we worked and by the time we were done he realized that my experience was limited solely to the sporting side, but it didn't seem to concern him any. He didn't know when he would be making his first commercial run of the season, but we did make plans to meet at Harborside Coffee in the morning (since he lived right there on his boat) and we would flyfish the Buskin together. I left for the apartment thoroughly soaked, but with a huge sense of relief and accomplishment.

In the morning, after a well-rounded, hearty breakfast of black coffee, Chuck and I headed to the Buskin. He had one small box of flies (which made me self-conscious of my bulging vest) and a yellow fiberglass Eagle Claw fly rod that was given to him by his father when the old man had retired. "He was looking for the warmer weather and willing women," Chuck said. "So he took off for the Philippines."

Chuck gave me a motorized tour of the length of the river, pointing occasionally out the window of his truck to show me different access points. The Buskin , a short river, originates from the tail end of Buskin Lake–only about three miles from the coast. The river has a few twists and turns, so it may be five miles from start to finish if it's lucky. We fished farther upriver than I had before, closer to the lake than the coast. Chuck came back an hour later with two red salmon, while I, again, had not even a strike.

Tonight Valerie and I devoured a hand-tossed salad, a bottle of pinot noir and almost all of the four-pounds of bright red salmon flesh

Chuck sent home with me. While we ate, I enjoyed telling her about the river and the fishing. She enjoyed hearing I had a job.

* * *

It is a foggy, drizzly Monday and Valerie is at work and has the truck. But the walk from the apartment down to the docks only takes twenty minutes and, no matter the weather, I like to savor the feeling and the view as I stride down the Lower Mill Bay Road hill in my black watchcap and folded down kneeboots, with my gear in an Army-issue laundry bag over my shoulder and my mind climbing to the peak of Pyramid Mountain. It's a grand feeling. I'm a care-free maritime hobo on the big rock candy island.

The price of halibut is still good so Chuck wants to make another run. He wants me at the boat around 3:00/3:30 and it was about 3:00 when I checked the travel alarmclock on the kitchen counter before I left.

The first two runs Chuck and I made together were good ones. We came home each time with roughly one ton of halibut and maybe two- to three-hundred pounds of gray cod. The price for gutted cod is fixed at 50 cents a pound (40 cents ungutted) but halibut is flexible and more valuable. Our first two deliveries went for $1.80 a pound, and now the price is up to $2.05. As Chuck's crewman, I get a 10% cut–which has come to about $370 a trip. Not bad for two days of fishing. They're easy days too, as far as commercial fishing goes. We only make one five-skate set a day (each skate is 1800 feet of line, holding approximately 100 hooks) and then let it soak for a few hours before picking it back up–like a giant trotline. This is quite the contrast to the halibut-opener stories Jack Koegle told. Back then the longliners would set and pick almost constantly for as long as they were permitted, leaving no time for sleep and precious little time for beer and food. The salmon seiners still fish this way, but the halibut openers have been scrapped and now each fisherman (usually the skipper or boat owner) has been allotted an Individual Fish Quota, which is measured in pounds. And they have all year to fish it, although most skippers fish their halibut IFQ early–before the first salmon opener–and when the price is usually below $1.00. Chuck, on the other hand, finds it more suiting to his lifestyle to work less and live frugally, so he leaves the salmon openers for the more ambitious and waits for the halibut price to get high. He then takes his time, scratching lazily away at his IFQ.

Needless to say, as his sole crew member, I'm as happy as a bear in the BFI dumpster behind the Buskin River Inn. And it shows by the content grin on my face as I stride down the noisy metal ramp and onto the wooden docks of St. Paul Harbor.

Chuck is nowhere around, but the cabin hatch of the *Bluefox* is unlocked, so I know he's not far. I stow my bag at the foot of my bunk and rub my hands together over the small oil-burning stove, letting them soak in what little heat it's emitting. There are four bunks in the cabin, two on either side, and they have zero head room–only enough space for an average-size man to squeeze into. If you are in one of the bottom two and roll over during the night, your shoulders have a good chance of becoming wedged. Because Chuck lives aboard his boat, only two of the bunks are clear to sleep on; the bottom port-side (mine) and the top starboard-side. The other two are loaded down with an emergency inflatable life raft, survival suits, marine navigational charts (with halibut hot spots penciled in, making them extremely top secret) assorted tools and tool boxes, radio parts, a suitcase of clothing and one small box of flies. The Eagle Claw fly rod and an ultra-lite spinning rod are hanging from the low ceiling along with two more rolled-up and badly weathered charts. There is a table large enough to accommodate only two people cramped into one corner, and behind the table is the hatch to the crawlspace that leads to the big diesel engine. Immediately inside the hatch is a five-gallon bucket and a plastic toilet seat. These are taken topside in times of need. You sit, grunt, watch the seagulls, and they watch you. Of course, if the boat is still in the harbor you would use the public restroom where there is absolutely *no* view, because there are no windows and the lights don't work–which makes stepping over the passed-out, snoring drunks very awkward.

There is room for only one person to move about the cabin at a time. In the mornings Chuck fires up the engine, turns on the weather radio and gets dressed, and I wait until he is out and pulling the anchor before I pry myself from my little wooden slot. The majority of time aboard is spent above, though, which isn't necessarily a hardship since the cabin never really smells that pleasant: a mix of stove fumes and that stale fish smell that reminds me of the old tackle box my dad takes out when the bullhead or catfish start hitting in the Huron River. Which is why I don't linger below deck now, either.

My hands have regained some of their previous warmth and flexibility, so I take down one of the four mugs swinging from its wooden peg and fix myself some instant coffee. The kettle on the stove is cast iron, built squat and sturdy to withstand heavy handed fishermen and the violent rocking from the waves, both of which weed out all but the most durable of equipment. The water may have been on the stove for hours, but is not in danger of boiling. The coffee will be cold long before I finish it.

I take my mug of lukewarm instant up on deck and peer around the harbor. The drizzling rain has eased off, but the fog is, if anything, a bit soupier. No sign of Chuck yet.

Where is he?

The skipper of one of the boats nearby–the *Monk's Habit*– walks by, towing a two-wheeled dock cart stacked with cardboard grocery boxes. He nods. I nod back.

Ahhhh. . .bet that's where he is. Gettin' us some grub!

With the riddle of Chuck's whereabouts seemingly solved, I set down my now cold coffee and begin organizing the hook racks. There are five of them, and I want one for each skate, so each rack needs 100 hooks. This will let me know if I am falling behind at any time during the hour or so it takes to set.

Some of the metal snaps are rusty and need to be replaced. I cut them from their two-foot, braided nylon gangions and replace them with shiny new ones. Some of the hooks feel dull, too, so I touch them up with a file. They are odd shaped circle hooks, like those some fly tiers use for single salmon-egg patterns. But these are much larger, about the size of my index finger crooked...*I suppose, with enough white chenille I could tie a chicken egg? Catch a racoon maybe?*

"Hey, we all set to go?"

It's Chuck. I had heard footsteps on the dock, but hadn't looked up. He isn't pulling or carrying any groceries, and appears to be in a hurry.

"Sure." I look up from a hook rack. "My bag's inside."

Chuck hops aboard and scoots into the cabin. A moment later the boat's engine rumbles to life and he comes back out and climbs up to the flying bridge, motioning for me to unleash us from the dock cleats. I do, but with a quizzical look–this rushing about is unlike him.

I get the scoop only after we have backed out of the stall and are on our way out of the harbor. At the wheel, he explains that he was on his way to Safeway for food, but decided against it when he heard that the fog was predicted to get even thicker than it already is. He wants to anchor over in Anton Larson Bay for the night, giving us an early start in the morning, but the fog could make navigating around the tip of the cape a tad treacherous. Not to mention Narrow Strait and all the rocks and points jutting from Spruce Island.

So, we're in a hurry. Which doesn't happen often.

No worries on the food supply. Chuck says he remembers having some canned goods in the cupboard, or if not there, under the table.

Before we brave the open ocean and ever thickening fog, we need to top off at the fuel dock and buy, or haggle for free, some ice from one of the canneries. And bait, too. Can't forget the bait. Usually we get a few frozen blocks of twelve-inch squid that I cut in half to make last for 500 hooks, but other times we'd be offered other things. Once we bought 65 fresh pink salmon for 30 cents a pound, which is three-times more than the fisherman who caught them was paid. I wanted to cry for sending 500 two-inch-thick salmon steaks over the gunnel that day.

We only buy the bait for the first set, the consecutive days I cut up whatever goodies we've managed to pull off the bottom of the ocean–octopus hopefully, and sometimes an interesting smorgasbord of gray cod, ling cod and a strange beast Chuck calls a monkeyface eel. Today we get squid again and luck out with a couple free tons of crushed ice. A Filipino cannery worker lowers a hard-plastic hose into the hold and blasts us full. The ice is light, fluffy and easy to move around now, but by tomorrow morning we'll be sitting on an alpine glacier shaped like a 38-foot seiner. And I'll be down in there with it, with a shovel.

It is almost midnight before the *Bluefox* cruises into Anton Larson Bay. Although the fog has given the trip a certain sense of eeriness, the sky has only gotten mildly dusky–the perk of an Alaskan summer. When fogged in on the open water, horizons are non-existent, and one loses all sense of perspective. It took me more than fifteen minutes to recognize the silhouetted object looming in front of us as we passed through Narrow Strait. At first I saw it as a rock outcropping, but before I could warn Chuck to steer clear, we got closer and I could see it was a fisherman in a skiff, mending his set net. I figured we were swinging by to say hello (Chuck knows about everyone out here). It wasn't until we were almost alongside it and the startled water bird took flight, that I realized just how mistaken I was.

Chuck idles the big diesel and we glide almost noiselessly into shallower water. As we pass the sheer face of one of the countless little rock islands that crowd the mouth of the bay, hundreds of puffin bail out of their nesting crevasses, flapping skinny wings and frantically trying to gain altitude before smacking their chubby bodies onto the water. Most manage, but more than a few have to make a second takeoff attempt from sea-level. I laugh out loud. It's like watching penguins trying to fly, and eventually succeeding. This world is still slightly foreign to me and full of surprises.

"Those are amazing birds," Chuck says climbing down from the flying bridge. "Funny, but amazing."

I nod and watch for more of the white and orange heads peeking out at us from inside their holes.

"They spend most of the year at sea," he says. "They're here on land now to hatch their young."

"Yeah?"

Chuck pauses on the deck with me, looking toward the cliff face. "I came in close to give you a look at them."

"Cool. Thanks."

"Happens to be a good place to hole up for the night, too," he says matter-of-factly and leaves to lower the anchor.

I linger awhile, gazing out over the dense spruce forest of mainland Kodiak. The fog seems to be lifting, or thinning (whatever it is that fog does when it's not getting worse). Or maybe it's just not as bad further inland, because I can make out the very peak of Pyramid Mountain. This is the peaceful, but desolate, backside view of it. On the other side is the crowded sea port. I don't long for it, I like it on this side of the mountain. I just long to wish a certain woman good night and then climb up to my loft with a good feeling in my chest.

She should be in bed by now. I hope work went well.

Beyond a large kelp bed I see two harbor porpoise breaking the smooth surface of the bay. The engine has been shut off and it is still and perfectly quiet.

"Good night, Valerie," I whisper over the graceful porpoise and the evergreens and the dark pinnacle of the mountain. It feels good to stand alone on deck and view life and the world from such a remote and majestic place. And it feels good to know I don't *have* to stand alone.

Then I clamber down into the cabin to have a beer and help Chuck look for the canned goods he *thought* he remembered having.

* * *

I wake to the sound of the engine and the weather radio, and I know it's early. I've slept well with the gentle rocking of my bunk. The radio voice is broken by static, but the news that does come through sounds promising. It should be a calm day. They're even calling for some sun, which will be a novelty–no one on the island has seen a trace of it in over three weeks.

I am dressed and out on deck before the anchor is up. Our slickers are bungee-corded to the side of the cabin, and I have to sort through them to find my bright yellow rain pants. I find and don them, pushing my rubber boots into the cold, stiff legs. There is dried blood and crusted fish remains in the creases of the bib that I missed when I scrubbed down last week. *No worries, I'll be a mess in a minute anyway.*

I pull the blue tarp off the top of the hold cover and heave up one of the four wooden slats. The boat is in motion already, and I know Chuck is at the wheel. I take a shovel, chip out the bags of squid and slide them onto the deck. We are still a ways from the prime fishing grounds, but I need to have all the bait thawed, cut and ready to go before we get there. I cover the hold, remove the frozen blocks of squid from their bags and use a bucket to splash seawater onto them. Once the salt has eaten through most of the ice, I am able to pry them apart in groups of twos and threes and dump them into the big plastic tote next to the baiting table.

After all the squid has been cut, I climb out of my slimy yellow pants, wipe my hands and relax. I am becoming more efficient and it means less work and more time to enjoy where I am. Today I stand on the hold cover, enjoying the sunshine and watching a pod of humpback whales surfacing. After a while they all submerge, first arching their backs above water, then airing out their giant tails. Then they are gone, and I am left alone to admire the rolling emerald coastline. I inquire, over the noise of the engine, the name of the large landmass off our starboard side.

"Whale Island," Chuck shouts back. "That's Raspberry Island out further," he adds, accurately predicting my next question. He turns in the other direction, points and is about to say something else, but is cut short. Two of the whales break the surface again, one on either side of us. One is close enough to snag with a fly rod. Chuck cranks down the throttle and veers the *Bluefox* away from it. It blows and I feel the wind bring some of the mist across my face...or maybe it was just bow spray. But it's cold and I let out a whoop. *What a life!*

When we arrive at one of the hot spots penciled in on the charts Chuck yells down for me to throw the buoys. I react smartly, heaving the twin blue, beachball-sized rubber floats off the stern. I pull off buoy line from the reel until there is enough out for the drag on the buoys to do the chore for me. Once the lead end of the first skate peels off the reel I tie it to the baiting table, secure an anchor to it and wait for Chuck's order to start the set. I have my yellow pants back on, as well as the matching top. My gloves are on too, and the hook racks are ready to go. Just waiting for the word.

Chuck watches the electronic depth reader, double checking the chart. Then he knocks down the throttle two notches and yells down at me to throw the anchor. I do, and the reel starts spinning again. I have to move fast, with no wasted movement–take a gangion from the rack and bait the hook in one fluid motion, throw the baited hook on the table and clip the snap onto the line as it's peeling out. If not done in the proper order; if the snap is clipped before the bait is thrown...well, the hook will get your hand, and over and down you go. And a healthy man might last twenty minutes in these waters before hypothermia kicks in. With this much at stake you would think it would be easy to remember, but, after over an hour any repetition can get muddled. Although, having one of my gloves yanked from my hand is a close enough call to wake me up.

When the end of the last skate comes off the reel, I clip on the last hook, tie another anchor at the conjunction of the skate and the buoy line, drop it over, and stand back. Once the end of the buoy line is off the reel, I tie on the last two blue buoys and give Chuck a thumbs up. He acknowledges with a wave, and turns the boat toward land.

Later, anchored in a larger, less protected bay, I scrub the deck with a coarse bristle utility brush and hose off the baiting table. The empty hook racks are stacked out of the way, but close enough at hand for when we need them. I sharpen my gutting knife–a long thin blade with a white plastic handle–and position it, the whetstone and a kidney-tissue scraper on the baiting table. While I'm busy with these things, Chuck is digging around in the cupboards looking for our lunch. He comes up with a half-dozen tortillas and an almost empty jar of salsa. We ate burritos last night and used the only can of refried beans, so today we have to settle for just plain *salsa* burritos. We eat these, as well as some borderline-stale crackers, and rack-out for a bit, so we can be fully rested when it is time to pull the set.

A couple hours later, five hours after I hooked the first squid through the eyeballs, Chuck swings us alongside the two blue marker buoys, and I pull them aboard with a gaff. The buoys are removed and secured at the aft of the boat, and the buoy line is run through two blocks before being tied to the loose end of backing on the reel. Chuck mans the reel controls on the starboard side and gaffs anything big that's winched up. I stand behind him with my knife nearby, ready to bleed out any cod or halibut. If the animal's aorta is severed without damaging the heart, the bled-out meat keeps longer and tastes better once it finds its way to someone's table in Seattle or L.A.

Today I don't do much throat cutting, and Chuck doesn't do much gaffing. Most of the hooks come up bare–no fish, or old bait – and Chuck shakes his head at every empty gangion he replaces on the hook rack. Any halibut we do haul over the rail is cause for mild celebration, and I have plenty of time to bleed and gut it before the next "keeper" comes up. But most are unwanted and released: arrowtooth flounder, big skate and bright red starfish–or "slurpies" as Chuck calls them–the size of baseball mitts.

At one point I am beckoned to the side of the boat, and I look down into the waves where Chuck is pointing. The shark that lies docile along us is almost half the length of the boat.

"Sleeper shark," Chuck tells me. "Or Greenland shark. Depends on who you ask." He leans down and cuts the gangion, and the giant creature senses it is free and slides back into the cold depths of the ocean. "They're harmless," Chuck says. "Feed on plankton. When they're not stealing our squid."

The first three skates produce a total of only ten halibut and about that many gray cod, but on the first hook of the fourth skate Chuck reaches for his gaff and yells for my help. I take up my gaff and join him.

"Pull it in quick, before it sticks to the side," he orders.

We bury the gaffs into flesh, and heave in unison. And thirty-five-pounds of pissed off octopus unfold onto the deck. One long orange tentacle wraps around my leg, fastening itself securely to my bright yellow rain pants. Another tentacle finds the plastic handled knife I left laying on the hold cover and waves it about menacingly. I try to disarm the animal, but fall down–it now has a hold of both of my legs. Chuck is laughing while he is freeing me from the grasps of the octopus, but I'm not. The tentacles make popping noises as they are disengaged from my pants. I take the knife back and kill the animal.

"Good bait for tomorrow," Chuck says.

A few hooks later we pull in another octopus, and I'm more prepared. From here on our luck seems to change for the better. There are thirty halibut on the last two skates alone. They are all around forty pounds each–the small side of medium–but I am kept busy gutting, at last. This means I'll be able to pay my half of the rent.

It takes us a solid two hours to pull our longline. It takes several more hours to get back to the safety of Anton Larson Bay where we finish gutting the halibut, packing their pokes with ice and stacking them properly into the hold. It's quite late before the hold covers are back in place and the deck is hosed down for the day. We are plenty whipped once we retire to the warmth of the cabin to scrounge the cupboards for dinner.

There are two soft taco shells left, but no more salsa, so we warm the shells on the stove and fill them with catsup. I'm hungry enough for this to be absolutely delicious.

* * *

I wake again to the same morning routine: the sound of the engine turning over and the radio turning on. Again the weather news is good, although the reports my body is sending me are wholly unpleasant. My bad knee has stiffened, my back aches when I move and my hands are swollen and cracking from the multiple knife slips and halibut bites. Before I dig the two dead octopus from the hold, I dip a bucket overboard into the frigid saltwater and soak my battered hands in it. My arms turn numb up to the elbows and the pain subsides. Then I clench my fists as tight as I can and the long scabs crack open, releasing the throbbing pressure and the pus.

I'm ready for a new day.

During our catsup supper last night Chuck and I had a couple beers, and he mulled over his charts. After some deliberation he came to the conclusion that our mistake with that day's set–and subsequent light haul of fish–was not with the location, but with the tide. The scent of our bait had been washed away from the prime area. Chuck drew a straight line with a little stub of pencil, showing me where the longline had been set. Near the end of the set was a cluster of converging circular contour lines showing a small underwater hill. That's where our last two, and most productive, skates had been. So today the plan is to set on the other three sides of that hill. According to the tide chart, if we set at the same time and let it soak for a solid six hours, the tide will wash the scent over the entire hill. Then an hour before we pull, the current will switch and carry the smell of any remaining bait over a ledge, into deeper water. This might lure in even more fish.

I gut the two octopus, being careful to avoid puncturing the ink sacks, and toss the organs overboard. The cape is cut into dollar-bill-size slabs and the tentacles sliced like rolled pastry. I also filet a lingcod and a few gray cod to make enough bait to cover the five skates.

Today's set is a bit tricky. Chuck has me tie an extra anchor onto the line before he makes each of the two ninety-degree turns around the hill far below us. This is to ensure that the longline is tight, and that it stays on the bottom. Currents can cause what is called "flying bait" where the gangions are whipping around well above, and out of reach, of any bottom-feeding fish. If an entire skate comes up with all the bait still intact, this is most likely the problem. We're able to set our gear and get back in calmer water without any trouble though, and Chuck has a good feeling about our luck.

Again I scrub and hose down the deck and Chuck finds lunch – the last of the half-stale crackers. And, after our mid-day nap, it's time to pull the gear and see how much money we've made. The first two or three hooks come up bare and we silently prepare for the worst, but we don't shake our heads for long. Soon the deck is alive with heavy, writhing fish. I no longer have time to gut the halibut as they are given to me, I have to bleed them and slide them into the area sectioned off by the bin boards. The larger fish need to be stunned (an aluminum baseball bat to the head) and then secured to the reel by the gangion snap so they won't catapult themselves off the boat.

"SOAKER!" Chuck yells, meaning there is an extra large fish coming up. I drop my knife, pull my gaff from the hook rack, slide over the blood-soaked hold cover and come to a halt next to him.

The giant head of the halibut comes out of the water and we both aim our gaffs for the cheek. We brace our feet against the bulwark, grab onto whatever is sturdy and close, and heave with every sore muscle we can muster. It takes us almost five minutes to drag the over-three-hundred-pound fish onto the boat, but once out of the water the fight turns serious. I wrap the gangion tight around my wrist and slide on top of the animal with all the determination and lack of decent sense of a bull rider. During a slight pause in the tussle I connect with a few good swings of the ball bat, which stops the action long enough for me to find my knife and bleed the giant fish.

Although the abundance of halibut means both Chuck and I will be slaving long into the night, we are in high spirits. The skipper, who I have become accustomed to working alongside in relative silence, is now muttering to himself happily and seemingly non-sequentialy. I make out some of what he is saying, snippets from Hemingway's *Old Man and the Sea* about loving the fish, but vowing to kill it before the day ends. I think, for a moment, that Chuck is being serious, repeating some strange personal rite, but when he switches from Hemingway to what sounds like a comic version of a Chinese-American dentist, I realize he is only having fun.

"Ah...toof ache. Ahhhh...I see," he says, wiggling the hook that's sunk into the mouth of a hundred-plus-pound halibut. "Vee hafe vays to help you vit dat!" he says, stroking the fish with the fat end of the baseball bat, now sounding more like Colonel Klink on *Hogan's Heroes*.

I shake my head and pretend not to notice, just in case he *has* lost his mind.

"Velcome to dee halibut hotel," Chuck says, and heaves another fish aboard with the gaff.

* * *

That night in Anton Larson Bay was a long and messy one. After the last halibut was washed off, slid into the hold and covered with crushed ice, and the deck more or less shipshape, we retired, once more, to the cabin. The cupboards were bare, but a last ditch food search came up with a large bag of white rice. Chuck found it stashed in a corner of an unused bunk, under the survival suits. There were holes chewed through the plastic bag, and that wasn't the only calling card left. There were droppings too; carefully (almost strategically) mixed with the rice that hadn't yet been eaten or crammed into a pair of over-stuffed, furry cheeks to be toted elsewhere.

I picked out all the "dark grains" I could find, poured the real ones into a pot of almost boiling water and proceeded to over-cook the bloody hell out of them–which, as it turned out, wasn't the smartest thing to do. The thick, white paste that Chuck and I choked down that night was made bearable only with liberal amounts of catsup.

The meal was salvaged by the shots of rum we had, along with a couple beers, to celebrate our fine haul of fish that day. I went to sleep with a good, warm feeling. And a full belly–full like I'd eaten three gallons of Elmer's Glue.

There was no fishing the next day. We never left the shelter of Anton Larson Bay. During the night nasty weather rolled in. I woke up occasionally with the more erratic movements of the boat and could hear the wind jangling the rigging and pressing its invisible face hard against the small cabin windows.

Chuck and I slept in that morning. It was wonderful to rest my poor, broken body, but once I was rested to the point of possible bed sores, the novelty ran dry. To break the monotony that day we engaged in bouts of highly intellectual discourse:

"Hey, Chuck. Ya fished the Buskin lately?"

"Nope. You?"

"Just a bit. Got a few Dollies up by the lake a few days ago."

"Any pinks coming in yet?"

"Naw. No salmon that I could see. They gonna be runnin' soon?"

"Should be."

After all suitable topics of speculation were exhausted–the start of the next salmon run, what flies work good on the rainbow trout in Lake Ambercrombie, and whether or not the anchor was dragging–our only sources of distraction were one copy of *Reader's Digest* and the radio. The latter was switched back and forth between the two channels coming in clear: The Weather and The Coast Guard. The Weather said that life on Kodiak was rough, the Coasties said that life was over, at least for the two set-netters whose skiff got swamped a few miles southwest of us. This news gave the howling wind and angry waves a more threatening tone. I peered out one of the rain-blurred panes of glass at the dark green coastline. Land never looked so safe and inviting. I wondered if Valerie would miss me if Chuck and I shared the same fate as the other two fishermen. I wondered if the men that died in the sea that day had loved ones in town praying for their miraculous return to port. I wondered how long the men struggled in the frigid water. *How long would I?*

When I got hungry I tried to persuade Chuck to sacrifice one of the smaller halibut we had iced and stored in the hold, but he would not allow it. I imagined what the Coast Guard would think when they boarded the *Bluefox* and found our starved and lifeless bodies guarding over two tons of fresh sea food. Out of sheer desperation I took Chuck's ultra-light spinning rod out on deck and braved the rain and waves. I found a few scraps of cut squid lodged in the scuppers that I had missed during the scrub down and used them for bait. I caught a small flounder that, once gutted and headless, fit perfectly into our cast iron skillet. And it tasted heavenly, so much so that I put my rain gear back on and fished for another.

The wind died down slightly the next morning, allowing us to brave our way out of Anton Larson Bay and get us and our load of fish safely into Kodiak. Standing up on the flying bridge with Chuck I watched the Dall's porpoise riding our bow waves, excited to be on my way back. Once we rounded Spruce Cape and sailed under the bridge to Near Island, I got down and carefully slid around the edge of the cabin and onto the very tip of the bow.

Pretty Valerie was waiting in the truck, eating a sundae and watching for incoming boats when the *Bluefox* cruised into St. Paul Harbor, riding low in the water from her heavy load, with me perched on the anchor and waving.

Office on the Buskin

I have never driven over a bridge without looking down, whether it's to watch the murky wrath of the Nenana River tearing spruce off her banks during spring runoff, or for a glimpse of one of those meeker streams back home that have rusty tractor parts submerged in their pools and white plastic shopping bags shrink-wrapped to the overhanging branches. There is always some luring beauty and remaining purity down there, straddled by the concrete pilings of progress, and it astounds me every time I don't see someone down there enjoying it. Where are the kids with their pockets of skipping pebbles? Where are the fanatics with their fly rods or kayaks? At school or at the office no doubt, being reminded of the dire importance of an A+, or sweating in a suit and wishing they had settled for a C- and gone into lawn care instead–at least they could be outside on a day like today.

No cars are behind me, so I slow down on the bridge over the Buskin River. These Alaskan rivers are wonderful. Any body of water has wonder if you suspect there are large fish hiding behind every rock, or lurking at the depths of every swift pool–strong and sleek ocean fish almost *waiting* for a good fight. *Weary here be the thin-wristed angler with light tippet!*

"I should have clocked in two minutes ago," Valerie reminds me from the passenger's seat.

I snap out of my river-gawker's trance and look at the time. She's right, it's already two minutes after six. "Yep," I say. "I'm on it."

As I accelerate off the bridge I turn my head to continue watching the river. There was movement down around the bend, small flashes of color through the trees, like fly line in the air.

"I thought I saw someone. They beat me down there."

Valerie yawns and covers her mouth. "Is that where you're fishing today?"

"I was thinking about it. Maybe I'll try further upstream."

We pull into the airport parking lot, joining only a half-dozen other cars.

"Are you coming in?" Valerie asks. "Heather will be upset if you don't."

"Yeah. Sure." I'm anxious to get on the water, but I turn off the engine and pocket my keys anyway.

I help Valerie with her bag and open the front door of the airport for her. She is walking faster than I am, so I have to hurry to get to the door first. She smiles and laughs as she brushes past me, closer than she needs to. I smell the lotion she put on after this morning's shower, and for the first time today I have a thought other than one involving fish or rivers. I want to reach out and grab her. I want to put my hands on her waist and pull her close and smell more of her.

She looks back quizzically. "I thought you were coming in?"

"Uh, yeah." I feel my cheeks get warm.

"Stacy is here with the coffee cart if you want some breakfast before you go."

I nod and pat my back pocket to be sure I have my wallet. *Breakfast. Yeah. Sounds good.*

I cruise over to the coffee cart and pick out a large chocolate muffin, order a tall black coffee and make funny faces at Jasmine in her crib while Valerie punches in and begins getting the Budget Rent-A-Car booth organized and ready for the first plane load of impatient tourists. Another day of "Whatta ya mean you're charging me extra for the rottin' salmon carcasses on the back seat?" and "I reserved a Ford Explorer three months ago! It's not my problem some idiot from Chicago buried your last one in the mud flats last night! I want my Ford Explorer!"

I couldn't cope with her job. I'd be in a fist fight at least twice a day. And, to be safe, I and my muffin will be long gone from here when that first plane taxies up to the gate.

I take my breakfast over to the car rental booths and chat with Heather, the blonde woman working at the Avis booth opposite Budget Rent-A-Car. When I see Valerie has her workplace situated I slide my food over to her counter.

"So, you'll be done at two-thirty, huh?"

She nods her head and makes pointed eye contact with me. "I would like to be *out of here* by then. There's a plane coming in at two-thirty. I don't want to get tied up here. You have your watch?"

I finger the lump in the breast pocket of my hold-over Army fatigues. The cuffs are worn thin and faded and there are threads sprouting from the name tag and unit patch.

"Sure do," I say. "What ya feel like for supper?"

"Are you cooking?"

"Yeah. Sure. How 'bout a fresh Dolly?"

"Fish again?" She laughs at her joke and smiles at me. The telephone rings and she picks up. Her day begins.

I gather my breakfast, wave good bye and mouth the words "see ya." But when I turn to leave Valerie reaches out across the counter and squeezes my arm.

"Good luck and have fun," she says.

* * *

I'm glad to be on my way to the river, but I can't get my mind back to fishing. I feel like a sixteen-year-old again. But this isn't just a high school crush, is it? I think I *love* this woman. So what now? Should I pick her a bouquet of fireweed and tell her all about it? How would *that* go over? Early on I told myself that she was off limits. She's my sister's friend along for the ride. Besides, we're partners in this adventure and that kind of mushiness would only make things difficult. And what if she has no such romantic ideas about me? That would make the whole flowers-and-heart-spilling a bit awkward.

I'm lost in thought, not paying attention and almost miss the gravel turnoff. I hit the brakes and crank the wheel and stones fly. This provides enough adrenalin to flush my mind of anything but the immediate, and that's the road, the potholes and the gorgeous river I'm now paralleling.

I pull off the road and park within sight of the water. I know I'm within a hundred yards of Buskin Lake. I'll be working upstream. This is a good stretch of water. The lake can produce a few Dollies too, if I'm not satisfied with my luck by the time I get up that far. I have all morning, so I just might give the big water a try today.

I don my vest, slide my rod out from behind the seat and get myself ready for work. There are no other vehicles in sight, I have the place all to myself. Nothing but me, the river and whatever I can conjure from it. *What a way to spend a weekday!*

My rod stays unstrung until I've left my truck and am standing in the water. This is in place of self discipline, or maybe it's just my own strain of discipline. It's the only way for me to control myself during the first five minutes on the river. If I walked down here with my rod ready for action I would be in danger of hyperventilating and losing all my flies due to the frantic thrashing nature of my casting. This act of walking to the water's edge with my rod in two pieces and the line all wound up snug in the reel forces a calm upon my natural anxiousness. It's like sneaking into the woods with an unloaded rifle, or sitting in a tree stand with an unstrung bow. The ammo is in a pocket only a second or two away; the graceful arc of the bow can be rendered lethal at any moment, but it's that deliberate unpreparedness and sense of reserve that brings about the feeling of calm–for me anyway. It makes my movements slower, steadier, and my observations more keen. It's what I have to force myself to do to fully absorb my surroundings instead of blindly crashing through the brush and doing a face plant into the cold river. The Buskin has that kind of drawing power over me.

There is no need for deliberating over what fly to use this far up the river, I have it all figured out. It's early August, so the pink salmon *could* be heading for freshwater by now, but if they already have they shouldn't be up this far yet. I'm after Dolly Varden today and this new fly I came up with, the Kodiak Peacock, is really deadly. It's a short-shanked streamer and I've tied a whole box of them in #8's. It's the size that seems to work the best.

I piece my fly rod together and thread the line and leader up through the line guides. Then one of my streamers is selected to be "first string." That's the thought that sometimes comes over me when I open my fly box at the start of the day, like a pee-wee football coach with all his excited boys in freshly bleached football pants crowding around him, eager and panting to get out on the playing field and cause some damage. Or at least to get some great grass stains to show off after the game.

I'm using a short leader with a sink-tip line. Well, actually it's just regular weight forward floating line with one of those five-foot lengths of sinking line looped to the end. They're instant sink-tip sections that sell for less than $15.00 for two. I can't afford new line, or the spare spool to put it on, so this will have to do. It works fine.

My knee boots allow me to get just far enough into the river to avoid snagging branches on my back cast, but just barely. I'm casting up and downstream, not directly across, so I can get away with long casts if I want–for the most part. The area I fish first is shallow. I can see the bottom of the gravel runs, but I don't see any fish feeding or making any moves for my fly. I cast quartering upstream first, letting the streamer ride the current back to me at about mid-river. When I can keep the slack line under control, as I'm supposed to, I give the rod some jerks. When my fly passes me, I can see it in the clear water and its action is good, the peacock Krystal Flash–tied as the wing of the streamer–glitters seductively from the bottom of the river. I'm fishing deep enough with the help of the sink-tip; I've positioned myself for proper casting (without killing myself) and I have my nerves under control. For once, all things are as they ought to be. I've finally gotten around to getting the hang of this.

When I'm satisfied that there are no gullible fish upstream from me I try a downstream drift and jerky retrieve. These antics usually work. I just need to move farther up, into deeper water. The Dollies will move out into shallower areas to feed on loose roe once the next salmon run heats up, but for now I'm finding them holding in deeper pools. Lately I've come across them in a variety of social contexts, from loners hanging by themselves, to small pods of a half-dozen or more. Other times, I've stumbled into Dollies by the hundreds–all rowdy and crammed together like frat boys at a kegger. I never know what the deal is going to be on any particular day. It's all trial and error, wait and see, and I love it.

There are no takers of my fly behind me either, so I reel in most of the line I have out and work my way upstream. I hug the near bank to avoid going in over my knee boots, but when I come to a jumble of awkward boulders I'm forced to choose one of only two routes: the safe one that entails breaking down my rod and busting brush, or the risky path on and around the rocks. The current looks tough, but if I can step in the right places and my coordination suddenly improves, the water should stay a good half-inch from the rim of my rubber boots. It's not a comforting margin for error.

The decision of which way to go is an easy one to make. I have plenty of time, there's absolutely no rush and the slight diversion from the river will further add to my overall sense of calm. I'm proud of myself. Not too long ago I would have been barging ahead without a thought and probably come out soaking wet up to my neck.

As I'm breaking my rod down and heading toward the river bank–to patiently search out a trail through the almost impenetrable thicket–something suddenly feels out-of-place...queer even. I freeze.

What's the deal here? You lost your nerve? Gone soft?

Yes. It's as I suspected. They're the demon voices of my recklessly impatient, go-for-broke youth resurfacing from somewhere deep in my subconsciousness. There's no use trying to ignore or suppress them. If I do they'll only get worse and the internal dialogue will eventually degenerate to the point where I'll be facing a wrestling match with a brown bear, or some other stupid event, to prove something manly to myself.

So I re-attach the rod tip and turn again to the slippery obstacles.

There ya go chickenshit! That's the ticket!

I make a gallant effort. After clambering to a one-legged perch on the first boulder I make a precarious leap to the second stepping stone, the slightly submerged one. Miraculously I make it, but only after a few seconds of swaying back and forth and waving my fly rod this way and that to regain my balance. The third, and last, foothold along my perilous path is the one that does me in. I slip momentarily and the current bulging at my shins finally wells over my boot tops and the added weight throws off what little balance remains. And into the drink I go.

On the river bank I roll up my wet sleeves and sit down to remove and drain the water from my boots. I'm not mad. I knew the probability of getting wet was high. The odds of my failure were great. But it appeased the demon.

Duuuuude! That was great! Ya almost had it!

Because I'm wet and slightly chilled, I bypass most of the pools between my fateful obstacle course and my final destination: Buskin Lake. I wade against the current and am warming up but not drying out, because the sun never spends much quality time over Kodiak Island. My dripping jeans are refilling my boots with every step. I feel the water accumulating, mixing with the once comfortable potency of my fishing socks to become the brine that will first try to freeze and then pickle my toes. But I don't care. I'm alone on a river, and that in itself is a powerful declaration. It says: "I'm beholden to no one." Despite the borderline misery, I don't have to kiss a boss's behind, I don't have to cram for midterms, and I don't have to play nice to cranky tourists. As long as I'm still on a good river I can continue to boast of my intact dignity and unfailing self-reliance. I do so regularly and with great pride, because it may not last forever.

When I finally slosh and stumble to within view of Buskin Lake I am not rewarded with the sight of hungry fish leaving feeding rings on the smooth surface. No. Not that. There are fish actually COMING OUT OF THE WATER! Every few minutes the lake pops out another Dolly, like it was squeezing infected slivers. This is a wonderful sight.

I try to act blasé. There is no one here to impress; it's more to fool myself than anything. *Yeah. Nothin' to it. Just another day at the office.*

I ignore the lake and make a few casts to the head of the first pool below the Buskin Lake outlet. I'm not concentrating on my retrieve. I'm not even sure where exactly I cast. My efforts are all focused on *not* paying attention to the random splashes coming from the lake. I'm not expecting any strikes, there are no jumpers here, but I get one anyway. The fly line stops abruptly and I raise the rod, almost startled (but not because I'm being blasé, remember?).

The Dolly fights out all of the line I have hanging loose and takes a couple runs worth from my reel, too. When I eventually tire the fish I tuck my rod under my arm, reach into the cold water and remove my streamer. The Dolly Varden doesn't yet realize it's free to go and I'm allowed to admire it longer. It's a good-sized char for the island–easily eighteen inches–with shiny silver sides interrupted only faintly by a smattering of pink dots. I have to kill at least one fish for tonight's supper, but it won't be this one.

In a flash the fish is gone. I wipe my hands on my shirt and prepare for another cast. My fly has held up well, the thread hasn't tried to unwind, and there's no tinsel hanging off the hook shank. My tippet doesn't feel nicked either, so I'm good to go.

Casting from the same spot, I'm able to catch three more Dollies. None are as nice as the first, but all are over fifteen inches.

They're stubborn fighters, never jumping, oddly, and always saving enough reserve for a last minute run, right after I'm sure the fight has been won. I move forward only after a half-dozen casts go unanswered. At the head of the pool I cast downstream, covering the same water as before, only from a different angle. The streamer slips down into the current and I strip line from the reel, letting the fly ride. When it reaches the tail end of the swifter water and slows down, I begin my retrieve. I'm feeling cocky and am expecting a fish to take–probably one that missed or passed over my offering swimming in the other direction.

A fish does take, but it's no Dolly. It hits hard and after a quick run the fish heads for the surface. I can feel what's coming a second before it happens. And there it is! Out of the water comes an Alaskan rainbow trout . . . its vibrant red flank twisting and hanging in midair, as if caught in slow motion, throwing a spray of water and then coming down with a splash. I guess the trout to be about the same size as the Dollies I've been playing with, but rainbows are a rarity in this river and I desperately want to get a closeup look at this one before I turn him loose. With this added motivation comes added stress and a faster heart beat. I nix the cocky facade I've maintained with the previous fish and get serious, putting side pressure on my rod to shorten the battle.

But then I hear the crunching of gravel up on the road. My privacy has been invaded. On a weekday no less.

I renew my "cool guy" impression and out of the corner of my eye I see that the vehicle has stopped at a gap in the foliage with a view of the river. They've seen me, and are watching. I can't help myself. I have to show off.

I stop putting side pressure on the fish and raise my rod high instead. This brings the trout out of the water again, splashing through a half somersault. I can almost hear the ooohs and ahhhs echoing around inside the vehicle.

Then I hear a door slam.

"HEY! QUIT SHOWIN' OFF!"

I recognize the voice. It's Chuck. *Shoulda known.*

My good acting...wasted on a friend who knows better. I stop provoking the fish to jump and fight it to within reach. As I'm sliding the hook loose without excessively rough-handling the fish, Chuck ambles down to the river in his waders.

"Hang on," he says, making his way into the water next to me.

"Hold it up. It's a rainbow, right?"

I smile and lift the black-speckled beauty from the water for just a moment. "Yup. Sure is."

"Good deal," Chuck says as I return the trout to its home current. "What'd he take?"

"Kodiak Peacock. Same as all the Dollies."

Chuck nods, unhooks his #14 beadhead Hair's Ear nymph from the stripping eye of his old Eagle Claw fly rod, and moves off out of my way. I've given him over a dozen flies of my own creation since we've been fishing together, so I know he has at least one in his box now. But I offer to give him another anyway.

"No, that's all right," he says over his shoulder. "I'm going to try what I've got on."

I shrug. He'll catch fish. Maybe not as many as he could, but he insists on using the one fly, no matter what. It's always a #14 Hair's Ear.

Chuck stands at the edge of the lake and surveys the flat water without casting. The Dollies have stopped jumping. There appears to be no feeding activity what so ever.

"They were jumping out of the water just before you got here."

I see him nod. "Yep. Hear that one all the time."

* * *

The two of us fish for several hours, not interrupted by any other fishermen. Chuck stands in the ankle-deep current spilling from the lake and concentrates his efforts out on the open water, letting his small artificial nymph slowly sink and mingle with the in-crowd. And from where I stand in the river, his fly appears to be fitting in. I look up to watch him fight some of the feistier ones. He's doing well, and his moustache can't hide his grin.

I'm not doing too bad either. I stalk the long pool, casting ceaselessly for several hours. And my persistence is routinely rewarded. I've lost count somewhere after three dozen Dolly Varden landed between the two of us. It's the fast and regular action that makes me nervous about ever fishing in Pennsylvania again. I hope I'm not spoiling myself.

When my casting begins to show signs of sloppiness, and the fish are proving to be better educated, I take a break on shore and check my watch. It's almost noon. I put the watch back in my pocket and look skyward. The sun is still well hidden. The rain has been holding off all morning, but I'm prepared. My rain jacket goes everywhere with me now.

Among many other things, I have found that the agitation of constant dampness must first be overcome before coastal Alaska can be fully enjoyed. Everyone wears knee boots here on Kodiak and has rain gear handy. Wives pushing shopping carts up and down the aisles of Safeway, kids walking home from school–none are exempt. I even see knee boots worn into the theater. Yes. It definitely makes a fisherman feel at ease. Actually, this may be the first time in my life I dress according to popular fashion. What a novelty!

Chuck notices me lounging on the bank and he stops fishing, reels in and hooks his fly back on the stripping eye. "You done fishing?" he asks once he has gotten close enough not to have to shout.

"Naw. Not done." I scratch my beard and lean back, sprawling out in the grass. "Just savorin' the day."

"You fished the campground lately?"

I run my fingers through a clump of long grass. "No. Why? Have you?"

He shakes his head. "No. I might try down there today."

"Yeah? Ya think the pinks are in yet?"

"Heard they were seeing a few," Chuck says. "Talked to some guys at the coffee shop this morning."

I jerk my head up and look at him. He doesn't seem to be kidding. "Really?"

"Yeah. Said they saw a few fresh ones at the mouth of the river."

All right! Salmon are back! By now I'm on my feet with my vest on and rod in hand. I try to calm down and act more casual. "Well, hell. Let's go see for ourselves," I say. But the little guy in my head is bouncing around and yelling: *Come on! Come on! Let's go! Wahoo! The pinks are in!*

* * *

Chuck gives me a ride to my truck and then I follow him out to the main road and on to the campground. We pass a pickup truck on the gravel road back to the campground and the two men inside look like fishermen. I take this to be a sign that there really *are* salmon in the river. But there are no other vehicles around us once we park, which makes me begin to question the now third-hand information. *Sure is desolate for there to be rumors of salmon. I don't know about this.*

I open the truck door and watch Chuck. He is already out and stringing his rod. "Whatta ya usin' for pinks? A Hare's Ear?"

He shrugs. "Sure. Why not?"

I slide off the seat, swing the door shut and fetch my rod from the bed of my truck. Chuck waits, and when I'm ready he leads the way down a grassy lane toward the river. I still can't get over his choice of fly. I always imagined something big, bright and gaudy for this kind of fishing.

"Something that small for salmon? No kidding?"

"Yeah. You'll see most guys down here using surf casters and spoons big enough to eat with. It's overkill."

I nod in agreement. I've seen it here myself–guys tossing hardware with treble hooks that would frighten away angry bears, tied on mono thick enough to probably get the bear in if it was hooked good.

Chuck continues. "Silvers are different. They feed on fish. Young salmon, even. But pinks and reds eat mainly plankton and crustaceans. Small stuff like that."

"So not fish, huh?"

"Well...pinks will go for a streamer. They eat fish, just little minnows mainly. Reds will take a streamer, too. If you give it to them right."

"But you do good with nymphs?"

"Yeah. These beadheads."

Once we're at the edge of the river, Chuck and I stop to have a look. From where we stand I can see down into the clear pools quite well. They're deep, though, so I can't quite see to the bottom. But I can see that there are no fish. Chuck disagrees with me. He points to the tail of the largest pool. "Right in there. At least six."

I squint and strain, but see nothing but water worn rocks shimmering back at me from under the current.

"No. More than that," Chuck says, still pointing. "Twice that. Heck, the river's full of fish."

What? Where?

Suddenly my eyes focus. One second I'm peering into empty water, then there they are, as real and alive as it gets.

Oh, man! Look at 'em all! I unhook my fly, pull out line and start looking for an easy way into the water. My hands and arms are shaking...my whole body's shaking! I've been dying for another chance at a salmon with my fly rod. And this is it. Oh, is this ever it.

I find a decent spot in the riffles at the tail of the pool and make several botched casts over the area where I last saw salmon. The ones in the shallower water spook before I can mend my Kodiak Peacock closer to them. My heart sinks. I just know I'm screwing this up.

Chuck has stationed himself at the head of the same pool and is drifting his same #14 nymph downstream into the school of pink salmon. On his third cast he hooks up. I'm too wired to stop and watch him fight it.

After almost an hour, and four more fish caught and released by Chuck, I become desperate enough to become humble. I change flies. It's hard to abandon one of my own creations and tie on someone else's pattern, but on my first drift a fish takes the beadhead nymph and my embarrassment is quickly forgotten. I set the hook hard and the pink rockets out of the water, throws the hook and crashes back into the pool.

"There you go," Chuck says.

I stand frozen in place, quivering. My line drifts limply back to me and wraps itself around my shins. For a tiny moment I feel like crying, but I get over it. *Come on. Saddle up. Try 'er again.*

I check my hook and leader. They're still good. So I cast some more.

But nothing will have a go at my fly.

"Well, that's enough for me," Chick says. "I can't play *all* day."

I glance up. He's reeling in and heading for shore.

"Uh...okay," I say. "I'm stayin' a bit longer." *Or* a lot *longer if I have to....*

He nods and waves and is gone.

And I'm alone on the river to continue waging, and losing, my personal war.

By two o'clock I have only hooked one other fish, and that one worked loose of my #14 hook just as easily as the first. I'm keeping track of the time because Valerie needs a ride home in a half hour, but I don't know which motivating force will falter to the other: my crush on my roommate, or this infatuation and frustration with these salmon. I might be late to the airport. After all, I did say I would be cooking fish tonight. I'm committed.

I wade closer to shore and find a comfortable rock to sit down on. There has got to be a way for me to rally for a last minute comeback here. I just need a minute to regain my head, reason things out. The opportunities are all only a roll cast away, holding patiently at the bottom of the pool. I need to think, and do something different.

I clip off my nymph and retire it to the felt patch of my vest and dig for one of my fly boxes. Chuck did all right with the little Hare's Ear, but he lost most of them right at the end of the fight. But they were close enough to the point of their capture for a catch-and-release fisherman to chalk it up as a fish landed. But I'm after meat now, not to mention my first salmon. The stakes are high. I need a bigger hook, and barb.

The fly I choose is tied on a #10 hook and has no name. It's a byproduct of a late night at the vise after a few too many Alaskan Ambers. It's an odd concoction of green yarn, orange feather and silver Krystal Flash. I don't have a reason or strategy for choosing this fly, other than that it's tied on the right size hook I'd like to use, and it certainly isn't something these fish have ever seen before.

The new fly draws immediate aggressive attention. On the first pass I get a hard strike but no hookup. While I'm making my second cast–back to the same seam in the current as my last one–I'm debating whether or not to quick switch to an even larger hook. I needn't bother. As soon as my mutant fly reaches the bottom of the river again it's eaten by another angry pink salmon. I set the hook hard and hold on. The fish holds tight to the bottom for a moment and I apply more pressure. Then the dramatic reel spinning starts. First I frantically try to keep the slack out of my line, then I worry about the salmon taking too much line. At this point the fight has moved downstream. I have to turn the fish at the next pool. I have to fight him, not just hang on to him. My wrist aches and my heart feels like it's ready to seize.

Then it's over.

I keep my rod high and reel in line as I wade downstream to intercept the beaten fish. I thread a shaking finger in behind the gill cover and lift my very first salmon out of the water... five pounds of fish, fresh from the ocean, sea lice still attached. *No kidding. I did it. Hot damn!* I'm ecstatic.

I kill and gut my prize at the river, then walk quickly back to the truck. I can still make it to the airport in time. If I hurry.

Salmon Mints

I struggled to catch my first salmon. That suggests that I'm not as good a fisherman as I thought I'd be by now. I've always been a slow learner. It's persistence and a bit of mental toughness, not natural grace and intelligence, that has gotten me through basic training, fifth grade and any other smaller versions of hell I've been faced with. But, on the other hand, I'm glad my first salmon was such a challenge (as was my first trout, come to think of it). If these fish came easy, I wouldn't attach so much romance to their memory. It would be like losing one's virginity in a whorehouse, as a few drunk privates in my old platoon found out in the red light district of Hamburg. Essential aspects of the feat are missing that would otherwise make it memorable.

Pink salmon aren't that hard to catch. Chuck Lewis told me most fisherman here in Alaska can't stand them, they crowd the water and hamper any efforts to pursue *real* salmon. He says these are the fish that even kids can have fun with, but for the most part they're ignored. So, they're almost the bluegills of the North, which is great to say after landing the fortieth fish of the morning, but downright agitating when they're playing hard-to-get.

I didn't migrate all the way up here to Alaska only to become a fish snob. I believe a good fisherman is someone who can find satisfaction in catching a five-inch chub, not someone who turns his or her nose up at a five-pound salmon. And, interestingly enough, tourist fishermen never bring a disdain for pinks with them. They usually pick it up after hanging around the locals, sometimes even before they've wet a line or seen a live salmon for themselves.

Just the other day two men (certainly non-locals) walked up behind me as I was releasing a bright female pink salmon of about four pounds. "All right! Nice fish!" I heard one of them say. "Good! The silvers are running!" said the other. I stood up, wiped my wet hands on my jeans and explained that the silvers wouldn't be in the river for another couple of weeks (also something I'd been told by Chuck). "But," I said, "the pinks are making a good show."

"Oh. Those are *pinks*?" And away they went, with dry lines and looks of utter disappointment.

I'm mighty defensive of pink salmon–and bluegill, too. Yes, I know they're a bit simple minded when it comes to self preservation. But, for me, they're like little cousins: I'll hold them down now and then and give them a good "noogie" when nobody's watching, but if some stranger pushes them around or insults them in my presence...well, watch out.

Pinks *can* be difficult. I've been down on the Buskin River fishing within sight of at least a half-dozen other adult anglers (some even fly fishermen) and none of us were getting a bump. And the river was holding enough pinks to sink a salmon seiner.

These are the times I anticipate, believe it or not. No matter the species I'm chasing, or the reputed ease with which said species is caught, there will always come a day when they just will not take a fly. As any innovative fly tier will admit, new patterns can't be realistically tested during a feeding frenzy. Any damn thing will work then. It's during the lulls that the boxes of prototype patterns get culled. Some are complete crap and are never allowed in daylight again. Others stay in the box, but will only get pulled out again when some jackass wades into the pool I'm fishing asking, "Whatta they bitin' on?"

Although, every so often a crazy new fly will prove itself worthy of further tinkering. And that, I swear, is the best part of tying my own.

I caught my first pink salmon two weeks ago on a "scrap pattern," meaning it was the last fly tied during an evening tying session and the sole purpose of its creation was to use up the larger clumps of scrap under the vise. I'm sure many decent trout patterns have come about this way–a bunch of leftover hackle and dubbing can be made to imitate almost anything squirming around in a lower-forty-eight trout stream. But after a round of Pacific salmon flies, the scrap pile can get a bit eccentric, and the scrap flies themselves look more like party favors.

Since then–the landing of my first one–I have had a lot of time off between commercial runs with Chuck and have been relentless in narrowing down exactly what made *that* gaudy fly work for me when nothing else did. After picking Valerie up at work and showing off what I'd gotten us for dinner, I cranked out several dozen spinoffs of the fly that did the deed (and that has now been honorably retired in a zipper-seal sandwich bag labeled "First Salmon").

The next morning I was back on the Buskin River field testing. I found an ideal spot: a shallow, clear pool with about fifteen pinks lined up in the main current. I could easily see them, my fly, and their reactions to my fly. It was extremely educational. I caught a lot of fish, but it took me three more days to perfect the fly. It isn't the fanciest, but it looks good in its own, simple kind of way. What really matters, though, is that it's absolutely irresistible to pink salmon. They swim over each other's backs to get at this fly. I'm proud as hell of it. I've used it to catch and release over one hundred fifty pinks in the last two weeks.

Yes, I'm bragging. Not about my great skill as a fly fisherman, because it just isn't so, but about the greatness of this new fly of mine. I call it the Salmon Mint. The hook shank is wrapped with green tinsel yarn and ribbed with white dental floss and the wing is made with silver Krystal Flash. It's a streamer, although it is tied on a #8 wet nymph hook. It's on the small side, as salmon flies go, but that's part of its magic. I've found that my success rate is reduced–as much as by half–if I fish a Salmon Mint tied one size larger. Even bead-chain eyes on the #8 hook messes with the mojo somehow. I don't know why.

Alaskan flies, like the people who tie them, are in many ways different from what has become archetypical. Which is to say, number-fourteen Adams dry flies these ain't. This is true, I suppose, of salmon and steelhead flies anywhere, from Oregon to Lake Ontario. Which, subsequently, reminds me: I picked up a magazine at the fly shop the other day and there was an article in it claiming the steelhead fishery in northern Ohio to be one of the fastest growing in the country. And, yes, I recognize the irony of it all. I came all the way to Kodiak Island to read about the great fishing in my old backyard.

Anyway, there are some excellent Alaskan tiers, and they produce beautiful stuff, but the flies actually *fished* up here are primarily large, flashy, and not entirely graceful. Which is great news for uncoordinated tiers like myself.

My flies may not be frameable, or even mildly attractive to admirers of such mediums of artistic creativity, but I do have high standards for myself. My flies must meet three important qualifications before I'm satisfied: they must be quick and easy to tie because I lose them at a rather fast pace; the material must be inexpensive and easily obtainable; and lastly–and definitely most importantly–they must be extremely durable. It's an enormous letdown to have one of my flies on the injured reserve, forced into early retirement, or otherwise shredded by the teeth of the animals I intended to chew on it. If I break the fly off in a fish, I couldn't give a damn about the fly–I 'm bummed about the fish. If I lose the fly to a snag, oh well, they're expendable, that's why I tie my own. But if that fly comes back with the tinsel dragging, or the wings bent, it's back to the drawing board. Or in this case to the old T.V. tray revamped with tying vise, drying rack and scrap baggy.

The Salmon Mint has passed all these tests: it's quick, cheap and can take one hell of a chewing. Its ability to fool large numbers of fish isn't included, it's a given.

* * *

Yesterday was a "no fish" day, which is the heading the pages in my journal get when the weather turns worse than normal, or commitments have piled up to the point where further procrastination is out of the question. But, yesterday was neither. The weather was fine, no rain and warm even (it may have crept into the mid sixties.) And it wasn't about commitments either, I dumped all that peskiness when I came to this island. I spent yesterday with Valerie.

My presence wasn't needed on the *Bluefox* (and won't be for another couple of days) and Valerie had a day away from the airport. So we hung out together. It started with grocery shopping, which we usually do together anyway, but soon led to other things. We walked around the square in town, checked out the shops, stood in line for the one-screen theater–but decided we were in more of a mood for a sit-down meal and a bottle of wine than a bag of popcorn and a movie we'd already seen. We ate at the Italian place just down the road from our apartment.

It was late by the time we made it home, but we stayed up even longer playing Scrabble on the livingroom floor and drinking wine. The interaction was fun, but I was afraid she would realize I can't spell very well and that would adversely affect her opinion of me.

"I'm kinda dumb," I said, figuring if I confessed my failings it would somehow negate them.

"How so?" she asked.

"Well...look at all the words I've played. The longest one's four letters."

"Get the dictionary," she said.

"But, that's cheating."

"So."

"So, you don't think I'm dumb?" I asked.

"No."

I rubbed my brow and fiddled with my wine glass.

"I think you're neat," she said. "I'm enjoying this."

I sat up straight and said, "I really like you, Valerie."

She smiled at me.

"Do you know what I mean?"

"Yes," she said. "I know what you mean."

* * *

So last night was interesting. At least everything's out in the open. We can go from there, I suppose.

Valerie had to work today, though (as did I, if you consider the self-appointed "river keeper" position on the Buskin a job). I was anxious to get on the water. My mind was set on one long, clear pool in particular. I can sight fish there all morning without spooking the newly arrived salmon. It's close enough to the ocean to hear the crashing waves and excited seagulls and kittiwakes.

A river is a pleasure meant to be savored in peace. That's why I get there early, to have her to myself. But this morning I didn't fish alone. I fished with a kid named Mike.

I'm telling you this story for two reasons: first, it's a testament to my new salmon fly, but second, I learned something that day from my young fishing partner. I'm not quite sure what it is that I've gained from him yet, but it sure felt profound at the time. It was one of those instances where I was smart enough to realize that if I weren't so dim, I'd be having a flood of life-altering insights. As it was, I thought to myself something like "Hey! Cool!" No visions with bright lights and singing angels.

I noticed the bicycle first, a kid's bike lying temporarily abandoned at the end of the gravel path I'd taken to the river. My heart immediately sank. There on the ground was the vehicle on which the violator of my solitary morning had rode. How long had my antagonist been at it? Had the sanctity of my precious river been thoroughly ruined? Had all my beloved fish been snagged, speared, or chased back to the ocean by this hideous yet unseen alien?

The boy never saw me approach, as I sat down quietly on a large rock and watched him fish the pool I'd wanted so eagerly to have a go at. The first few minutes were painful. At least once I had to restrain myself from crowding the kid out. A few close back casts would have worked wonderfully, I'm sure. But I didn't. I just sat on my rock and watched. And I could have moved as far as I wanted along the river in either direction and not run into a single other fisherman–it was still early enough that we were the only two on the Buskin. But I didn't leave, I sat there, drank the coffee I'd brought from the airport and watched the boy fish.

What kept me there after the initial realization that someone had beaten me to my favorite spot was curiosity. Up the riverbank a ways, on the dry pebbles, the boy had set a backpack. It was full and zipped shut. Set neatly on top of it was a portable radio with earphones and a half-eaten candy bar. The boy looked to be about twelve or thirteen, too young to be this organized. There didn't appear to be any parental units lurking about either. *Odd this one is*, I thought to myself using my best Yoda impression. I was intrigued.

His fishing technique wasn't as original as he himself seemed to be. He was casting some sort of large Mepps-looking lure with a sturdy spinning rod and not having the slightest bit of luck. He would cast and crank over and over again with repetitive determination, without a twitch of creativity. I observed all these things–from the neatly organized gear to his failing attempts at catching fish–from the vantage of my rock, and I pondered them. This was obviously a boy who loved to fish, that's why he was here alone. This was no forced trip to bond with a son for one weekend in the summer, either. This was private passion...and it looked all too familiar. He knew how to use his rod. It wasn't a lack of proficiency in casting that was hindering his efforts. I could see what he was doing wrong: the lure was too big and he wasn't fishing it deep enough, the same problems a lot of adults have on this river. His problem wasn't my dilemma, though, it was what to do with the knowledge I possessed that could help this young stranger catch a salmon.

As I sat there on my rock, finishing my coffee, I guess I went through a transition. I didn't suddenly become a saint, or anything that radical, but I slowly changed from impatient, self-serving loner battling between self-regimented codes of edict (and the more primeval urge to bully a kid out of a fishing spot) to a guy content to sit, watch, and really hope to see someone else catch a fish.

If by the time my coffee was gone he hadn't had anything at least *attempt* to hook itself to the end of his line, I would intervene, but I wanted to do it delicately.

When the time came I broke the large styrofoam coffee cup into a sloppy triangle, slipped it into my fishing vest and then tried to get noticed. I zipped and unzipped a few vest pockets, shuffled my feet, but had to resort to the fake cough before my presence became known.

The boy jerked his head around and took a step forward into the water.

"Hi," I said.

"Oh...hi."

I fiddled with an open zipper, peering into the vest pocket like I was intent on finding something important. "Nice mornin', huh?" I commented without looking up.

"I didn't see you over there," he said.

I nodded.

"Are you fishing?" he asked.

I looked up quickly. "No. Not now." I hesitated, "I will later. Gettin' geared up here. I'll be out of your way in a bit."

The boy seemed all right with that, and made another cast. "There's lots of fish right out here in front of me," he said.

Uh-huh. I know.

"They won't bite, though," he added.

I see.

It all played out beautifully. Within minutes I had him telling me his name and that he was in the seventh grade. His dad was in the Coast Guard and they had moved to Kodiak from Florida and had only been on the island for two months. I stayed on my rock and told him a bit about who I was, and I think it put him more at ease knowing I was ex-military. It made me almost family.

I asked if he had any flies and, of course, he said no. So I pulled out the old metal film canister where I kept my freshly tied Salmon Mints and administered a palm-full. I gave him a few heavy split shot as well, so he could cast the fly with his spinning rod. Then I instructed him to lob the fly upstream and reel in the slack as it drifted back to him.

And on his second cast, Mike caught a pink salmon.

I was happy as hell. So was Mike. After he landed the fish he pranced around on the pebble riverbank clenching his rod with both hands. "My mom's gonna be *so* proud of me!" he kept saying.

I killed the fish with a rock–one quick whack on the head–and I showed him the best way to gut it. He watched closely and when I was done he produced a metal stringer from his backpack and eagerly clipped the dead salmon onto it. Then it was back to the pool for another cast.

After I wiped the blade of my pocket knife clean and put it away, I again retired to my rock. Mike then quizzed me as to why I wasn't fishing yet. "You brought your pole, didn't you?" he asked. I told him I had, but explained that I didn't want to get in his way. I said I'd be on my way shortly, but I wanted to see him catch one more.

"There's all kinds of them right here!" he said, pointing out into the pool. "You won't be in my way!"

Well, heck. Why not? I suppose I can make a cast or two.

So I strung my rod and tied on my own Salmon Mint.

All I wanted was for Mike to catch some fish; I never intended to get him psyched about fly fishing. The poor kid. I already had him sold on flies, and it didn't take long before I saw him watching me and pretending he had a fly rod of his own. It looked difficult, but he was trying to false cast a fifteen-foot length of ten-pound mono with his spinning rod. I pretended not to notice.

We fished together for an hour or so, both bringing in some good salmon. I was planning on leaving the river once more anglers began showing up, but it was hard. I was having fun. At one point Mike pulled a little point-and-shoot camera out of his backpack and took photos of me landing a good five-pound male humpy. I asked to borrow the camera, and took a few shots of him holding up the two salmon he decided to take home to impress his mother. He had noticed that I was letting my fish go, and questioned me about it. I summarized the catch-and-release philosophy, and it must have made enough sense to him because he let his next salmon go.

When I could see at least two other fishermen on down the river, I knew it was time to leave. I shook Mike's hand and thanked him for letting me fish with him.

"Thanks a lot for the flies!" he said. "Maybe we'll see each other on the river again....I'll look for you."

"Sounds good," I said, and headed back down the gravel path to my truck.

I didn't realize how big my smile was until I got back and saw my reflection in the glass of the driver's side window. It meant something. I was learning something important about myself.

I like seeing people happy–maybe only because it's contagious. I like to tell them stories and make them laugh, and maybe think a bit, too. I like to share with them what small things I've learned to make my own life better. I'm no yoga guru, or financial consultant. I'm a fisherman. The best I can do is help others catch fish. And maybe tell some entertaining stories about it when it's all said and done.

I like that.

Silvers and the Styrofoam Hatch

Red. . .right. . .returning. . . .

I stand confidently at the wheel of the *Bluefox*, but still repeating the phrase Chuck taught me to remember how to approach a port. The big green buoys mark one side of the channel, the big red ones mark the other.

Red. . .right. . .returning. . . . I repeat it again to myself and look over the opaque windshield along the front edge of the flying bridge, looking for a channel marker as we near Spruce Cape. I could get the boat back safe without the aid of buoys or memorized phrases. I know now all the routes we usually take, but I'm bored, because we're moving slow–into the wind and under the weight of three day's worth of cod and halibut.

For most of our trips this past month Chuck has had me at the wheel while he goes down below with the charts to plot new sets, or, as this evening, to work on the paperwork due in with the load of fish –routine fisheries management stuff we have to provide whenever we make a delivery.

I'm always excited when we get close to rounding the corner of Spruce Cape because it means we're almost done for the week. Within an hour I'll be home and with Valerie again. This is the same shoreline I peered out at through a little porthole of the ferry when she and I first arrived here. The dark stone crevices and crashing waves so foreign and intimidating then, are now comfortably familiar.

Further inland I can vaguely make out roof tops, homes of people I've met, out along Monashka Bay Road. I can see the usual snarls of driftwood on the beach just west of Mill Bay–pale and glowing back at me through the ever-thickening dusk. They are large enough to require two hands and some concentration to climb over, like primitive jungle gyms. I know them because they mark where Lake Abercrombie spills out over the sand and pebbles and into the saltwater. I've walked the fern-lined trails around the lake many times, flipping small dry flies out under the spruce branches and in between the lily pads, to catch rainbow trout.

I can't see many details on land, though. It's been dark when we come back to port lately. We're down to about eleven hours of daylight now, from the eighteen hours we were having four months ago. The first long winter nights are only a calendar page away. The halibut are starting to move out to deeper water, too, and the seas are even less predictable than ever. Chuck only needs a couple more trips to finish off his IFQ, so we're doing all right. We just have to keep a close eye on the weather and squeeze in those last trips whenever we can.

Chuck said he was thinking about selling the *Bluefox* once we've finished this season's quota. He told me about it yesterday evening after we were cleaned up and back in the warmth of the cabin. I sipped my beer and listened to his grand retirement scheme involving nothing but day trips in fair weather. His plan is to buy a good skiff, one of those small metal boats with an enclosed wheelhouse just big enough for one man to squeeze into with a cup of coffee.

Listening to him I thought about my own future. What will I do to get through the winter? Who will I fish for next season? How long will Valerie be here with me? How long will *I* be here?

I got a letter from my folks the other day. I stuffed it in my laundry-turned-sea-bag, along with my warm wool sweaters and spare pair of jeans, before we set out on this fishing trip. I haven't reread it yet, but I remember what it's about. Deer archery season is open back home and Dad was giving me a detailed scouting report from one of the areas down in southern Ohio where we hunt. He says he has several new tree stand locations picked out. Lots of fresh buck sign, too. That's the kind of news that makes me fidgety.

It's not the deer, necessarily, that keeps Ohio in the back of my mind. I think it's family. I can hunt anywhere, really. The snow is going to be pushing all the blacktail down from the mountains here on Kodiak at any time. Deer season has been open on the island for a while now, as far as I know. Chuck and I passed a guy toting a .30-06 not long ago. We were hiking up to a high country lake to catch some trout and escape the insane Buskin River crowd that materialized out of thin air as soon as the first silver salmon was reported. I smiled and nodded in passing, and the guy with the rifle gave us a funny look. Not many people walk so far to go fishing here, I guess.

My bow and a couple dozen arrows are up in my loft bedroom, but I haven't had the urge to take it out and string it yet. I guess I associate bow hunting with family. It wouldn't be the same.

Not a lot of bow hunting goes on here from what I can gather. I hear the stories about how venison is acquired, though. The local trick, they say, is to hire one of the commercial purse seiners and have the skipper cruise the coast glassing for deer on the beach. Once a herd has been spotted, the anchor is tossed, the rifles loaded into the skiff (which is towed behind the seiner, normally used to control the other end of the purse seine) and then the "hunt" begins. The skiff is motored directly at the unsuspecting animals, and the shooting starts as soon as the boat hits the beach. That way everyone has a good chance to fill a few tags on the first sortie.

Ahhhhh! It's the Alaskan experience!

The winters are harsh enough up here to keep everyone in subsistence mode. They seem to favor whichever method of hunting or fishing puts the most meat in the freezer the fastest. Although I find it very difficult to condemn these people and this way of life, it's stories like that one that make me long for my family's deer camp. The months of practice and scouting, the weeks motionless and freezing in a tree stand or ground blind, and the ecstatic nature in which the stories of a deer within bow range are told back at the tent–even if a shot never was quite possible.

Oh, but it could always be worse. The natives up in interior Alaska are still allowed to hunt using their traditional methods. The government figures they've screwed them over enough already, so maybe it's fair. But keep in mind, this doesn't translate to atlatls and flint spearheads. They park themselves at river crossings in the migratory routes of large herds of barren-ground caribou, waiting for the opportune time to zip out and intercept the middle of the herd with their flat-bottomed aluminum dugouts. They tie the antlers of the swimming animals to the side of the boat before putting a .22 rimfire to as many heads as possible.

"White man want to be *sporting*!" they muse.

It rocks my whole perception of what being a Native American means, although that's certainly not their fault. When I was a kid I always let my sister play the cowboy, because I liked being the Indian. This progressed from carrying around a little plastic bow everywhere I went, to collecting arrowheads from the fields, to studying anthropology. I had fallen in love with the culture because I thought my own ideals reflected theirs. Out of misconception, I had respect. What I didn't know was that the only thing different from man *then* and *now* is firearms, fossil fuels and a few million more of us. Human nature, regardless of race or era, is still the same.

But, really, how can I stand here, balancing on the saddle of my high horse like a moral circus act, and preach to you about recurve bows, fly rods, catch-and-release and the mainly unwritten rules of fair chase, when I'm currently making a living out of killing fish by the ton? Maybe you've been thinking that, and I don't have a good answer. The best I can do is say that I'm trying hard to live a life void of hypocrisy, but I'm finding it tough to pay the rent with idealism.

What we need is an "Employment Opportunities for Fanatic Fishermen" column in the classifieds. It would help those of us uncomfortable with mining living resources, or dressing up like a clown to promote eighteen brands of crankbaits on the pro bass circuit.

So maybe, if I'm lucky, I won't have to fish commercially next season. Then I can go back to being idealistic. Wouldn't that be nice.

* * *

Chuck comes out of the cabin and climbs up next to me on the flying bridge. I step aside, relinquishing the wheel, and let him slide in behind it. There are a few other fishing vessels about, both coming and going, and the bridge spanning the channel to Near Island looms before us, then over us, as we cruise into port.

This is such a great place to return to. What an enormous feeling of homecoming, gliding into a busy seaport at night after the hustle and bustle has subsided to a steady and quiet rhythm. No airport or train station can conjure the same emotions I have as we pass the dry docks, the mountainous stacks of cage-like crab pots and the rows of large wooden pilings along cannery row–standing out of the water as tall as our own rigging. It's all so simple and utilitarian...and real. Nothing fancy, just how life happens out here on the islands off Alaska. And I'm a part of it. I'm the crew of this fine wooden vessel, and for the moment I'm not dwelling on the fact that I'm part of something, an institution and way of life, that might not completely jive with the ideology gestating inside me. For now, I'm just a fisherman, doing what I do well. The pride I have standing with Chuck on the *Bluefox* as we slip her neatly back into St. Paul Harbor is immense.

"Good enough," Chuck tells me after we have all the lines tight and coiled around the dock cleats. I don't waste a minute. I jump into the cabin, grab my seabag from my cot and scoot back out and onto the dock with all the fervor of a man in love.

I hesitate only for a moment, looking back over my shoulder at Chuck silhouetted against the lights from town. "When do you need me in the morning?" I ask.

"Oh, I wanna get to the cannery early." He pauses, thinking. "I'll call you," he says after a bit.

I nod, wave and trot down the dock toward dry land, glad to be home, and anxiously wondering if Valerie is still awake.

I dig some change from my pants pocket as I head for the phone booth by the Harbormasters Building. I dial my own number and listen to the rings, hoping I'm not disturbing Valerie's sleep, but at the same time pining for the sound of her soft voice on the other end. The phone continues to ring. Six times. Seven times. *Not there?* Eight times. *Where is she? At work still?* Nine times. I hang up and my change clatters noisily down to the coin return slot.

A woman's voice behind me says, "What's the matter? She's not home?"

I spin around, and there, waiting in the shadows with bright eyes and a beaming smile, is Valerie.

* * *

She took me off guard. I wasn't expecting her to be lurking in the shadows waiting for me when I came in off the docks. Who would have? It's not as though she knew what day we would return. We aren't on a schedule. But that wasn't the only surprise I had that evening.

I got a good deal more than just a welcome home hug from my sympathetic roomie. No. What happened out there behind the Harbormasters Building was highly platonically incorrect. Do you remember that famous Second World War victory photo of the sailor planting a kiss on the unsuspecting nurse out in the middle of the street? Well, it was along those lines, but my nurse wasn't putting up much of a fight.

Now the funny thing was–and really I'm trying not to get too carried away here in self indulgence–but this was a scenario I'd been imagining all summer. I daydreamed about gazing into her eyes, and fantasized about touching her lips and feeling her breath on my face. You know, all that sappy romantic stuff that doesn't usually get mentioned to a fishing buddy. But there we were, both letting out a little something that had been pent up and brewing between us, and all I could think about was how bad I smelled. My wool sweater alone must have had at least a pound of condensed fish guts smeared into it. She apparently didn't mind. She told me I looked sexy with my scruffy beard and tan face, leaning against the phone booth.

Incidently, I was ordered to the shower as soon as we got back to the apartment. My stench must have finally become intolerable once we were indoors and away from all the romantically handy sea breezes.

When I was in the bathroom scrubbing out dried halibut blood from my hair and digging cod remains out of my fingernails, Valerie was taking the dish of pasta shells she had made out of the refrigerator and putting it into the oven. She lit some candles around the apartment and popped the cork on a bottle of red wine, too.

What a great situation to come home to.

We ate on the livingroom floor, with the lights off and two of the fat, stubby candles burning off to the sides of our plates. I asked her how it happened that she was down at the docks when I arrived, and she admitted she had been going down there every evening after work to watch the boats coming in, waiting for the one with me. Usually she would only stay for an hour, but sometimes she would enjoy a book or a hot fudge sundae while she watched the sun set.

I don't recall what the rest of our conversation consisted of, though. We spent most of the meal just passing smiles and suggestive looks back and forth in the candlelight.

Chuck called early in the morning, as he had warned, and I met him down at Harborside Coffee. I walked to the coffee shop so Valerie could sleep in and still have the truck to drive to work. I left her a note by the alarm clock telling her how happy I was, how beautiful *she* was, and how thoroughly she had ingrained herself into my mind.

* * *

Delivering fish to the cannery can be interesting. If there are some big halibut onboard we'll oftentimes draw a crowd. The Filipino cannery workers come out and hover at the edge of the dock, peering down, and a team of about four of them (usually the younger ones) swarm into the hold after the fish. A crane lowers a big net for them to put the halibut in and then hoist up to be processed. Once the last halibut is off, the net gets switched out for a heavy metal drum to toss the cod into.

The whole unloading process takes about half an hour. Then I have to shovel the rotten ice out of the hold and scrub the deck. Chuck is always up in the cannery filling out papers, getting a receipt, and whatever else. He has me stay back to make sure the *Bluefox* doesn't get beaten up too bad during the unloading. As he's climbing the ladder up to the cannery he always warns me to be careful. "This can be the most hazardous part of the profession," he says, shaking his head. "These people have no respect for human life."

I stand back as far as I possibly can, grimace, and try to remember as much as I can from the combat-lifesaver classes I had in the Army. What *can* be done for someone crushed by a five-hundred-pound barrel of gray cod, anyway?

Out of sheer luck alone, I have yet to see any teenaged grease spots get created on our deck. Just some minor skull dents (that looked as though they hurt way more than the recipients admitted) and a cracked bin board that really got Chuck riled up.

It's dangerous, this knack for getting riled up, especially for two abnormally stubborn and opinionated fishermen confined to a small area for a long period of time. It has been known to spark a "sea-debate," which is a lot less civilized than it sounds. We've had some real dandy sea-debates this summer, actually. The issues are usually diverse: religion, female psychology, and where the world-record largemouth bass was caught. This last one is undoubtedly the longest running, and often the most heated.

I've been getting agitated with people quickly, and more often, it seems. Not so much with Chuck (although I know he's wrong – about the bass, anyway) but with people who just don't circulate in the same veins as myself. We may live in the same town, even fish in the same rivers, but it's all in different dimensions. Sure we see each other and all that, this isn't the sci-fi channel, but our personal view of the flowing water, or, on a larger scale, the planet we live on, is vastly different. How can two people in this situation communicate effectively? Or, better yet, how can they live in the same place, or frequent the same bodies of water, without contemplating severe acts of violence on one another?

I've been able to reign in my temper, for the most part. Although, I've noticed it's getting harder to maintain my cool. It's the residual effect of prolonged exposure to what I see as idiocy. Sometimes things just happen at the wrong time and I lose it. Not long ago some guy waded right through the middle of the pool I was fishing, and I zinged a rock at his head before I remembered to just do breathing exercises and laugh about it.

I guess I react more violently to things like that–the severe breaches in common sense and etiquette–because they're directly affecting me. But, I suppose if I had to choose between sharing a river bank with a guy who has no regard for me, or one with no regard for the river, I'd go for the guy that picks up after himself, even if he does cast over my line while I'm fighting a fish. I'd just be sure to have a few stones handy.

A large percentage of my passion (which, unlike patience, I have a surplus of) gets directed at the environment. I guess it's because I've always been an outdoorsman, and by this I mean not only do I enjoy being outside participating in a nationally-acknowledged outdoor activity, but that I actually appreciate what makes the out-of-doors different from say, the inside of an abandoned warehouse. I appreciate that this planet is beautiful, and that it can sustain me, so I respect that. And I gracefully take what is given. But surrounding me are my peers who are trying to squeeze every last drop of comfort, pleasure and wealth from this planet, the origin of their very existence, like a lot of ungrateful little shits exploiting their own selfless mother.

And because I'm a fly fisherman, most of my soapbox-tirades begin with rivers. I see some of the other fishermen on the Buskin who have absolutely zero love or respect for the thing that is bringing them both sustenance and enjoyment. I would like to say this saddens me, and I imagine eventually it will, but for now it just makes me mad.

All this animosity isn't new; I've boiled about similar things for years. Like the time a bunch of idiots decided to host a dirt bike race through the middle of Ohio's Wayne National Forest. Many of the hiking paths and deer trails were turned into two-foot-deep muddy rills that looked like bulging, infected gashes on an otherwise gorgeous woman's face. Or, for another example, the couple who lives down the street from my parents. They own some acreage behind them that used to be ideal rabbit and whitetail habitat, but they were disappointed because they could never see the deer from their back window, so they took a chainsaw and Bush Hog to it all–you know, to tidy it up and unobstruct the view. Well, now it's one big lawn. The rabbits have moved on, of course, and the deer stay away. As a replacement, they bought a pair of ceramic deer lawn ornaments.

This annoyance with derelicts en masse in the outdoors has been a relatively new thing for me up here in Alaska, though. Mainly because there are fewer overall people here. But, I have now learned that with the silver salmon come the problems. And it's a real shame, too, because I'd been looking forward to sharing the river with a heavy run of thick-bodied coho's. I couldn't wait, really. Now I'm so fed up I can't even stomach the sight of the poor Buskin River. I don't even slow down over the bridge anymore.

Okay. So there's a lot of people down there now, I guess you'll have that. This close to town it should be expected. But this is sick. Not only are there masses of people, they have completely trashed the place. All the tall grass and brush along the bank is hacked back or matted down. There's garbage strewn everywhere–pop cans, beer bottles, plastic wrappers, empty lure packages, cigarette butts and gnarls of monofilament. Then there are the salmon remains–guts and heads, and eggs, lots of eggs, dried out and cemented to the tops of rocks and spewing from plastic bags along the trails. I could go on, but I won't. It's killing me.

Oh, I did have some fun before the word got out. The beginning of the silver run started slow, but let me tell you, what a rush! The best way to describe hooking a large silver on a light fly rod is to have you imagine standing on the berm of a highway and tossing a rope with grappling hook out into traffic. It's terrific. And a little scary at first. The fly line starts whipping around between the reel and stripping eye like a loose electrical wire in a rainstorm, and the reel's screaming away, and the bright flourescent backing is running downriver. Or, sometimes, they head against the current when they feel the prick of the hook, blasting through riffles and blowing out of the water, going end over end and then back into the river. They're supercharged, chrome-colored missiles. High-octane, adrenaline fish.

I took my first silver salmon on a #8 Salmon Mint. I was after pinks at the time, but saw a larger than usual shadow drift into the pool and, miraculously, the fish took my fly on the first drift past it. The next few minutes are a blur. I almost broke my thumb on the crank handle of my reel. I had to wait until the rpm's eased a bit before I could try palming the spool again. It was all a matter of how long I could hang on. I never thought landing the fish would be possible.

The Salmon Mint pattern worked for a few fish. Then they changed their fickle, pea-sized minds and I had to switch to my Bloody Yolk steelhead fly. That did the trick for a few days, and quit, as well. I'd gotten real cocky after figuring out the pink salmon so fast, so I was a little frustrated. I assumed I could pull off a repeat performance and create a super lethal silver salmon fly. They proved to be a lot more difficult. Then I came up with the Animal, a purple number with orange yarn as hackle and a gold bead head, that they really liked.

But that's about the time the word got out. The next morning I had to fight for a parking spot in the campground, and as the sun was coming up I could see Styrofoam coffee cups drifting by out in the river. They looked like giant white mayflies bobbing along the current seams. They were hatching thick, too.

Chuck and I only lasted another week before we gave up and headed way upriver after Dollies that are spawning and getting really pretty. Their pink spots are very distinctive now, and their bellies bright red. Beautiful fish. But the silvers moved up and so did the mob. Now we don't even get near the Buskin.

The other rivers on Kodiak accessible by road are inundated now, too. I drove all the way to the very end of the road system, down to Pasagshak Bay, and still couldn't get away from the crowd.

The last time I've been out was with Chuck about a week ago, and it was a wild goose chase. He showed me a hand drawn map penciled in on a napkin stained with brown coffee rings. The guy he'd talked to worked for the department of fish and game and said there were some big rainbows in this lake up in the high country. So we geared up, hid the truck in the brush along the road and climbed for glory. And it was so refreshing not to have to share the water with anyone. We passed only one person on the way up, and that was the deer hunter who gave us a funny look. Other than that, the only discouraging signs were fresh bear tracks and menacing claw marks on rocks.

We found the lake all right, and fished it until well past dark. Neither one of us caught anything. And that was just fine.

End of the Run

A gust of wind shakes the large pane of glass in the bay window and creeps in with a whistle under the door. I have my wool socks on and Valerie is wearing two sweaters. We sit close to one another on the couch, our feet tucked under the cushions and our hands touching under the afghan we share. We sit sideways, heads turned and leaning on the back of the couch, watching the northern lights in the night sky out the window and feeling the cold draft that's fluttering the curtains. It spars with the small hot flame of the candle by the telephone.

Outside, a light dusting of snow is being blown around in circles on the frozen surface of Lily Lake. All the float planes have been warehoused, and all the tourists have taken their photos, bought their trinkets and gone home. Everything that remains on the island has been tied down and covered up for the winter.

Valerie fidgets under the afghan, trying to pull more of herself under its warmth. "We need to put a towel or something under the door," she says.

I listen to the whistling and nod.

"We're going to have to do something about insulating this window, too, if we're really planning to stay," she adds.

I nod again and sigh.

She leans back against my legs and looks at me. "Are we really planning to stay the winter?"

"Yeah, I guess," I say watching the sky. The Aurora Borealis has painted large swaths of green light from somewhere behind the black outline of Pyramid Mountain to an area of the night sky directly above us. The light appears to be motionless, but if you watch one green brush stroke long enough, you can see that it's moving. Ebbing and flowing. Vanishing slowly and gradually reappearing somewhere else.

"Are you going to get work on another boat?" Valerie asks.

"Oh, I don't know. I don't think so."

We sit awhile without saying anything.

"I was thinking about asking around," I finally say. "Maybe A-1 Tire down the road. Just for the winter."

"Then what?"

"I don't know." I close my eyes and take a deep breath. The green sky still sways across the backs of my eyelids. It remains beautiful.

I open my eyes and look at Valerie. "What would we do if we left?"

"I could teach," she says quickly. "I didn't go to college to rent cars."

I can tell that she has already thought a lot about this.

"You can teach here," I say as conversational filler to buy myself more time to brainstorm about my own employment options. I can hear Valerie explain, again, why that's not such a super viable idea. I know she has already inquired at Kodiak High School; there were no openings and probably wouldn't be for awhile. This island has proven not to be the best place for job opportunities. If you're not catching, counting or cutting up fish, chances are you're unemployed.

"Okay," I interrupt. "But what would *I* do back in Ohio?" This is thrown out as proof that we have to stay, disregarding the fact that I have no clue as to how to make a living here either.

"You could try going to school."

Huh?

"The Army will help pay for it, right?"

"Uh, I guess. All of it, I think."

I have a flashback to sitting in a recruiter's office trying unsuccessfully to convince the sergeant to swap my G.I. Bill for the cash equivalent of a couple cases of beer. The military has a fine money-saving strategy: if the kid looks like he can barely read the back of a box of macaroni and cheese, give him money for college, he'll never use it; if there is a hint of intelligence behind the glazed eyes of the recently graduated teenager, give him a token wad of cash. I guess it's the government's way of making up for the cost of toilet seats.

"And what would *I* do with college?"

The wind outside dies for a moment and the snow settles cold and still on the ice of Lily Lake. The silence inside is telling.

"Well, okay," she says. "But you like to tell stories. You're good at it. Maybe you can write a book?"

"*Valerie*, I don't even know how to *spell*, let alone write a complete sentence!" I sit up straight on the couch and the afghan slides off me. "I almost failed second grade because I couldn't learn how to spell my own last name!"

She rolls her eyes and laughs. "So what *are* you planning to do?"

"I don't know." I look back outside at the green sky and smile. "Maybe I'll go fishing in the morning."

* * *

My black wool watchcap is pulled down over my ears and I'm wearing polypropylene long underwear that zips up to my chin, but none of it keeps the sting of cold from my face as I step out of the truck and into two inches of new snow. I was confronted by the same chill when I left the apartment earlier this morning, but the truck's heater had lulled me back into a comfortable state of drowsiness. I pull my rod from its aluminum tube, attach the reel, and string the line through the eyes. I notice my leader is a bit short and has rough abrasions near the butt section. I need to rebuild it. But by now my fingers are too numb to tie the proper knots, so I prop the rod up in the bed of my pickup and thread the end of the fly line through the smallest crack of an opening in the truck door window. I sit inside with the engine and the heater on again until my hands become pliable enough to function.

I'm not in a rush. There's absolutely no one else about, mine are the only vehicle tracks anywhere around. The fishing will be very slow this morning anyway, I already know that. It will be slow all day, actually, and it will stay that way. I'd almost rather stay in the truck and keep warm. *Almost*.

When my hands are operable again I dig through my fishing vest, pulling out several spools of leader material. My salmon leader is about six foot long–nothing fancy. I usually build it with only three pieces of different diameter material, and it's quick, but this time it takes me much longer to get it all tied up. It's partly because my hands are cold, but mainly it's because I'm preoccupied with last night's conversation with Valerie.

What *am* I going to do with myself, anyway? Where *am* I headed? I feel that I'm at an important crossroads of life with enormous consequences. Good or bad, I don't know yet–it's still up in the air. But the more I think about it the less clear it all becomes. It's more like I'm stuck spinning around a roundabout with a dozen roads leading a dozen directions with no street signs. For quite awhile now I've had the hunch, lurking somewhere in the back of my brain, that this day would sneak up on me. So what now? Is it really the end of the run? Will my life from here on out mirror the lives of the salmon I spend so much time getting to know? Is it time now to leave the magnificent uncertainty of the open ocean, find a nice cozy river, procreate and then hang around for as long as modern medicine will allow me while the flesh slowly rots off my bones? Are the best parts of this adventure already over?

I finish my leader and think about stepping out of the truck again, but decide to first tie on a fly. I shove my hands into a pair of thick and warm wool mittens–the type that flips back to expose my four finger tips when I need to do something delicate. These are shooting mittens I bought the last time it took me into January to finally arrow a deer. I never thought I'd be fanatic enough to need them for fishing. I open the truck door window an inch more, flip the fly and leader out into the snow and cut the engine. The warm air stops blasting my face, it's time to go get cold.

I'm still preoccupied enough to almost forget to grab my rod out of the bed of the truck. And I'm still agitated enough to find it irritating, not laughable. But not forty yards from the truck everything stops. I find fresh bear tracks. It's like a whistle was blown and every bit of straggling concentration jumps to its feet and reports in. All other topics drop. It's not that bears and their tracks are a rarity in these parts, it's just that when they're this fresh and this big they get my undivided attention. It only stopped snowing twenty minutes ago. And, no, there's no snow on the tracks. Just how big, you ask? I can stand in the pad print with both feet and not come close to obscuring the outline in the snow.

The bear had taken the same path down to the river, so I move forward slowly and deliberately. I should probably drive downstream farther, or at least be making noise to alert the animal to my presence, giving it time to duck and run without causing a gruesome scene when the two of us bump into one another on the trail. But I don't make a sound. To hell with safety. He's just another fisherman. I don't want to crowd him out, though, so if he's still there, I'll just move down a few pools.

Then I hear a splash.

I'm close enough to the river to be able to hear running water if it weren't so low, but I can't actually see it yet.

Was it a couple old buck silvers fighting in shallow water? Or was it. . .?

Suddenly safety is sounding a lot better.

But. . .I'm already this close!

So I go on, and when I get to the river there's not a soul around –four-legged and furry or otherwise. There are signs, though. The snow on the opposite bank is heavily stained by the blood of a fish. The bear tracks lead back from there on into the bush. I must have spooked him off. For a moment I feel a bit guilty.

Then I spot the dark red shimmers of mature silver salmon through the clear, shallow waters. They help me get over it. *It's my turn at them now.*

* * *

There's still quite a few fish in the river, and they're easy to spot. They're just not all that excited about eating anymore. They've been in freshwater for so long now that even the instinct to eat is gone. The weather doesn't help, either. Every second cast I have to stop and break the ice out from the eyes of my rod, and sometimes off the entire length of my fly line and leader. I resort to a 2x tippet, as well, because anything thinner keeps snapping off when I cast. And with my numb hands and the thick, ice-encrusted mittens over them, I can't even feel the rod handle, let alone a subtle strike.

The fish I do take is a good one, a twelve-pound male, but he fights me like a fat man trying to win a wrestling match by just laying down on his opponent. The real fight is spawned out of him. The hard part is getting the hook up. It takes me over two hours to coerce him into taking my fly, and when the strike does come it's a quick, slashing one made out of pure aggression. I have to bounce a big, flashy streamer off his nose and past his face for twenty minutes before he lashes out.

I follow him down a few shallow riffles, then use the current's assistance to drag him ashore. He flops twice and then lays still in the snow. I remove my fly and stand over him and try to capture the memory of this forever–his beautiful, dark red contrast against the pure white of the snow; his hormonally-distorted face and patch of teeth, the teeth the shape of cat's claws curling back from his lower jaw. For a moment all that moves is one pelvic fin, slightly, and the cloud-like vapor from my excited breathing drifting over the beautiful salmon and the cold, clear water.

I grasp him gently by the wrist of the tail and slide him back into his river. He rights himself and slowly cruises to the nearest eddy, regaining his composure to tackle the rest of his short life. I stand up, clip off my fly and reel in the slack line. For today, I'm done. I'd gotten what I came for long before this salmon.

It's not that fishing has answered any questions, or resolved any of my problems, but it certainly sets the right size stage to confront them. I don't think about anything while I'm on the water, other than what's pertinent to catching my next fish, but the act itself clears room in my mind for the perplexities nagging to be addressed. When I'm finally done and my rod is unstrung, the world around me is fresh again. It's like waking up in the morning after a good night's sleep and having forgotten what was so damn serious about life the night before. I feel stronger now. Things seem so much more simple. And maybe even plausible.

Jay Zimmerman is a hunter, woodsman, and writer with a passion for rivers, fishing, and good stories. He was born and raised along Lake Erie in Ohio, among a family of fishers, hunters, and storytellers. He served in the U.S. military, then traveled to Alaska and back to Ohio to write the story of his life as a fisherman and his growth as a person. This is his debut book.

Titles in the Harmony Series
from Bottom Dog Press

In Neck Deep: Stories from a Fisherman by Jay Zimmerman
0-933087-90-X 256 pgs. $15.00

America Zen: A Gathering of Poets
eds. Ray McNiece and Larry Smith
0-933087-91-8 224 pgs. $15.00

O Taste and See: Food Poems
edited by David Lee Garrison & Terry Hermsen
0-933087-82-9 198 pgs. $14.00

When: Poems by Don Moyer
0-933087-81-0 96 pgs. $10.95

Songs of the Woodcutter:
Zen Poems of Wang Wei and Taigu Ryokan
by Larry Smith & Monte Page
0-933087-80-2 (CD & Booklet) $15.00

Song That Fathoms Home: Poems by Ray McNiece
0-933087-85-3 124 pgs. $12.00

Hymns and Songs of Purandaradasa
translated by Dinesh Hassan
0-933087-89-6 88 pgs. $12.95

Bowl of Water: Poems by Allen Frost
0-933087-88-8 136 pgs. $12.95

Homepage for Ordering
http://members.aol.com/Lsmithdog/bottomdog
Include $1.50 with any order for shipping.